BABIES
with DOWN
SYNDROME

❧

A New Parents Guide
Edited by Karen Stray-Gundersen

WOODBINE HOUSE • 1986

Copyright © 1986 Woodbine House, Inc.

All rights reserved under International and Pan-American Copyright Conventions. Published in the United States of America by Woodbine House, Inc.

Figure 2 in Chapter Six reprinted by permission of Siegfried M. Pueschel, M.D., Ph.D, M.P.H. and Andrews, McMeel and Parker from *Down Syndrome: Growing and Learning* (1978). All rights reserved.

Karyotypes courtesy of Lillian D. Killos, Ph.D., Director of Cytogenetics, Columbia Hospital for Women, Washington, D.C.

Library of Congress Catalogue Card Number: 85-052007

ISBN: 0-933149-02-6

Cover Design: Sicklesmith & Egly

Cover Illustration: Annie Lunsford

Charts and Graphs: Jay Townsend

Book Design and Typesetting: Wordscape, Inc., Washington, D.C.

Photographs: Gayle Krughoff, National Down Syndrome Congress, and parents

Library of Congress Cataloging-in-Publication Data

Babies with Down syndrome.

  Bibliography: p.
  Includes index.
  1. Down's syndrome—Popular works. 2. Mentally handicapped children—Care. I. Stray-Gundersen, Karen.
RJ506.D68B33   1986   616.85'8842   85-52007
ISBN 0-933149-02-6 (pbk.)

Manufactured in the United States of America

   7 8 9 10

With deep affection and admiration, this book is dedicated to babies with Down syndrome and their parents.

TABLE OF CONTENTS

Foreword

LOWELL P. WEICKER, JR.
CONNECTICUT

𝔘𝔫𝔦𝔱𝔢𝔡 𝔖𝔱𝔞𝔱𝔢𝔰 𝔖𝔢𝔫𝔞𝔱𝔢
𝔚𝔞𝔰𝔥𝔦𝔫𝔤𝔱𝔬𝔫, 𝔇. ℭ.

July 31, 1986

Dear Mom and Dad:

Sonny Weicker was born in the wee hours of June 13, 1978. He has been fun and work ever since.

Sonny is indeed lovable, which trait is attributed to all Downs children. And he is also

> Stubborn
> Resilient
> Street smart
> Bossy
> Open

Some of these traits according to my wife have nothing to do with Down's Syndrome, but are inherited from his father.

So my congratulations to you for a life experience that few parents will lay claim to. Don't look back. Rather, prepare for your child's future -- a future that one day will have to be lived without you. So start today.

Affectionately,

Lowell P. Weicker, Jr
United States Senator
Connecticut

Introduction

When our little boy was born, my husband and I were told that they wanted to test his chromosomes; the doctors said they wanted to check for "Trisomy 21." We suspected that we should be worried about something, but didn't know what; we didn't know that Trisomy 21 meant Down syndrome. A few days later we knew.

Our first image was a desperate one, primarily because we had literally no information or knowledge of what Down syndrome was. We expected the worst. We immediately tried to learn more about Down syndrome, but found little to read. What we did find was a collection of outdated and often insensitive material. But over time we learned a lot—mostly from doctors, teachers, Down syndrome organizations, other parents, and of course, our son, with whom we fell madly in love.

This book was compiled to provide new parents with a complete introduction to Down syndrome. Hopefully, you can avoid the time we spent searching for information and worrying over inaccuracies. The book is intended to provide you with what we missed: up-to-date facts about what Down syndrome is and information about how to start dealing with it. Most importantly, this book will tell you that kids with Down syndrome are kids first and foremost. Once you understand Down syndrome you can get on to loving your new baby.

The chapters in this book cover the full range of things you need to start thinking about for your baby's early years. They explain what Down syndrome is, how to cope with the fact that your baby has Down syndrome, and how to deal with potential medical concerns. Those are the basics; from there you need information on daily care, your family life, your baby's development and education, and finally, your baby's legal rights. Each of these important subjects is covered in the book. Children with Down syndrome present great challenges, and even greater rewards. This book will help you to see your baby's great potential.

A special part of this book is its Parent Statements at the end of each chapter. In them parents who have gone through what you are going through now share their experiences, thoughts, and advice. You will find that every parent has a different slant on the same problem or experience. Combining the Parent Statements with the basic information in each chapter gives the book a real-life perspective.

You cannot do it alone and you don't need to. This book contains an extensive Resource Guide that will help you get in touch with parents like yourself, with doctors, teachers, therapists, and other professionals, with federal, state, and local government agencies, and with a variety of organizations that can give you the support and information you need. This book gives you the facts you need to take full advantage of the programs and services available to help your child.

Down syndrome has its own language, and parents need to learn it to best help their baby. At the end of this book is a glossary of key terms. There is also a Reading List with books the authors and the editor recommend for further reading for new parents.

Our book also contains photographs of children with Down syndrome, at play, at home, and at school. Most of the children are age three and under.

No book can mend a broken heart or shattered dreams. But it can give you the facts you need to begin dreaming once again of the bright future all parents want for their children.

Throughout the book we use the personal pronouns alternately by chapter. We felt uncomfortable about referring only to either boys or girls, and felt that constantly using "he or she" to refer to children would become unwieldy. When the references are to the parents and professionals, we were able to use both pronouns because it happened less frequently. Hopefully this arrangement will be clear.

This book is obviously the combined effort of many people. Each chapter was written by a parent or professional highly respected in their field. Each was motivated by a desire to inform people about the reality of Down syndrome. We gratefully acknowledge their generous contribution. In addition, we would like to thank the following people for their contribution and support in our efforts: Lawrence Cohen, M.D., Maureen Flanagan, Seymour Hepner, M.D., Marshall Keys, M.D., Kathy Rodriguez, and Ruth Wells. Both the National Down Syndrome Congress and the National Information Center for Handicapped Children and Youth provided essential information and assistance for the book, and we would like to express our appreciation. Our sincere thanks also go to Marshall Levin for his fine work on the book's manuscript.

We owe a special thanks to the many parents who allowed us to interview them and to photograph their beautiful children. Lastly, we want to thank all those people–parents and professionals alike–who have shared their lives out of a deep commitment to help babies and their parents.

All children require care and hard work. Children with Down syndrome do too. Raising any child can be very rewarding; raising a child with Down syndrome will be equally rewarding. Your baby will never quit on himself, and you won't quit on him either. He will always try hard to please you and will work extremely hard during lessons and therapy. He will inspire you to do the same in learning, teaching, and advocating for him. And as you work, live, and play with your child, you will fall in love.

Everyone associated with this book wishes you a happy and fulfilling life with your new baby.

Karen Stray-Gundersen
September 1986

ONE

What Is Down Syndrome?

CHAHIRA KOZMA, M.D.*

The best way to understand Down syndrome–what it means to your baby and what it means to you–is to get the facts. For a condition that has for so long been shrouded in fear and darkness, the facts are far better than the myths. The worst enemy facing parents of babies with Down syndrome is ignorance. Before you do anything or decide anything about your baby, learn about Down syndrome.

This chapter introduces Down syndrome to people who may never have heard of it before or who may know little about it. It addresses the basic questions parents have about Down syndrome and gives the foundation of knowledge you need to begin properly caring for your baby.

The technical terms in this chapter may be unfamiliar to you. The glossary at the back of this book includes all of the important terms. Use it to understand the terms you don't yet know and refer back to it as often as you need.

No one will say that raising a child with Down syndrome is a picnic. The thousands of parents who have done it successfully will say that there is a lot of hard work and patience involved. But with today's medical and educational advances, the myths and stereotypes of the past that so deprived children with Down syndrome are giving way to facts and realistic expectations.

*Dr. Chahira Kozma is Assistant Professor of Pediatrics and a Clinical Geneticist at Georgetown University Hospital in Washington, D.C.

What Is Down Syndrome?

If you are like most people, you probably had little understanding of what Down syndrome meant before your baby was born. Basically, Down syndrome means that your baby has one extra chromosome in each of his millions of cells. Instead of forty-six, he has forty-seven. Over six thousand babies with Down syndrome are born in the United States every year and thousands more in other countries. It is one of the most common birth defects. Everyone has heard of children born with other disorders, such as spina bifida, cerebral palsy, muscular dystrophy, and Tay-Sachs disease. Of these, only cerebral palsy is more common than Down syndrome. Other chromosomal disorders are far less common.

Because genes and chromosomes play a large part in determining your child's characteristics, this extra chromosome will affect his life. His appearance may be a bit different from other children, he may have some unique medical problems, and he will likely have some degree of mental retardation, although the severity of any of these problems varies tremendously from child to child.

Two things about Down syndrome are clear. First, parents do not cause Down syndrome; nothing you did or did not do before or during pregnancy caused your baby to have Down syndrome. Second, like "normal" children, each baby with Down syndrome is unique, with his own personality, talents, and thoughts. There are few absolutes governing your baby's destiny; like other children, he is an individual and will grow to become a distinct personality.

Parents frequently are amazed at how often conception results in abnormal chromosomes. In general, chromosomal abnormalities of one kind or another may occur in as many as four in one hundred conceptions. Most of these pregnancies end in miscarriage. In fact, a quarter of all miscarriages result from chromosomal abnormalities that do not allow the embryo to develop.

Down syndrome, the most common chromosomal abnormality in humans, is one that *does* allow the embryo to develop. Down syndrome occurs in all races and in all countries. Recent figures place the frequency in North America at about one in eight hundred to one in one thousand births. It can happen to anyone. It happens in both girls and boys evenly.

What Causes Down Syndrome?

To understand what has caused your child to have Down syndrome, you need to know something about genetics. Every person has genes located in every cell of the body; they are the blueprint of life. Almost all of a person's traits—from eye color to the size of one's hands to the sound of one's voice—are coded in the genes. Genes are located on microscopic, rod-shaped bodies called chromosomes. How genes control the human body and its functioning is only now being discovered. Figure 1 shows a picture of a set of random chromosomes. Called "karyotypes," these pictures are made from blood samples taken from babies after birth. The blood samples are "cultured"—allowed to grow in a petri dish—and the chromosomes are then isolated by a microscope or a camera.

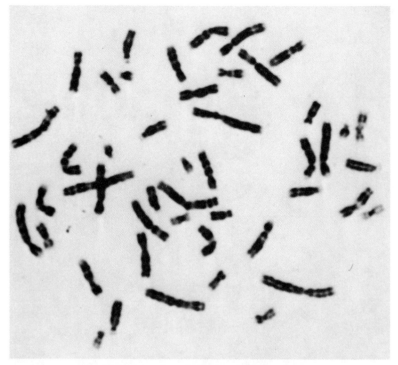

Figure 1. Karyotype of Chromosomes

Most people have forty-six chromosomes in each of their cells. Each chromosome is grouped into pairs, with twenty-three sets in all. One chromosome of each pair originally comes from the mother's egg; the other comes from the father's sperm. These cells are known as germ cells and have twenty-three chromosomes each. As germ cells mature, a process called meiotic division occurs, splitting the chromosomes exactly in half, with each new cell–called a daughter cell–receiving one pair of one set of chromosomes instead of two.

At conception the sperm and egg cells combine, yielding a fertilized egg with a set of forty-six chromosomes. As the fertilized egg begins to divide, it duplicates its genetic material so that each new cell receives the same chromosomal material as the original cell. Because all cells duplicate the genetic structure of that first fertilized egg, its genetic content is crucial to the genetic makeup of the baby. Figure 2 illustrates this process of cell division.

Figure 2. Meiotic Division Fertilization > Normal Cell Division

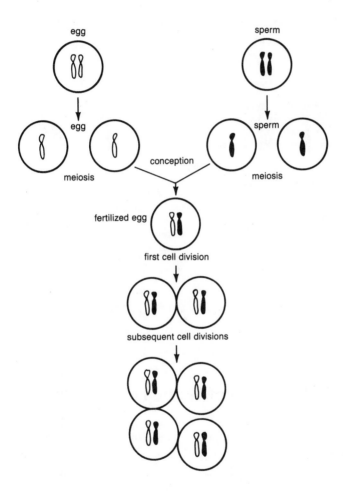

Diagram illustrating normal meiosis or cell division of the germ cell with each daughter cell receiving 23 chromosomes. Upon conception the fertilized egg contains 46 chromosomes. This leads to the development of a baby with 46 chromosomes in each cell.

Figure 3 shows a picture of normal chromosomes. As you can see, the chromosomes are grouped into pairs for analysis. They are believed to function in tandem, with each set carefully balanced. If for some reason, an extra chromosome is present, the genetic balance is thrown off. Doctors refer to this as a "trisomy," which means three chromosomes. When the cells contain three number-21 chromosomes, Down syndrome results. This is known as Trisomy 21.

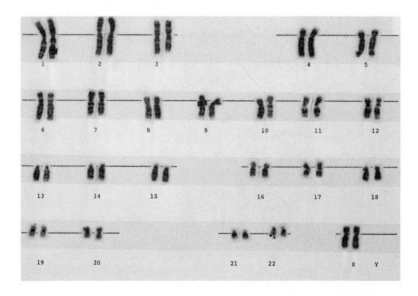

Figure 3. Karyotype of Normal Chromosomes

The mystery of procreation persists, but this much scientists know—babies get their genes from their parents, half from their mother and half from their father. What scientists do *not* know is what causes the extra chromosome to be present in Down syndrome. Several theories have been suggested. Possibly when sperm or egg cells are created, something causes the chromosomes to stick together with the number-21 chromosomes separating incorrectly. Then later, when the germ cell is fertilized, an extra chromosome becomes a part of the new living embryo, giving it forty-seven instead of forty-six chromosomes. This process is demonstrated in the diagram in Figure 4.

Figure 4. Nondisjunction Cell Division

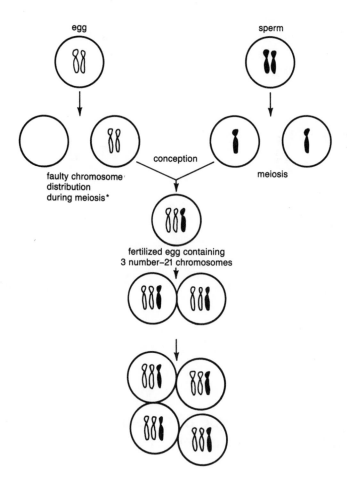

Faulty chromosome distribution during meiosis in the egg or sperm causes Trisomy-21 in the fertilized egg. This leads to Trisomy-21 occuring in all cells of the baby, resulting in Down syndrome.

* Can occur in the development of sperm.

As the newly created embryo begins to grow, the extra chromosome is duplicated and transmitted to each new cell. The result is that all of the cells contain an extra chromosome. Because this type of Down syndrome probably results from some genetic material sticking together—failing to separate or "disjoin"—it is called Nondisjunction Trisomy 21. What this means is that your baby has an extra twenty-first chromosome. Figure 5 is a picture of the chromosomes of a baby with Down syndrome, and shows the extra number-21 chromosome. Ninety-five percent of babies with Down syndrome have Nondisjunction Trisomy 21.

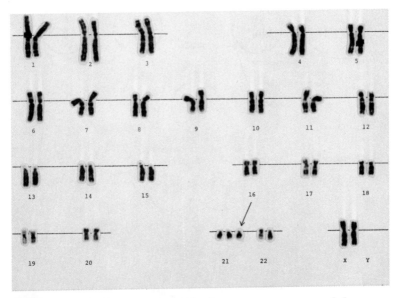

Figure 5. Karyotype of Chromosomes with Nondisjunction Trisomy 21

The five percent of babies with Down syndrome who do not have Nondisjunction Trisomy 21 have one of two other types: Translocation or Mosaicism. In Translocation Trisomy 21, a part of the number-21 chromosome breaks off during cell division and attaches to another chromosome, usually chromosome 14 or the other number-21 chromosome. Either way, there is extra genetic material.

Two to three percent of babies with Down syndrome have Translocation Trisomy 21.

About two-thirds of translocations occur spontaneously during fertilization; the rest are inherited from a parent. This is the only type of Down syndrome that can result from a condition in the parent's genes. When this happens, the carrier parent is normal, but two of his or her chromosomes are stuck together, and the total chromosome count is forty-five instead of forty-six. The reason this is important is that if the Translocation Trisomy 21 is inherited from a carrier parent, the risk of the same thing occurring in future pregnancies is higher. The karyotype of a baby will reveal whether or not he has Translocation Trisomy 21.

The least common form of Down syndrome is known as Mosaicism. Only one to two percent of all people with Down syndrome have this type of Trisomy 21. In Mosaicism, a faulty cell division occurs in one of the early cell divisions after fertilization. As in Nondisjunction Trisomy 21, something causes the chromosomes to divide unevenly. But when this occurs in the second or third cell division, only some of the cells of the growing embryo contain the extra chromosome. As a result, not all the cells have the extra chromosome, and the baby may have fewer of the identifying features of Down syndrome. The percentage of affected cells differs from child to child. Some children may have the classic Down syndrome features, while others may have fewer of the usual physical features as well as higher intellectual capacities.

Although babies with Down syndrome possess an extra number-21 chromosome, all of their other chromosomes are normal. In fact, the material in the number-21 chromosome is normal as well; there is just too much of it. This additional chromosomal material causes a genetic imbalance that alters the normal course of development. But the rest of the chromosomes function normally, and that is why your baby seems so much like any other baby. Some of his features are affected

by the extra number-21 chromosome, but most of his characteristics are determined by the remaining forty-six chromosomes in his genetic blueprint.

One of the many myths surrounding Down syndrome is that a child can have only "a little" Down syndrome. With the exception of Mosaicism, a child either has Down syndrome or does not. It is simply all in the genes.

Why Does My Child Have Down Syndrome?

Scientists have investigated the causes of Down syndrome for decades. So far the exact cause of Down syndrome—what makes the number-21 chromosomes stick together—has eluded discovery. With the exception of the age of the mother, the occurrence of Down syndrome appears to be random.

The mother's age is the only established factor related to the likelihood of having a baby with Down syndrome. Women are born with a fixed number of eggs and do not produce new eggs during their life. It is possible that as eggs age in the ovaries, something happens to cause nondisjunction. Possibly the mother's chromosomes become stickier with age; possibly there is some other reason, but the precise cause still awaits discovery.

Figure 6 charts the likelihood of having a baby with Down syndrome. As you can see, the chance increases dramatically as women age. Yet many young women with no history of Down syndrome in their families have babies with Down syndrome. A surprising fact is that seventy-five percent of babies with Down syndrome are born to mothers *under* thirty-five years of age.

Recent studies have shown that nondisjunction may come from the father's sperm—about twenty to thirty percent of babies with Down syndrome. Even though a man produces new sperm throughout his adult life, scientists have suggested the possibility that some people may be genetically predisposed to "sticky" genes. However, the hard fact remains that we don't know how Down syndrome occurs and we don't know how to prevent it.

What Are Babies with Down Syndrome Like?

Doctors are often able to spot babies with Down syndrome im-

Figure 6. Likelihood of Having a Baby with Down Syndrome Based on Maternal Age

MATERNAL AGE	FREQUENCY OF DOWN SYNDROME AMONG BIRTHS*
20–24	1/1450 (Average)
25–29	1/1347 (Average)
30	1/885
31	1/826
32	1/725
33	1/592
34	1/465
35	1/365
36	1/287
37	1/225
38	1/176
39	1/139
40	1/109
41	1/85
42	1/67
43	1/53
44	1/41
45	1/32
46	1/25
47	1/20
48	1/16
49	1/12

*This chart lists only the *approximate* frequency of babies with Down syndrome based on the mother's age. The figures are based on the *average* of the findings of four separate population surveys. (Hook & Lindsjo, 1978; Trimble & Baird, 1978)

mediately after birth. Newborns with Down syndrome often have features that trigger the doctor's suspicions. Karyotypes and other tests are usually ordered. Bear in mind, however, that there is tremendous variety among babies with Down syndrome; not every baby possesses all of the characteristic features. To dispel one common myth: no connection has been shown between the number of Down syndrome features a baby has and that baby's mental ability.

The following list of characteristics are those most commonly associated with Down syndrome.

Low Muscle Tone

Babies with Down syndrome have low muscle tone. This means that their muscles appear relaxed and feel "floppy." Low tone affects all the muscles of the body. It is a significant physical feature that alerts doctors to look for other signs of Down syndrome. More importantly, low muscle tone affects the baby's movement, strength, and development. Most of the physical features linked to Down syndrome do not affect a baby's ability to grow and learn, but low muscle tone can complicate all areas of development. Accordingly, great importance is placed on good physical therapy to help children with low muscle tone develop properly. Physical therapy will be discussed thoroughly in later chapters.

Facial Features

Your baby's face may have some features characteristic of Down syndrome:

Nose. The nasal bridge is flatter than usual and the nose is smaller, giving the baby's face a flat appearance. The nasal passages may be smaller as well, and can become congested more quickly.

Eyes. The eyes appear to slant upward, giving a slightly oriental look. Your doctor may call these "slanting palpebral fissures." The eyes also have small folds of skin, called "epicanthal folds," at the inner corners. The outer part of the iris of each eye may have light spots called "Brushfield Spots." These spots do not affect the baby's sight and are not readily noticeable. It is very important to have your baby's eyesight checked, however, because vision problems tend to be more common in children with Down syndrome than in other children. This will be discussed in more detail in Chapter 3.

Mouth. The mouth may be small, and the roof of the mouth may be shallow. When these features are accompanied by low muscle tone, the tongue may protrude or appear large in relation to the mouth.

Teeth. The teeth may come in late and in an unusual order. Babies usually get their teeth in the same sequence, but the teeth of babies with Down syndrome seem to have a sequence all their own. The teeth may also be small or unusually shaped.

Ears. The ears can be small and the tops may fold over. Occasionally they may be set slightly lower on the head. The ear passages tend also to be smaller, which can make it very difficult for your pediatrician to check your baby's ears for fluid. Because they are smaller, the ear passages can become blocked, causing a hearing loss. For this reason it is important to include early audiological exams in your infant's check-up schedule.

Head Shape

Although babies with Down syndrome have smaller than normal heads, usually the difference is not noticeable. Studies have shown that the head, while smaller than average, is still within a normal range relative to the rest of the body (Pueschel, 1984). The back of the head may be flatter. Also, the neck may appear shorter, and in newborns there may be loose folds of skin on the back of the neck, but these folds tend to disappear as the child grows. The soft spots of the head (fontanels), which are present in all babies, may be larger in babies with Down syndrome and so may take longer to close in the normal course of development.

Hands and Feet

Hands may be smaller, with fingers that are shorter than normal. The palm of each hand may have only one crease across it (a transverse palmar crease), and the fifth finger may tend to curve inward with only one crease. In most ways, the feet of babies with Down syndrome appear normal, but there may be a gap between the first and second toes. Frequently there is a deep crease on the sole of the feet in this gap.

Most newborns with Down syndrome do not exhibit all of the physical features described here. In general, the most common features are the low muscle tone, the upwardly slanting eyes, and the small ears. With the sole exception of low muscle tone, these features will not hinder either the health or the proper functioning of your baby. There are, however, some medical conditions associated with Down syndrome that do affect your baby's health. These will be discussed in detail in Chapter 3.

Because babies with Down syndrome all have the extra chromosome, they often may have features that resemble other babies with Down syndrome. However, because these babies also have twenty-two sets of completely normal chromosomes, they will also resemble their parents, brothers, and sisters, and will possess their own unique physical characteristics.

What About My Baby's Intelligence?

Babies with Down syndrome are mentally retarded. The degree

of retardation, however, varies tremendously. Your baby *will* learn; and what he learns, he will not "lose." You need not expect any regression or loss of skills over time. Most importantly, remember that both the intellectual and the social skills of babies raised at home are far superior to those of infants raised in institutions.

The human brain controls almost all of our bodies' functions. Muscle coordination, the five senses, intelligence, and behavior are all controlled by the brain. Differences in chromosomes presumably cause differences in brain function, and these differences cause what we refer to as mental retardation.

Intelligence has been measured for many years by standardized tests. Scores are computed into a measurement called an "intelligence quotient" or "IQ." This gauges a child's ability to reason, conceptualize, and think. Parents should remember that low IQ scores do not preclude a child's ability to take care of himself, perform useful tasks, and learn. One of the myths that has plagued children with Down syndrome is that because of their relatively low IQ scores they cannot learn. This is simply not true.

Among the general population, there is a wide range of intelligence. Studies find that ninety-five percent of the population have what is called "normal" intelligence, with IQs in the range of 70 to 130. Two and one-half percent of the population have what is called superior intelligence, with IQs over 130. And, two and one-half percent have intelligence below the normal level, with IQs of less than 70. Individuals who score below the normal range are considered to have mental retardation. Those who are mentally retarded range in measured intelligence from mild (55 to 70) to moderate (40 to 55) to severe retardation (25 to 40). Figure 7 shows the full range of human intelligence on a bell curve, and shows where most children with Down syndrome score relative to the rest of the population–generally within the moderate to mild range of retardation. Some children are more severely retarded; some possess intelligence in the normal or near-normal range.

Scientists do not yet understand how the extra chromosome affects mental ability. Research indicates that the excess chromosomal material in the number-21 chromosomes prevents normal brain development. Both the size and structural complexity of the brain are diminished in babies with Down syndrome. But just how (or if) re-

Figure 7. Range of Human Intelligence

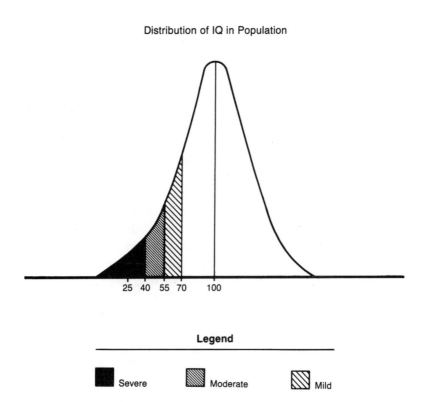

Distribution of IQ in Population

25 40 55 70   100

Legend

Severe   Moderate   Mild

duced brain size and complexity affect mental functioning remains unknown.

Mental retardation has been misunderstood for centuries. As a result, society has consistently underestimated the intellectual potential of children with Down syndrome. Today, however, with early infant intervention, better education, and higher expectations, mental achievement for children with Down syndrome is on the rise. Parents should be cautioned about old studies and statistics about the mental ability of children with Down syndrome (usually gathered from people in institutions), for these studies tend to indicate lower intelligence than the more current studies show.

Children with Down syndrome have long suffered from low expectations and self-fulfilling negative prophecies. In the past, lower IQs condemned these children to institutions where, segregated from society, isolated, given little education, and quite often ignored, they could not surpass the low expectations held for them. Too often, low expectations yielded low performance. We know today that this negative cycle is both unfortunate *and* avoidable. With early infant intervention, advanced medical care, better special education, and greater social acceptance, children with Down syndrome are functioning at increasingly higher levels. Not only are IQ scores on the rise, but new skills are learned and fuller lives are realized.

How will mental retardation affect your child? Although its effects are different in each child, mental retardation will generally slow development. Your child will learn new skills more slowly than other children. He will also find learning advanced skills harder. Skills requiring fast judgment, intricate coordination, and detailed analysis will be more difficult for him. This does not mean he can never develop advanced skills; but it will be harder and will take more time for him to learn these skills.

Children with Down syndrome *can* learn. Parents often want to know precisely what skills their children will master. Will he be able to read? Will he learn to write? Will he be able to attend a "normal" school? None of these questions can be answered unequivocally for any child. Many learn to read and write. Many are being "mainstreamed" in school. Remember that "normal" children also have a wide range of abilities, just as children with Down syndrome do.

There is much more to good development than reading and writing, and babies with Down syndrome do quite well with help. Although they may not excel in academic subjects or in complex reasoning, they can experience learning, achievement, and pride.

What About My Child's Future?

Generally speaking, children with Down syndrome can grow up to function semi-independently. With the trend toward community group homes that foster independence and self-reliance, fewer and fewer people with Down syndrome are remaining at home. They take care of themselves, hold jobs, and enjoy family and friends. Achieving independence and self-reliance, however, takes a lot of effort. The essential foundation that will enable children with Down syndrome to grow into capable individuals is laid through hard work in the first years of life.

As children with Down syndrome grow up, parents often worry about their child's reproductive capacity. The concerns are different for male and female children. Men with Down syndrome cannot produce children, due either to a low sperm count or some other as-yet-undiscovered cause. They do, however, mature sexually. Women with Down syndrome are fertile, but their eggs are likely to possess the extra number-21 chromosome. Consequently, they run a very high risk of giving birth to a baby with Down syndrome. Sex education and proper birth control methods are important subjects for you to discuss with your child as he grows.

Future Babies

Parents often wonder if their chances of having another baby with Down syndrome are higher after giving birth to a child with Down syndrome. The answer depends both on the type of Down syndrome their child has and on their particular family history.

In general, the risk of having another baby with Down syndrome is one in one hundred (Thompson and Thompson, 1986), regardless of the mother's age, unless the woman is already over forty. This represents a large increase in risk for mothers under thirty. As we saw in Figure 6, the risk in the general population does not approach one in one hundred until approximately the age of forty. After forty, the probability increases markedly. These figures apply to families with a child with Nondisjunction Trisomy 21, or roughly ninety-five percent of all families with a child with Down syndrome.

For most types of Translocation Down syndrome, however, the risk of recurrence is higher, and depends on the type of translocation and the sex of the carrier parent. If the mother is the carrier, the risk is about one in ten; if the father is the carrier, the risk is about one in twenty. To find out what type of Down syndrome your baby has, ask your geneticist. He or she can tell from looking at your baby's karyotype and will counsel you accordingly. Parents can also have their chromosomes tested.

Families having a higher risk of giving birth to a baby with Down syndrome can monitor future pregnancies. Today there are sophisticated techniques to test the fetal chromosomes during pregnancy. In the sixteenth to eighteenth week of pregnancy women can undergo amniocentesis. During this procedure a needle is inserted into the uterus through the mother's abdomen. Doctors use ultrasound to continually monitor the location of the needle. A small amount of amniotic fluid is drawn out and analyzed. Because the amniotic fluid contains some cells from the fetus, doctors are able to thoroughly examine the chromosomes of the baby.

A newer and more experimental method is called chorionic villus sampling, or CVS. In this procedure a narrow tube is inserted into the uterus through the vagina and cervix. Tiny pieces of the chorion—which develops into the placenta—are harvested. Doctors use ultrasound throughout this procedure as well to guide their work and to protect the embryo. The chorionic material is then tested for chromosome structure. What makes CVS very different from amniocentesis is that it can be performed from the ninth to the eleventh week of pregnancy, and the results are generally available within two to four days of the test. With amniocentesis, there is often a two to four week wait for the results.

Some risks are associated with each technique, and parents should investigate all aspects of the procedure they are contemplating. One of the risks resulting from amniocentesis is miscarriage, but the risk is very low—only about one in eight hundred. Doctors believe that the risk for miscarriage due to CVS may be somewhat higher—about two to four in one hundred—but more studies must be performed to verify this figure.

Other experimental methods are being tested for detecting Down syndrome in pregnancy. Studies are underway to determine whether blood samples from the mother can be analyzed to reveal Down syndrome. For example, researchers are testing whether a special protein, alpha-feto protein (AFP), commonly used to detect spina bifida, can also indicate the presence of Down syndrome. Statistics show that if a baby was born with Down syndrome, more often than not the mother's AFP level was low. This test is presently used only to indicate a need for further testing. Researchers are continually studying these and other leads in the prenatal detection of Down syndrome.

While these tests may permit parents to learn the chromosomal make-up of their future babies, that pre-knowledge can create a dilemma. If the test comes back showing Down syndrome, a painful decision may be forced on the parents. Of course, intimate personal decisions are involved, and this book does not presume to recommend what to do about future pregnancies.

The History of Down Syndrome

Well before the genetic link to Down syndrome was discovered, John Langdon Down described it in 1866 as a distinct set of characteristics. He distinguished Down syndrome from other conditions by noting some of the common features associated with it, such as straight, thin hair, a small nose, and a broad face. Down is also responsible for naming the condition "mongolism." Through the years, terms like "mongoloid idiot" have been used. These and other derogatory labels are no longer commonly used today, though people still need to be reminded that Down syndrome does not refer to someone who is unhappy or inferior. It seems that too few people realize that Down syndrome is named for the man credited with first describing it.

In this century, advances in genetic research led scientists to begin to understand the cause of Down syndrome. By the early 1930s, some researchers began to suspect that Down syndrome might be caused by a chromosomal abnormality. In 1959, Jerome Lejune, a French cytogeneticist, discovered that cells grown from individuals with Down syndrome had an extra chromosome. Later, the exact location of the extra chromosome was found to be at the number-21 chromosome. These findings led to the discovery of the other forms of Down syndrome, including Translocation and Mosaicism.

The treatment of people with Down syndrome has also advanced remarkably over the decades. Life spans have increased dramatically with advanced medical care, and the education and care of people with Down syndrome have also improved markedly. For years children with Down syndrome were thought to have no potential to learn. Denied the opportunity to learn, they seemed to substantiate society's mistakenly low estimation of their abilities. Thankfully, today's world is very different for children with Down syndrome.

Recent Progress in Down Syndrome

Doctors, scientists, and researchers continue to explore the

causes, effects, and treatment of Down syndrome. With technological advances in the field of modern genetics, scientists are isolating some individual genes and studying their specific functions. Researchers are also probing to discover just how the extra chromosome causes the characteristics of Down syndrome. Scientists have already identified over ten of the thousand genes on the twenty-first chromosome. Their goal is to pinpoint the gene or genes that cause Down syndrome so that they may then "decode" its biochemical process.

Over time, much will be learned about Down syndrome. Some doctors are working on ways to alter the appearance of children with Down syndrome to reduce some of the features associated with it, such as the slanting eyes and protruding tongue, in order to lessen the stigma that has often accompanied the condition. If this interests you, consult your child's pediatrician or geneticist. Generally speaking, plastic surgery is not performed on infants or very young children. Your specialists can keep you informed of the most current treatments in this area.

Parents need to be wary, however. Often parents and doctors hear of "cures" for Down syndrome. People have claimed that megavitamins (huge doses of vitamins), enzymes, amino acids, and experimental drugs can reduce the degree of mental retardation. *None* of the claims has yet proved true. Some experimental treatments can even be dangerous to your child.

It is possible that some of the ongoing research in these areas may yield solid results in the future, but so far no treatment or cure has been found. Although there is room for experimental, creative treatments designed to help children with Down syndrome reach their potential, false claims and empty promises only serve to hurt families.

Conclusion

I recommend that parents learn as much as they can about Down syndrome. Many books about Down syndrome, mental retardation, and exceptional children are available. But be careful: *avoid books that are outdated*. The Reading List at the end of this book contains a list of useful current sources.

Down syndrome has its own language and its own dictionary. Understanding the terms used in connection with your child's care and development is important for good communication with doctors, teachers, and other professionals. The glossary at the end of this book will help. You will be surprised by how fast you will become an "expert" in Down syndrome and by how much a good understanding of Down syndrome will help you and your child.

REFERENCES

Anneren, G. "Metabolic and Endocrinologic Abnormalities in Down's Syndrome, With Reference to the Growth Retardation and Presenile Dementia." *Down's Syndrome Papers and Abstracts for Professionals.* Vol. 8, no. 1, January 1985.

Committee on Sports Medicine. "Atlantoaxial Instability in Down Syndrome." *Pediatrics.* Vol. 74, no. 1, July 1984, 152–53.

Diamond, L. S., Lynne, D. & Sigman, B. "Orthopedic Disorders in Patients with Down's Syndrome." *Orthopedic Clinics of North America.* Vol. 12, no. 1, January 1981, 57–71.

Knox, E. G., ten Bensel, R. W. "Gastrointestinal Malformations in Down's Syndrome." *Minnesota Medicine.* June 1972, 542–44.

Mearig, J. "Facial Surgery and an Active Modification Approach for Children With Down Syndrome: Some Psychological and Ethical Issues." *Down's Syndrome Papers and Abstracts for Professionals.* Vol. 9, no. 2, April 1986.

Mikkelsen, M. "Parental Origin of the Extra Chromosome in Down Syndrome." *Down's Syndrome Papers and Abstracts for Professionals.* Vol. 7, no. 3, July 1984.

Nora, J. J., Fraser, F. C. *Medical Genetics, Principles and Practice,* 2d ed. Philadelphia: Lea and Febiger. 1981, 37–47.

Pueschel, S. M. "The Child With Down Syndrome." in Levine, Carey, Crocker & Gross, *Developmental Behavioral Pediatrics.* Philadelphia: W. B. Saunders Co. 1983, 353–62.

Pueschel, S. M., ed. *Down Syndrome: Growing and Learning.* Kansas City: Andrews and McMeel, Inc. 1978.

Pueschel, S. M. *The Young Child With Down Syndrome.* New York: Human Sciences Press, Inc. 1984.

Rogers, P. "A Program of Preventive Medicine for Down's Syndrome Individuals of all Ages." *Down's Syndrome Papers and Abstracts for Professionals.* Vol. 8, no. 2, April 1985.

Smith, D. W. *Recognizable Patterns of Human Malformation,* 3d ed. Philadelphia: W. B. Saunders Co. 1982.

Spicer, R. L. "Cardiovascular Disease in Down Syndrome." *Pediatrics Clinic of North America.* Vol. 31, no. 6, December 1984, 1331–43.

Thompson, M. & Thompson, J. *Genetics in Medicine,* 4th ed. Philadelphia: W. B. Saunders Co. 1986.

Parent Statements

I remember my image of Down syndrome before Michael was born – the Psych. 101 films of insane asylums and state institutions, bleak, black-and-white films. The reality is radically different.

I'd never known a child with Down syndrome. I had worked a little with adults with Down syndrome, and it was horrible. They were very poorly functioning individuals. No speech, minimal comprehension of receptive speech or language, just very low functioning. But those people were institutionalized since birth. Whereas my husband knew a family who raised their daughter with Down syndrome at home and he has followed her progress for many years. She is now about fourteen and does very well. Also, we had good information. We had a geneticist who knew what could happen, that a child could function very well or very poorly, and explained the need for early intervention right from the beginning. I think we need more health professionals who are educated to push parents in this direction.

We were real surprised to find out how common Down syndrome is. We thought it was just women over forty who gave birth to babies with Down syndrome.

When Josh was born, we were surprised at how common Down syndrome was. And not only Down syndrome, but mental retardation in general. We wanted to pick up a lot of information. Of course the biggest question is the one they can't answer: "What's causing this? How does Down syndrome make him the way he is?"

We had even talked about adopting a child with Down syndrome. That was probably a year and a half before Julie was born. I think we thought about it so hard we split a chromosome.

My image of what Down syndrome was before our son was born was not very clear. I don't think I knew the connection between the word "mongoloid" and "Down syndrome." I remember there was a boy with Down syndrome who lived in our neighborhood before Christopher was born, and he perplexed me because he seemed able to get about by himself, but he looked retarded at the same time.

I had a fear of having a child with a disability, and when our child was born with Down syndrome, I was scared. Mental retardation or mental problems were very foreign and strange to me.

I knew the incidence of Down syndrome was about one in six hundred. That meant it wouldn't happen to me – right? Now I tend to think that things *will* go wrong. I mean, when someone says to me, one in six hundred, it's like saying, "Well, there's a great possibility that it will happen."

If I had any impression about Down syndrome when he was born, it was that he'd just be a blob and he would never walk or talk and he'd just be a total vegetable. But then I found out that's not true, and it isn't true. He has a very definite personality.

I haven't really worked with kids with Down syndrome but I've seen lots of them. I was working in special ed centers but with older children. None of the kids I worked with had Down syndrome. But I just loved the kids with Down syndrome. I liked being with them and I liked their vivaciousness and just lots of things about them.

After Chris was born, we wanted to learn. All we had to go on was half of a column of a page about Down syndrome in a medical book. The book said that these children are quite sociable and if possible, parents should try and bring them up at home – they make wonderful pets. You know, it didn't say that, but could have. We were really thirsting for knowledge.

I know a lot of women who are well into their thirties. One of them was pregnant and close to forty. She was having her first baby, and was having amniocentesis. She came and asked me for counsel, and flat out said she would probably abort if she found out the baby had Down syndrome. I don't like to get into the abortion issue, but I was just real candid on the fact that Julie is the joy of our lives. She's brought such an added dimension to our lives. In a lot of ways she's difficult, but it's a different type of workload. But boy, she's not a liability; she's a definite asset.

It was a struggle to get good information. We were lucky because I was in the special ed business. I had friends who had friends who immediately could refer me to parents or doctors or books. I think that a lot of parents have to seek those out and don't know where to go to get them.

I can't imagine putting a child in an institution. When I look at my little boy and see how he takes my existence so absolutely for granted, it's impossible to imagine my not being there for him. It's not so much that he's mine, but that I'm his. He has no concept of belonging to me less than his sister just because he has Down syndrome.

I keep putting Julie into a historical perspective of generations who were sent off to institutions or who were kept in the closet. They were lumps on logs—you kept them clean and that was about it. And now, we're moving into an era where the whole generation is being mainstreamed. We're bringing them out in public and loving them. Even if we stopped doing anything special for Julie, just the fact that she's in a family where she's accepted, she's light years ahead.

You learn day by day. I imagine we'll always be learning. There's something new around every corner about her and about how society reacts to her. It's a constant learning process. And you have to educate doctors, friends, and neighbors. We're still kind of new in this neighborhood. A lot of the neighbors are real interested, and that's nice, but it's a constant education process.

TWO

◈━━◈

Adjusting to Your New Baby

MARILYN TRAINER*

Getting the News

It is painful beyond belief to be told that your precious new baby has Down syndrome. Instead of that special sense of joy, all those months of waiting end with your world turned upside down. During those months you didn't care whether it would be a girl or a boy—you just wanted a healthy baby. But the baby you were expecting never arrived.

Your baby has Down syndrome. And you have another kind of syndrome: "Why us?" It is a syndrome that strikes virtually every family who has had a retarded child. It's almost as if a stark, impenetrable wall has dropped from somewhere and with a terrible force cut off the future, not only for the small new baby, whom none of you yet really know, but for all of you in ways you cannot explain, but instinctively know are there.

You are in shock. In a minute or so after you first hear the term "Down syndrome" a strange, almost warm feeling envelops you. You

---

*Marilyn Trainer is the parent of a nineteen year old with Down syndrome. She has been active for many years with the Association for Retarded Citizens and Parents of Down Syndrome Children. Her writing has appeared in the *Washington Post* and in other publications.

27

are sitting inside a bubble; you can hear voices, and you can respond to them. But somebody else is sitting in that queer bubble. The real you is outside, far above, watching and listening. You feel calm, except that you're trembling from head to toe. If you could just stay there above the bubble, if you could just stay there safe and untouched–but of course you can't. And so reality begins.

This chapter addresses what the reality of having a baby with Down syndrome feels like and what you can do about those feelings. No one should tell you how to feel right now: there is no preprogrammed response to being told your baby has Down syndrome. Soon you will begin to notice all the little things that are just like any other baby–soft warm skin, tiny fingers and toes, cries for Mom or Dad–and your need to care for your baby will take over.

Your Emotions

All kinds of emotions well up at once: anger, despair, guilt, shame, rejection–yes, rejection of the baby–and perhaps most of all, a terrible fear of the future. You wonder how you are going to cope with this overwhelming burden for the rest of your lives?

Will life ever be even remotely light and carefree again? Will there always be a feeling of never-ending responsibility with no light at the end of the tunnel? Will there ever be laughter again or has the funny side of life been lost forever along with happiness? Many parents in the days following the birth of a handicapped child are plagued by these and other fears.

Grief

Often the first reaction to the news that your baby has Down syndrome is intense grief and sorrow. You may grieve the loss of that ideal baby you dreamed of or the loss of your family's normalcy. You may not even know exactly why you are grieving. What you do know, however, is that sorrow sits on your chest like a ton of bricks. This sense of grief is, for parents who have received such shocking news, completely normal. And as with most parents, your grief will pass eventually.

It's easy to let your grief rob you of the joyful feelings you can experience at your baby's birth. You went through all those months of pregnancy; you delivered your baby. You *have* achieved the miracle of life–your baby, alive, loving, and entirely trusting in you. Your love for your baby will grow spontaneously and will conquer the grief.

Ego

Ego can be the biggest obstacle to accepting your child. Its interference is perfectly normal, and, as with other negative feelings, will diminish over time.

There is no denying that for many parents the birth of a handicapped child is a tremendous blow to self-esteem. How could *we* produce a child with screwed-up chromosomes, they ask? *Other* people have handicapped children, we don't. It is simply not in *our* life plan. Along life's way it may be that some of our own goals will not be met, but one thing is for sure: Our children will be bright and beautiful and excel in all they do. When our children make it, we make it too.

Give your baby a chance. Your love will grow naturally and you will realize that your baby has great potential. Children with Down syndrome work so hard to achieve. Rather than a blow to your ego, you will feel tremendous pride at what your child accomplishes.

Resentment and Depression

Parents usually experience other painful emotions that they would consider less than noble. Jealousy, resentment, depression, and rejection are all common emotions to people who receive shocking news. You may resent parents with "normal" babies, begrudging them the joy you know they feel. You even resent that they appear to take their baby's normalcy so much for granted. It can be especially difficult when others seem to treat the birth of your own baby as a death. Instead of flowers sent to your room in the hospital, you get silence or sympathy–no congratulatory cards or baby presents.

You wish you could feel joy over the birth of your baby but the pain is too strong. You may even wish your baby would die–that you could wake up freed from this nightmare. These feelings may strike you as contemptible. They are not; rather, they are your mind's way of coping with a situation you cannot fully grasp or control. Time and love will heal your wounds.

How to Adjust

Address Your Emotions

It is deceptively easy to ignore the emotions brought about by the birth of your baby. You are bringing a baby home feeling more than the usual newborn baby stress. The house is a mess, work responsibilities have fallen by the way, your other children need attention: there is always too much to do. Don't let the press of work prevent you from sifting your thoughts and emotions. Time spent on yourself now is essential.

Take Time to Adjust

You know best what you need to do first. Some people need to organize their lives. Others deal with their problems by jumping in head first. Still others need to be alone and withdrawn. Above all, take the time you need to adjust and recover. Don't make irreversible decisions immediately. You can't solve all the problems for your baby's life or your life right away.

Don't Feel Personally Responsible

Do you torture yourself in the belief that you have somehow "given" your child Down syndrome? We have all heard of babies who are born with problems because of things mothers did or did not do during pregnancy. We've all read how drugs, poor nutrition, or lack of prenatal care can affect a baby. Self-indulgence, ignorance, or plain stupidity can take a terrible toll. But the chromosomal abnormality of Down syndrome is not caused by any of these. You are not personally responsible for your baby's extra chromosome any more than you are responsible for the last raindrops to fall in your neighborhood.

Underneath the feeling of personal responsibility is that old feeling of guilt that you are somehow at fault for producing a damaged baby. And below that are feelings of guilt for rejecting this baby while longing for the baby that never was. It hurts even more when we see or hear of a mother who didn't do everything "right" during her pregnancy. Maybe she smoked, drank too much coffee or too many glasses of wine, or worse. Her baby turned out perfectly fine anyway. Your baby should have been born as fully endowed as any other baby. But fate or nature—call it what you will—cheated her, and in doing so cheated you too.

Quirks of fate or nature happen every day—often in worse ways than conceiving a baby with Down syndrome. You are no more responsible for your baby's Down syndrome than other parents are for their child's leukemia. So relinquish that guilt and put your energies where they are needed: in getting your strength back and helping your baby to reach her full potential.

Allow Yourself to Grieve

Right now all you may want to do is cry. Spill all the tears you want; you have the right. Rant and rave if that is your way; you have the right to that too. Or go somewhere to lick your wounds alone.

Whatever you do, there is something you should keep in mind: Hardly a parent of a child with Down syndrome has not experienced these very emotions with wrenching anguish. And although you may find it impossible to believe right now, almost every one of those parents will tell you that despite the initial heartache they would choose to have their child again a thousand times over. It's almost a sure bet that in not too many months you will be saying the same thing.

Sometimes old truths do well by us: Let some time pass. You *will* laugh again; your baby will see to that.

What You Should Do

Get to Know Your Baby

This might sound utterly banal considering what you are experiencing now, but ask yourself whether you are thinking more about the baby or more about the baby's condition. When you look at your baby do you see your child or do you see Down syndrome? Take your cue from a youngster with Down syndrome who when told he was "a living doll" replied indignantly, "I'm not a doll—I'm a person!" He's right; that baby of yours is a person and as you come to *know* that little person you will feel less grief. As you take on the pivotal role of helping your baby to develop, wounded pride and bruised ego become irrelevant. As a matter of fact, expanded horizons often bring a mature kind of pride: pride in what your baby is achieving and pride that *you* are in large part responsible.

Tell Your Friends and Family

There is no doubt that one of your most difficult tasks is to break the news about the baby to friends and relatives, particularly grandparents. Unfortunately, there are still those who are steeped in ignorance and prejudice. They may have grown up at a time when mental retardation was considered in the most negative way. They feel hurt just as you do, but may cast about for someone to blame, saying, "There's never been anything like this in the family before."

Sometimes grandparents can be particularly trying. For example, it's not unheard of for grandparents to pressure parents to place the child in an institution. When this doesn't work, they may ignore the child as much as possible, never mentioning the baby to friends, much less bragging about the baby as only grandparents can. This attitude can be devastating to parents who are in a very vulnerable state themselves and are struggling to cope and to accept their child.

Give grandparents, aunts, uncles, brothers, sisters, and friends time to overcome their shock. Just as you needed some time to process the unexpected information, they need time to adjust as well. Their first reaction may not be their last.

Happily, people with negative attitudes about Down syndrome are in the minority. You must catch your breath, get your facts straight, and explain the situation in due time as forthrightly as possible. Give these people a book or pamphlet to read that presents an accurate picture of Down syndrome. They may know absolutely nothing about Down syndrome and may suffer from a distorted picture. Moreover, people will take their cue from you and most will become sincerely interested and involved with you and your baby. A good number of advocates for children with Down syndrome are friends and relatives who have no handicapped children of their own.

Some people may never "come around"; they may always suffer from old myths and stereotypes, excess pity, or other emotions. These people cannot matter—you have more important things to do, more important people to care for. Seek out people who will help *you* cope.

Contact Other Parents

One of the very best sources of support is other parents of children with Down syndrome. Down syndrome parent groups are forming in all parts of the country and throughout the world. Parents in the same boat can be tremendously helpful. Seek out an acquaintance, a small group, or an organization when you feel ready.

There are many ways to make contact. Try calling your local Association for Retarded Citizens (ARC), your local chapter of the March of Dimes, or your school system. Ask to speak with a staff member who works with parents of handicapped children. These and other groups who can help are noted in the Resource Guide at the end of this book.

If you feel put off by the idea of suddenly becoming involved with an organization, be assured that parent-to-parent groups are usually small and informal, and no one is going to try to "recruit you." Tell them you need someone to talk to who can give you some basic information. Your greatest support will almost always come from other parents. No one is going to understand you better. It's just a phone call; you have nothing to lose, and potentially a great deal to gain. Aside from support and valuable information, many parents develop lifelong friendships with other parents because their children happen to have an extra chromosome in common.

Round Up Your Professionals

Get as much help for your baby as you can. When you have a baby without special needs, you're on your own. But when your baby does have special needs, you will be surprised at the number of experts out there who can help you. In fact, some parents, after benefitting from the phalanx of professionals lined up to help their baby, expressed the wish that they could have used a little of this help for their "normal" children.

Throughout the book we describe the different kinds of people who can help your baby, along with what they do. They include educators, therapists, and a wide variety of doctors. There are pediatricians, cardiologists, internists, geneticists, ear, nose and throat specialists, and ophthalmologists. Each plays a key role in screening your baby for possible problems and in helping ensure that your child stays healthy.

You may find it helpful to use one doctor to coordinate the medical services your child might need. A pediatric geneticist who specializes in Down syndrome and other chromosomal conditions can be very helpful as a coordinator and information source. Ask your pediatrician, hospital, or obstetrician to refer you and your child.

Be prepared in case a doctor expresses outdated, negative and inaccurate information. Unbelievably enough, there are a few who still recommend institutionalization or inaction. If your doctor suggests this, change doctors. Parents are sometimes frustrated in trying to find a doctor who cares, but good doctors are out there. The search is worth the effort. Shop around, be selective, and get what is best for your child.

Keep Your Baby Home

Experienced parents will give new parents one essential message: *keep your baby home!* Resist any pressure to do otherwise no matter who is doing the pressuring. Even if you are inclined to send your baby away, *don't do it!* There is absolutely no reason not to raise your child at home. Very few people with Down syndrome are severely retarded; most are considered to be moderately or even mildly retarded. *Any* baby's intelligence, even a "normal" baby's, will be lowered if that child is raised in an institution. What parents would want to limit their child's potential?

You are in the best position to raise your child, to help her grow, to protect her rights. There are people out there to help you. Don't throw away the chance for a very fulfilling family experience, not to mention a lot of love.

Get the Facts

Ignorance is your worst enemy. Don't let outdated assumptions about what the future holds for children with Down syndrome get the better of you. The prognosis for your child is much more positive than it would have been just ten to twenty years ago. In part this is due to advances in medical care, but it's also because the people who work with these kids know a great deal more about achieving the best possible developmental path for your child. One of the first priorities is to get some of this information. Read books, consult professionals, and talk to parents.

But be careful what you read. Although information about Down syndrome has improved within the past ten years, there is still much antiquated material on library shelves. Some of this old information is enough to scare the wits out of new parents. Instead of the public library, check with your ARC or one of the Down syndrome organizations to find out about reading matter. And don't forget these groups are very good about mailing brochures, packets, and information to people in isolated areas. Sometimes a small fee is required, but it is well worth the cost.

Teach Your Baby

The importance of early intervention cannot be stressed enough. Neither can the fact that you can motivate your child better than anyone. Early intervention means parents and professionals helping a child grow to reach that child's greatest potential. The normal developmental sequence of children is used as a guide. Early intervention requires professional help, but much of it can be done right at home. Chapters 6 and 7 will address some of the fundamentals of development and how important early intervention is for your baby. It's not just a matter of encouraging your baby to keep trying new and "harder" things, but to do them right. At home, and with help, you can truly enhance your baby's potential.

The goal is to devise ways to increase your baby's learning abilities every chance you get. There are opportunities everywhere in your baby's daily life, if you think about it. For example, a cat or a dog can be a great incentive for a child to move, or just to actively observe. Think about the family who gives tender, loving care to their ancient diabetic cat because years ago as a frisky kitten she enticed a baby to follow her—to roll, to hitch, to crawl, and to walk. (Today guess who most often feeds her and holds her and loves her?)

Your brand new baby obviously is not going to be chasing the family cat. But a new baby can do exercises and be introduced to playing games. Just remember that early intervention is crucial in the development of a child with Down syndrome and it should begin immediately. But don't get nervous; use your common sense and try to have fun with it.

Don't Despair

Above all, the experienced parent will want to tell you, "Do not despair." Don't even think of those things your child might not be able to do. At this point there is almost nothing you can rule out of your baby's future repertoire. Focus on what your child can and will do *now*—all the better to help her seemingly small achievements build toward future milestones.

It is important to keep your perspective and sense of humor. Minimize stress by having fun when you can. Get yourself a baby sitter—a close friend might really enjoy the opportunity—and go out to dinner, a movie, whatever—regularly. A baby is a baby after all, and there's no reason yours won't be just fine with a reliable sitter.

What about My Family?

Many parents ask whether a baby with Down syndrome will affect their other children. Chapter 5 addresses that question in detail, but a quick and easy answer is a resounding yes. Siblings of babies with Down syndrome will most certainly be affected.

One mother recalls the day she and her husband brought their baby home from the hospital. With sadness and great apprehension in her heart she wondered what this was going to mean to the lives of their three older children, a boy of ten and two girls, eight and four. The baby was placed in his bassinet in the parents' bedroom as the children gathered around to see their new baby brother. The baby needed changing so the mother removed the wet diaper. Before she could put on the fresh one, the baby urinated in a beautiful streaming arc that hit the wall and trickled down. The children's eyes widened in undisguised admiration. "Wow! Look what he can do!"

Overcome by a tremendous sense of relief, the mother didn't know whether to laugh or cry. It didn't matter in the least to those children that their baby brother had Down syndrome. In their eyes he had performed a fantastic feat and was a wonder of a baby. They loved him, and that was that.

Many years have passed since that significant day, but no member of the family has ever forgotten it. Today that baby is a capable, high-functioning teenager, thanks in large part to his brother and sisters who with each goal he achieved said, "Wow! Look what he can do."

Certainly the lives of your other children will be changed now and in the future because their sibling has Down syndrome. No one in life is immune to change, but children adjust to it surprisingly well. It becomes a natural part of their world. There may be times when they are annoyed, bothered, or even ashamed of their sibling with Down syndrome, but with good communication, understanding, and a lifetime of shared experiences, the deepest bonds will form.

Your Work Will Pay Off

Kids with Down syndrome can do just about anything any other child can do. It might take them a little longer, but they can do it. They can learn to read, and some parents report a positive genius in their children for reading logos and road signs that will take them to McDonald's or Burger King. And they have a persistence that, with some delay, can enable them to learn to write.

They play the piano, swim, ride horses, play basketball, baseball, and soccer, take ballet lessons, you name it. They do chores around the house, catch the school bus on their own, help the neighbor carry groceries, feed the family pet. And someday they will grow up, hold jobs, and be contributing members of society.

These things *will* happen. Your hard work with your baby and child will be rewarded. Just remember that your baby is first and foremost a child. With your courage, encouragement, and—most of all—your love, that child is going to blossom.

While your child is growing and learning, so are you. If you gain nothing else, you will at least develop a point of view that might be somewhat different from one you've held before. To some it will seem slightly askew; but it is nothing more than rejoicing at life's small victories.

For example, one particular family had worked so diligently to expand their little girl's vocabulary. One Sunday morning as various family members were sitting around reading the paper the two year old lost her temper and, clearly enough to please Professor Higgins, shouted, "Damn it! Damn it! Damn it!" Mother, father, brother, and sister jumped up and down for joy! Only hours later did they remember that perhaps instead of jumping they should have been saying "No-no!" But on further reflection they decided it was better to hear her say a nice clear "Damn it!" than to not hear her say anything at all.

The Future

As time passes, you will begin to look at the birth of your baby very differently. Far from the grief and despair you felt at her birth, you will feel joy and pride. You will come to see the precious little baby you originally dreamed of, and Down syndrome will take on a different—and proper—perspective.

Many parents will tell you that if you are going to have a retarded child, be glad it's Down syndrome. Compared to many other types of disabilities, Down syndrome seems almost minimal. Remember, children with Down syndrome are much more *like* other children than *unlike* them.

It is important to note that the dictionary definition of the verb "retard" is "to cause to move more slowly." Retardation does *not* mean "unintelligent." People who still link retardation with "unintelligent" are often at a loss when they meet children with Down syndrome and find they do not fit their preconceived notions. Children with Down syndrome may have some limitations, but within those limitations they are bright, inquisitive, and often surprisingly erudite.

This was not always thought to be so. Perhaps no other group of mentally retarded persons has been so stigmatized. It may be that because of similar physical characteristics, it has been easy to lump them together and put a label on them. They were automatically consigned to the bottom of the barrel. More often than not, the diagnosis of Down syndrome was a passport to an institution or a back room. Sadly, these children then lived up to the dreadful images remembered from old biology books or exposés of institutional life; they became victims of a self-fulfilling prophecy.

Today there is a new generation of children with Down syndrome who are leading very different lives. This is a generation of potential. Old stereotypes are being laid to rest. Your baby is of this new generation.

Consider the youngster who while waiting to get his hair cut in an Italian barbershop, suddenly stood up and sang out at the top of his lungs, dreadfully off key, "Figaro! Figaro! Figaro!" His

mother didn't know whether to stare transfixed at the ceiling, deny all kinship and claim a quiet child as her own, or express the triumph she felt that her son could equate grand opera with a happening in his own life. The misgivings she felt about any possible ethnic misunderstanding, mixed with pride in her son's perception, were dissolved when barbers and patrons alike applauded as the impromptu performer climbed into the barber chair.

There is no getting away from it. Although generalizations are as difficult with kids who have Down syndrome as with any others, the child with Down syndrome is often "the personality kid." Endearing, compassionate, exuberant, often stubborn, just as often mischievous, the child with Down syndrome has a genius for bringing out the best in people. Families who think they will never smile again find that life centers around their child in a joyous way they could not have dreamed possible when the baby was born.

Your baby has Down syndrome. It's a fact of this fresh little life and of yours. The birth of this baby has given a new challenge to your life and quite possibly a new set of values as well. A different dimension has been added, partly frightening and partly sad, but also beautiful. You wish with all your heart that your baby had been born normal; you wish it for her and you wish it for you. But you don't have time to dwell on that. Right now, above all else, your baby *needs* you. Someday, probably as you are giving a bath, spooning in the spinach, patting up a good burp, or even walking the floor in the wee hours, it will hit you how very much *you* need your baby.

Parent Statements

I found out Amanda had Down syndrome right after she was born. I asked the doctors what it was, 'cause I wasn't real familiar with it, and they said there would be some retardation. They were encouraging; they told me she'd be able to read, and they gave me a little brief of what to expect. But I was just so happy about having a baby that it didn't really hit me right away. I'd seen her when she was born; she was really healthy and everything.

We were not told right away. There were a couple days there where we actually hoped that he didn't have Down syndrome. We knew just enough to be very worried.

My family and relatives were very supportive. Initially my husband took the news harder than I did, but he rallied really well. And then we had lots of support from close friends and our church. I was disappointed, of course. I didn't want her to have Down syndrome. For a long time, when I would think about what she might grow up to be, I'd have a really hard time with it. But it never struck me as being a terrible tragedy. See, everybody was very accepting; nobody said "Oh no, this is awful." They were very encouraging. Not one person acted negatively. It was "Well, it's too bad but, hey, it's great you had your baby, and that's wonderful."

My initial reaction was total shock, but soon after, I wanted information. What did this mean, what is going on, why? But we didn't really push the why. We wanted information, but realized that we had to hold together for Laurie, even though she was this minute-old baby. And we had to be together for other people who were going to take our lead on how we reacted and accepted her. If we acted unaccepting, so would everybody else. Or if we tried to deny it in any way—or tried to delay it. We didn't know the best way to explain it to people, because there is no best way. You just have to say it.

When the doctors told us at the hospital that our son had Down syndrome, we both just thought the world opened up and swallowed us right then.

Our whole approach from day one has been that we accepted this right away and the question was not "why was it?" or "whose fault was it?" or "why did we deserve this?" but "what do we have to do to make her the best person she can be?"

I wanted people to say congratulations, and they didn't. It was like my baby had died.

I kept wanting people to act like they were just happy that I had a baby. You know, not like it was terrible that he was born.

We thought it would be harder to tell people later. So we told everyone right away. And the outcry from family and friends was just really wonderful. They came to see us. They showered her with everything under the sun. To us it really meant, "She's an important person and we're glad she's here." Because that's how we felt.

Everybody was sympathetic. I don't remember any harsh or negative comments. Everybody was just as nice as they could be. They didn't treat him or us as weird. They didn't always know how to approach him, but I put myself in their position. I'd feel awkward too, so I wasn't offended.

My wife was most upset about Christopher having Down syndrome and I think particularly because we'd been so hopeful that it wouldn't be. You see, we'd been told by several doctors who were really experts, just on the basis of a quick examination, that it probably wasn't Down syndrome. It made it even worse because we had held out hope for a long time. And after we found out, the first things that came to mind were the worst images because we really didn't know—we knew more bad things about Down syndrome than good. We didn't know the mitigating factors.

I've talked with a lot of parents who weren't as lucky as we were. They didn't have a diagnosis on their child until the preschool years because it wasn't a clear-cut diagnosis like Down syndrome. They're just now beginning to realize that their child is retarded. It's much easier when you know from the beginning what you have to deal with. The other parents were always holding out the hope that their child would end up normal.

The nicest times are when people treat Chris like any other baby. They say, "Oh, what a beautiful baby!" And that makes us proud because he is a beautiful baby, and we feel very happy about that. One time we were in an airport and someone came up to us and said, "Down syndrome?" When I said yes, he said, "Wonderful children. I've got one myself." It was nice of him.

One part of me was extremely sad—I couldn't stop crying. It took me a year to stop crying. And the other side of me wanted to be really happy and take her for walks and enjoy my new baby. It was a strange situation. Other people had a hard time because outwardly I probably looked really together and happy. Since then, some people have said to me that it was really weird. And it was.

Sometimes I have feelings of resentment. I don't think against anyone specifically, but when I go to the grocery store and I see people all concerned over some little thing like the diaper not being on right, I feel like saying, "Come on, give me a break, save it for something really serious."

We weren't particularly interested in why the cells didn't separate properly. We didn't really look back. Various people go from doctor to doctor and ask, "Why did this happen to me?" But we figure, he's here, he's got forty-seven chromosomes. Nothing is ever going to change that, we'll deal with it as it is.

I think it made a big impact when people wanted to extend condolences, and we came back at them very positive and optimistic. We had to let them know that this wasn't a sad moment and they kind of backed off with their condolences.

My reaction now when I see a baby with Down syndrome is, I think, "Oh, how nice." But it makes me feel strange if somebody says, "Oh they are wonderful children," because that's stereotyping. They aren't all wonderful any more than any other children are all wonderful.

One of the things that I remember right after she was born, and it kind of irked me, was that lots of people acted as if it was a real tragedy, like it was a real sorrowful moment in our lives and they had to apologize for us. The flowers came in like it was a wake, not a birth. But I remember one guy who came in and he was all grins and congratulations, and he shook my hand. It dawned on me that this guy's reaction was different. He was reacting the way someone's supposed to react when you give birth to a child. That put everybody into perspective.

I think it takes a long time for parents to accept other people looking at their child. And now that I've had another child,

I realize that people look at *any* baby. They don't just look at the baby because she has Down syndrome or is handicapped. People stare at babies.

I still have trouble telling people about my son. You know, I say I have a child and I think to myself, now do I have to tell them he has Down syndrome? I don't want to introduce that to people I don't know. I don't want to say he's mentally retarded, he's got Down syndrome. That's something I still have to work through my system.

One day I took Laurie to the park. There was a couple there with a little boy around two and his grandmother. The little boy kept pointing at us. He'd run over to Laurie from a distance and pull her hair and run away. Our little girl just started screaming—naturally. The grandmother looked back and said, "Well, that little girl is retarded." I just thought, "Well, your little boy isn't very nice." Of course she was screaming—her hair was being pulled. It took me by surprise, but I just thought, "Why should I say anything? It won't change anything." It was the first time that's ever happened to me.

I had a particularly hard time with one neighbor. She had a little girl just about the same age as mine. I really had a hard time when that girl first sat up, when she crawled, when she walked. She was talking a blue streak in a year, and that was really hard for me. It took me a long time to like that little girl—isn't that awful?

One time a woman came up to us and said, "Oh, what a nice little child. Just think, he'll always be childlike. What a wonderful thing, he'll never grow up." I thought it was funny because she was trying very hard to say something nice and yet she completely misunderstood.

When he was smaller, not many people said anything to me about the baby. We were at an evening dinner, and the baby was with us, and a woman invited us to her new babies parent group that she'd just started. When I said he had Down syndrome, she looked like she had a hot potato. She looked sort of horrified as if she were recoiling, and then she never got in touch with us afterwards. I always felt a bit bitter, and I thought she was a bit stupid anyway, to have that kind of reaction.

I've run into strange reactions on the part of parents whose kids aren't quite perfect in some minor way. I have a little bit of impatience, but then I think they're just families who haven't experienced the full range of perspective. People get all upset because their kid has an ear infection. When your kid has open-heart surgery and some other kid has a minor infection, you think well, no big deal.

Now that Chris is older, people ask, "How old is that lovely baby?", and I say twenty months, and they say "Ten?" And I say twenty, and they say "Oh." And then they say "Can he say his name?" because he is so old and he doesn't walk yet and he doesn't talk well, so people notice. I don't feel embarrassed, just a bit withdrawn.

Some people acted like the baby was dead. I didn't get a lot of presents for him—not that you care about the presents themselves, but I cared about what it meant. My aunt didn't even tell her friends we had a baby.

Initially we thought there would be a million decisions to make right away, but we found that the decisions were spread over a long period of time, like with any other child. The decisions aren't knocking at your door every day.

THREE

⊜══⊏══⊐══⊜

Medical Concerns and Treatments

CHAHIRA KOZMA, M.D.*

Babies with Down syndrome can have special medical problems. Although some of these problems can be quite serious, the good news is that medical treatments have improved so much that today the vast majority of babies with Down syndrome can grow up healthy and active.

As with other characteristics of children with Down syndrome, exactly how the extra chromosome causes medical problems is not known. But it is clear that extra genetic material can cause a wide variety of medical conditions, including heart, intestine, and eye problems.

In the past, the medical problems associated with Down syndrome resulted in shortened life spans and premature deaths. Sometimes decisions were made not to perform life-saving surgery. Today, however, there are advanced medical treatments for virtually every medical problem babies with Down syndrome may have. Life spans are increasing. More importantly, the quality of life for these special children is much improved.

This chapter reviews the medical problems babies with Down syndrome may have. Because early detection and treatment is often

*Dr. Chahira Kozma is Assistant Professor of Pediatrics and a Clinical Geneticist at Georgetown University Hospital in Washington, D.C.

47

crucial, learning the basic facts about medical conditions can help parents spot problems, ask the right questions, communicate well with doctors, and make important decisions.

All babies have a chance of developing any number of diseases or conditions, but parents of newborns are usually not presented with the statistics as soon as their baby is born. Yet those statistics exist for every infant. Every baby has a possibility of developing heart problems, vision problems, hearing problems, infections, or anything else you care to name. But when your baby has Down syndrome, doctors come to tell you the statistics. It may seem insensitive and unfair, but the reason for raising the issue so early is simply that babies with Down syndrome have a higher incidence of certain medical problems and these problems are usually best dealt with as soon as possible. Most importantly, medical problems are best cared for before they have a chance to delay development. This chapter will point out those conditions parents of babies with Down syndrome need to look out for.

Before we start, however, remember as you read that not every baby has the medical problems covered in this chapter. Some have none, some have few, and some have many. These are conditions that babies with Down syndrome statistically have higher chances of developing than do babies in the general population. And remember also that in medicine, forewarned is often forearmed.

Heart Defects

Over forty percent of babies with Down syndrome are born with heart defects. For decades these defects meant early death, but today advanced medical treatment with drugs and life-saving surgery are common, even almost routine.

First, some background about hearts. Hearts are divided into four chambers. These chambers are separated by walls made of heart muscle. As blood is pumped into and out of each chamber and then out to the lungs and the body, it delivers the oxygen the body needs to live.

When a baby has a heart defect, there may be a hole in the walls between the chambers, or the walls between the chambers may be poorly formed. A hole can cause blood to squirt through the walls between the chambers. The result is that too much blood is pumped to the lungs and not enough blood is pumped to the rest of the body.

Because a hole can disrupt the flow of blood within the heart, this condition can raise the risk of serious cardiac infections.

There are several types of heart defects. The most common is called an endocardial cushion defect. This means that the walls (or septa) between the two upper chambers (the atria) and the two lower chambers (the ventricles) of the heart, as well as the valves between them, may be deformed. There may also be a hole between the two lower chambers. This condition is called a ventricular septal defect or VSD. There are other less common heart defects, involving holes between the two upper chambers (atrial septal defect or ASD), problems with the heart valves, and the major arteries attached to the heart.

Heart defects are serious problems. In their most severe form, they can threaten your baby's life at birth and require emergency corrective surgery. Even defects that do not need immediate surgery can drastically shorten a child's life if left untreated. If, because of the heart defect, excess blood is continually pumped to the lungs, high pressure in the blood vessels in the lungs (pulmonary hypertension) will result. Over time, the blood vessels will become scarred, and eventually will become so narrow that not enough blood can reach the lungs. This condition is fatal.

A pediatric cardiologist—a doctor who specializes in heart defects in children—should be consulted as soon as Down syndrome is recognized. If possible, he or she should examine the baby immediately after birth and continue to monitor the baby closely for some time afterwards. Through a stethoscope, your doctor will listen for murmurs that might indicate a congenital heart defect. He or she may also use electrocardiograms, ultrasound, and X-rays to closely examine the heart and its structure. One technique called cardiac catheterization actually allows doctors to view the inside of the heart to evaluate in detail any defect that might be present. Repeated examinations are crucial. Some heart defects may not be detected at birth, but can appear later on—within the first few weeks, or even years, of life.

Babies with heart defects may show the symptoms of what is called "heart failure." Heart failure does *not* mean the heart is stopping, but rather that it is not functioning efficiently. The clearest symptoms are poor feeding, a change in color during feeding, poor growth, and easy fatigue. Sometimes the baby's skin may turn blue (cyanosis), especially during times of physical exertion. Other signs include labored, accelerated breathing and frequent upper respiratory infections.

If your baby has a heart defect, he may be more lethargic than normal and may tire easily. Eating—the most strenuous activity in which any infant engages—may exhaust a baby with a heart defect. He must be closely observed by parents, doctors, and teachers.

There are two ways heart defects are treated by doctors. First, drugs are used to treat minor defects and to help babies with more serious defects survive until they are ready for surgery. For example, drugs that reduce the amount of water in the body are used to ease the heart's job. These drugs, called diuretics, are monitored carefully by the cardiologist. Other drugs to prevent infections and to help the heart function more efficiently may also be used.

Second, open heart surgery may be necessary to correct a defect. If possible, this surgery may be postponed until the baby is about one year old in order to give the baby a chance to grow and gain strength. Although in the past open heart surgery was very risky and consequently was considered a last resort, the risk is far less today. It is important, however, to find the right specialist for this type of surgery. Look for a cardiac surgeon with experience in pediatrics for whom this type of surgery is routine. The Resource Guide at the end of the book contains listings of Down syndrome clinics, university hospitals, and organizations that can refer you to the right doctor.

For over one hundred years doctors have known that heart defects are associated with Down syndrome. In the past, there was little, if anything, that could be done in the way of treatment. Today, however, heart defects claim far fewer lives. If doctors and parents closely monitor their infants and provide them with proper treatment, then the prognosis for most babies is greatly improved.

Intestinal Problems

Babies with Down syndrome are more likely to be born with some type of intestinal malformation. Although intestinal problems occur three hundred times more often in babies with Down syndrome than in other children, still only about ten to twelve percent of babies with Down syndrome have an intestinal problem.

These problems can take several forms. Blockages in the esophagus, the small intestine, the large intestine, and the rectum are the most common. The symptoms of intestinal blockage, which usually appear within the baby's first week, are bloody stools or no stools at all and vomiting. Today all of these conditions can be permanently corrected with surgery.

Some babies with Down syndrome have a rare intestinal defect in which the intestinal tract and the respiratory system are connected. Called tracheo-esophageal fistula, this is a serious condition that requires immediate surgical correction.

Respiratory Infections

In the past, one of the most common causes of early death in children with Down syndrome was respiratory infection. It was believed that children with Down syndrome had abnormal immune systems, leaving them vulnerable to infections. This belief, however, has lately been disputed (Pueschel, 1984). In any case, your child will develop respiratory infections; virtually every child does. A respiratory infection is usually a viral or bacterial infection of the nasal passages, throat, bronchial tubes, or lungs. Bronchitis and pneumonia are both serious respiratory infections. Today, however, with modern antibiotics and better general medical care, fewer respiratory infections become serious or complicated.

Researchers have found that children with Down syndrome who also have heart defects have more problems handling respiratory infections than do other children. Contrary to prior belief, however, children with Down syndrome *without* heart abnormalities seem to tolerate infections as well as other children.

Vision

Children's eyes are not fully developed at birth. In fact, all babies are nearsighted during their first few weeks of life. Their sight and eye control will improve, but at first they do not see very well. For this reason it is often difficult to determine if there is a problem with a child's sight. Most children with Down syndrome have the same quality of sight as other children and develop the same control of their eyes, but because eyesight can affect other facets of development, it is especially important to make sure your child's eyesight is normal as early as possible.

Early eye examinations will ensure that poor eyesight does not become an obstacle for your baby. There are new techniques available to check a baby's vision. Later, when your child is older, the more standard vision tests can be used. A pediatric ophthalmologist – a physician specializing in vision in children – should be consulted when your baby is approximately six months old. Earlier consultation may be necessary if you or your pediatrician suspect a problem.

Children with Down syndrome often have vision problems. These are the same types of problems any child can have, but they may occur more frequently than in the general population. These problems include crossed eyes, nearsightedness, farsightedness, and cataracts. Each of these problems can be detected early and can be corrected so as not to hinder development. Let's briefly review the types of vision problems and their treatment:

Crossed Eyes. Crossed eyes, also known as strabismus, occurs when one or both eyes tend to look inward. It is caused by incomplete or abnormal development of the coordination centers that control eye muscle movements. If an eye remains crossed, that eye may lose sight. This condition is known as lazy eye or amblyopia (partial blindness). An ophthalmologist must evaluate this condition and prescribe treatment, which may include glasses, an eye patch, or surgery on the eye muscles.

Nearsightedness and Farsightedness. Eyes are like cameras; they take in a picture through the lens and display it on the retina in the back of the eye. With nearsightedness (myopia) and farsightedness (hypermetropia), the eye is either too long or too short, causing the image projected through the lens to be out of focus. Objects in the distance (in nearsightedness) or objects close-up (in farsightedness) appear blurred. Children with either of these problems have difficulty focusing, locating objects, and following moving objects.

Nearsightedness or farsightedness may only affect one eye. If one eye focuses but the other does not, amblyopia (partial blindness) may develop. Complicating this problem is the difficulty in knowing when only one eye is being used. This is why early vision exams are so important. The treatment for these conditions is glasses – a simple solution for a potentially major problem.

Cataracts. As people age, sometimes the lens of one or both eyes becomes cloudy. The result is deteriorating vision. The treatment today is surgery to replace the damaged lens with a new one. Rare in young children, this condition is slightly more common in children and adults with Down syndrome.

It is vital for children with Down syndrome to have regular eye examinations. One recommended schedule is to have your child's eyes examined at six months, three and one-half years, five years, and every four years thereafter, depending on the examination findings. With modern techniques and corrective glasses, eye problems need not – and should not be allowed to – interfere with your child's development.

Hearing

Newborn babies can hear quite well. As parents quickly learn, they respond to loud sounds by blinking, becoming startled, or crying. Soon the baby can tell the difference between the voices of his parents and siblings and the voices of others, and will also try to locate the source of sounds.

The ears of babies with Down syndrome tend to be smaller than normal, which can cause some problems. The middle ear is smaller as well, and that is where most ear problems start. Again, effective treatments are available to correct these problems, but close monitoring and frequent check-ups are essential. Dr. Siegfried M. Pueschel, a leading authority on Down syndrome, has found that approximately forty percent of children with Down syndrome have some form of mild hearing loss. At least an additional ten to fifteen percent have a more severe loss. He recommends that all babies with Down syndrome receive frequent hearing tests. Other studies indicate even higher percentages. Most children with a hearing loss have a mild degree of loss, but treatment is important whatever the extent of loss.

Even though a baby may not be able to indicate when he hears faint or high-pitched sounds, tests allow hearing to be evaluated very early in life. There are even advanced techniques that can measure electronically the brain's reception of sound; these tests can evaluate the hearing of infants. Later, standard hearing tests can be used. Another test used to evaluate middle ear function is known as tympanometry. This procedure can confirm the presence of fluid in the middle ear, or if no fluid is found, can detect a blockage of the Eustachian tube.

The middle ears of children can often become filled with fluid. This can happen sooner and more frequently to children with Down syndrome. The middle ear is connected to the back of the throat by a small tube called the Eustachian tube. This tube can become blocked, resulting in increased risk of infection and in retention of fluid in the middle ear. Fluid in the middle ear interferes with the vibration of the eardrum, which reduces hearing sensitivity. The hearing loss should be temporary; when the fluid clears, freeing the eardrum, hearing should improve. If the fluid remains in the middle ear for a long time, however, significant hearing loss can occur. For these children, sounds may be muffled and language development may be delayed.

Treatment of ear infections ranges from medicine to surgery, depending on the severity of the ear congestion. Antibiotics can help cure bacterial ear infections, decongestants can help reduce symptoms, and in more severe cases, doctors can implant small tubes through the eardrum that help the eardrum function more normally. Implanting the tubes is a relatively minor surgical procedure.

Hearing is vital for childhood development. With early detection, medical care, and, if necessary, hearing aids, there is every reason to expect children with Down syndrome to hear normally.

Thyroid Problems

The thyroid is a tiny gland located in the neck. By the release of certain hormones, the thyroid gland controls the rate of some of the body's chemical functions.

Doctors have found that babies with Down syndrome are more likely to have a thyroid problem. The most common of the thyroid problems is called hypothyroidism, which is a decreased production of the thyroid hormone. This is a potentially serious problem and, if undetected or untreated, can cause developmental delays and other serious complications. Today, however, hypothyroidism can be controlled with medicine.

Babies with Down syndrome should be screened for thyroid problems every year because symptoms of the disease are often not apparent until the damage is done. Only blood tests will reveal if there is a problem *before* the symptoms of hypothyroidism appear.

Vertebrae Instability

Between ten and twenty percent of children with Down syndrome have instability in the upper two vertebrae, the bones of the spine. This condition is caused by the low muscle tone and flexible joints common in babies with Down syndrome. Children who have this condition run a risk of spinal cord injury because their two upper vertebrae allow too much bending of the spinal cord.

Because newborns and infants under three years of age are not as active as older children, doctors usually wait until they are at least two years old to X-ray the spine to detect the problem. The X-ray will show if the two top vertebrae are unstable.

Detection of the condition is important. Spinal cord injury resulting in paralysis can occur if a child with unstable vertebrae falls on his head or neck. Consequently, the activity of children with this problem has to be restricted to prevent injury until the condition is treated. Treatment may entail surgery to fuse the unstable vertebrae. This repair does not significantly affect movement or development.

Children with Down syndrome like to be active, as do all children. Many participate in vigorous activity and sports programs. To guide parents in supervising their child's activity, the American Academy

of Pediatrics recommends: 1) all children with Down syndrome who wish to participate in sports involving possible trauma to the head and neck should have X-rays to assess the cervical region; 2) children with Down syndrome should have an X-ray of the spine between the ages of four and five; 3) children with any signs of instability should be restricted from strenuous activity and surgical stabilization should be considered; and 4) children with Down syndrome who have no evidence of instability may participate in all sports.

Weight

At birth, babies with Down syndrome usually are of average weight. Initially, the baby may feed and gain weight slowly because low muscle tone makes eating more exhausting or because of a medical problem such as a heart defect. Later, weight gain usually is normal, but occasionally obesity becomes a problem. Researchers have found that approximately twenty-five percent of children with Down syndrome develop obesity.

In the past, many children with Down syndrome were overweight. This was due to a number of causes. Children with Down syndrome were less active and given fewer opportunities for active play. Also, other problems—such as low muscle tone, low thyroid function, and heart defects—hindered activity. Thus, the familiar equation of too many calories and not enough activity equalled obesity.

Today there is no reason why children with Down syndrome who are in good health cannot maintain normal weight. A good diet and plenty of activity are essential, and both should be watched carefully. The same common sense we all should follow to control our weight applies equally to children with Down syndrome.

Leukemia

Leukemia is a type of cancer that attacks the white blood cells, leaving the body open to infection. Although uncommon even in children with Down syndrome, it is slightly more common among children with Down syndrome than the general population. Leukemia is a very serious disease, but treatment has improved dramatically. Some patients may now be cured. More and more children are now surviving leukemia, especially when the disease is detected early.

Feet and Ankles

Because of low muscle tone and flexible joints, children with Down syndrome tend to have flat feet and weak ankles. The arches of their feet cannot support their body's weight. Flat feet can be treated effectively with shoe inserts or arch supports. Weak ankles, which can make it harder for children to walk, can be supported with corrective shoes or orthopedic inserts.

Umbilical Hernia

Many children with Down syndrome have a condition known as a navel or umbilical hernia, in which the navel sticks out. This is caused by incomplete muscle development around the navel. There is no reason to worry about this condition. Most umbilical hernias close by themselves and, in any case, they rarely cause medical problems.

Medical Problems and Your Baby's Development

Proper medical care is absolutely essential for any baby, but particularly for yours. Medical problems left undetected or untreated can seriously slow development and prevent your child from reaching his full potential. For example, a child with poor eyesight will not be able to walk, play, or explore as he should. A child with poor hearing won't learn to talk as soon because he simply cannot hear sounds well enough. Even respiratory infections that occur too frequently can hinder development by keeping your baby inactive and away from his developmental program. For these reasons, rigorous medical care is necessary. No child deserves less.

Effective treatments are usually available for each of the medical problems facing children with Down syndrome. There are also special clinics that specialize in treating children with Down syndrome. In these clinics, doctors who specialize in Down syndrome can oversee and coordinate all of the various medical services your baby may need. The many children's hospitals and university hospitals located around the country are good places to start. The Resource Guide at the end of this book lists some of the major Down syndrome clinics and child development centers around the country. Do not hesitate to contact one for help.

Life-Saving Surgery

Like many parents, parents of babies with Down syndrome sometimes are faced with the terrible decision of whether to authorize life-saving surgery. Some parents have chosen not to allow surgery, while many more others have chosen to save their baby's life.

This book and this chapter are obviously biased in favor of doing everything that can be done for babies with Down syndrome. Down syndrome alone should not be a reason for allowing a child to die. With advanced medical care and the great progress being made in education, the vast majority of parents are authorizing life-saving surgery. When you read the statements by parents at the end of this chapter you will see how natural and automatic their decisions were.

If you are facing the possibility of life-saving surgery on your baby with Down syndrome, the best advice is to first learn as much about Down syndrome as you can. Learn what it means to you and your family, but most important, learn what it means to your baby.

Concerns for the Future

Although this book focuses on the first three years of life, parents often want to know what medical problems may occur later. In the past when life spans for people with Down syndrome were shorter, there simply wasn't very much information about their later life. Now, thankfully, information is building as people with Down syndrome live longer.

One issue often debated is whether people with Down syndrome lose some of their mental ability as they get older. Some doctors have diagnosed Alzheimer's disease in their patients with Down syndrome. Recent studies have shown an increased incidence of Alzheimer's disease among older people with Down syndrome. Although Alzheimer's disease is a serious condition, researchers believe we are close to finding either a cure or effective treatment.

Older individuals with Down syndrome may have two other health problems. First, they are more likely to develop cataracts on their eyes. As mentioned above, this condition is treatable and should not cause blindness. Second, gum disease often occurs as people with Down syndrome age. Although the teeth of children with Down syndrome seem to be unusually resistant to cavities and tooth decay, gum disease can cause tooth loss later. That is why it is so important to teach proper oral hygiene early so that good habits are carried into later life.

Children and adults with Down syndrome will benefit from medical progress in the areas of concern for the future. Remember that the problems affecting people with Down syndrome also affect others; they may be more common in people with Down syndrome, often only slightly more common. So, as medical research discovers new cures and treatments, many problems will become less serious.

Dealing with the Medical Profession

Parents with babies who have medical problems must face additional hardships. On top of dealing with the medical problem itself, parents also have to learn to deal with the medical profession. With conflicting schedules, multiple appointments, and an entirely new language to learn, confronting a medical problem for the first time can be quite stressful. Here are a few hints:

Get the Facts. It is tremendously helpful to be able to understand what a doctor is saying to you about your child. Be it heart defects, vision problems, or just dry skin, there is a new language to learn. Learn that language by reading books, asking doctors, nurses, teachers, and other parents, and getting deeply involved in your child's care. The basic facts about a particular problem can enable you to ask the right questions, and to communicate well with your child's doctor. Remember, *you* are the most critical member of the team treating your baby.

Ask Questions. When discussing your child's medical problem and treatment with a doctor, *do not* be afraid to ask questions–lots of questions. Ask until you are satisfied that you understand enough to make informed choices about your baby's medical care. Do not be intimidated. Every doctor should be able to explain medical problems and treatments in plain English. Demand full and complete explanations, including explanations of potential side effects and contingency plans.

Avoid Excessive Waiting. There is nothing harder on parents and children than sitting in doctors' waiting rooms. It must seem that every doctor in the world runs behind schedule and that waiting around is taken for granted. Many things delay doctors, including emergencies, difficult cases, and a routinely busy schedule. Call ahead to find out if your appointment will be late. If you do have to wait, be sure to bring along something for your baby to play with.

Batch Your Doctor Visits. Sometimes babies need a series of tests, such as blood tests, X-rays, and a physical examination. Try to take care of all of these things at the same time and at the same place. Try to set aside a morning or an afternoon to take your child from test to test, rather than spreading it out over days. This eliminates constant shuttling to and from your treatment center.

Watch Out for Outdated Opinions. Doctors have come a very long way in treating babies with Down syndrome and in recognizing their great potential. There are some, however, who may cling to stereotypes and outdated information. Be sure you pick a doctor who is current in both knowledge and attitude. Switch doctors if you find your doctor has beliefs and biases that make you uncomfortable. Do not hesitate to get second opinions, or third opinions if you feel they are necessary.

Coping with Paperwork. Being sick today is not what it used to be. To parents, it must seem there is a sea of forms to fill out, and a sea of bills and statements to decipher. Complex insurance forms are often very difficult, as well as time-consuming, to sort out–and they usually descend upon you in the middle of your trying to deal with a medical problem. Do not feel pressured to stay on top of your forms. There are no more stressful times for you and your child than when your child is ill. Although it is not advisable to be late on medical bills, be sure to take time for your child *and for yourself* before attacking that mountain of bills. If possible, wait until after your child's treatment is over—at least until it is less intense. Take some time to

breathe, *then* tackle the pile of papers. Also, do not be afraid to call your doctor or your insurance company with questions. They are there to help *you*.

Keep a Notebook. Because there are so many specialists that you and your child might need to see, it may be very helpful to keep a notebook. List questions and addresses and telephone numbers, and take notes on your consultations and meetings. This notebook can also be used to keep a record of your written observations of your child, along with tests and evaluations.

Conclusion

After reading this chapter you may think that babies with Down syndrome are always sick and in need of medical care. That is simply not the case. Instead, babies with Down syndrome generally enjoy good health. Problems can come up, but there are effective treatments for virtually every one of them. And most children do not have all of the problems discussed in this chapter.

In the last two decades, medical science has come a long way in helping children with Down syndrome lead more healthy and vigorous lives. Problems that not too long ago meant premature death are now treatable. Problems that hindered development and prevented children from reaching their full developmental potential now pose far less serious threats. With better overall health, improved medical care, and close monitoring by parents and professionals, there is every reason to expect children with Down syndrome to lead full, healthy lives.

REFERENCES
See references for Chapter 1.

Parent Statements

We have been quite pleased with the medical attention he has gotten. The children's hospital here has been very understanding; they seem to be assertive about their medical practice. You know, they would make sure that he got tests for his heart and all the things that could happen that we wouldn't have known about. They made sure that he had tests and they followed up.

When we found out she had a heart defect, it almost didn't matter. That's really awful to say, but we almost couldn't have felt worse. We had just found out she had Down syndrome, and we felt the heart thing was something we could take care of. We felt we could manage it better.

We feel it's extremely important to get vision and hearing check-ups. You need to know there is a problem to help the problem. Many children with Down syndrome speak later than other children and you need to give them every chance to speak and to hear what you're saying. It is the same thing with vision.

I think physicians have a responsibility to give you all the options and let you make the decisions. But I don't think anyone ever suggested that she not have her heart surgery. Even with her failing to thrive and with her not gaining weight and doing absolutely awful, it was never recommended that we give up in any way.

I can't understand *not* allowing life-saving surgery. I was shocked once when a doctor actually gave me the option of not authorizing emergency abdominal surgery. Mike deserves the same chance to live his life as any other child. For heaven's sake, he's my child.

Our little boy has hypothyroidism. We were so glad it was diagnosed early because we were able to start medication immediately. Otherwise, he'd have other problems on top of Down syndrome. But we caught it early enough, and now we just give him medicine once a day.

She had no colds, no pneumonia, no nothing, until this year, until she was three. The doctor feels it was not related to having Down syndrome; it was just a bad year. She had high exposure to many children this year, because she was in nursery school.

The medical professionals have been very thorough. Sometimes it has caused him too much pain for the end result. It's a function of his having Down syndrome and therefore he has to suffer being probed a bit more because he has higher chances of this or that. Now he just breaks into hysterical sobs whenever he sees a doctor.

I've always felt that it's open season on Mike. I mean the kid's been x-rayed a lot. He has had heart problems and he had abdominal surgery. They are really quick to order medical procedures and tests they might not otherwise order.

I spoke to a parent not long ago who had just given birth to a baby with Down syndrome. That woman had five different doctors. She had a two-day-old baby, and they all had something different to say. None of them were conferring with the others. She was already the team leader and didn't know enough to lead the team. It was just overwhelming for her.

Certain things worked well for us in dealing with the doctors. We ask a lot of questions, and don't let them get away with not answering or putting things in language we can't understand. We're paying them to help our child and we need to understand what they're saying. People shouldn't be embarrassed to not understand.

I wanted somebody who, even if they didn't know, would help me find out. I think an important function of a pediatrician is to coordinate your child's care. Some programs do this for your child, but many do not. The pediatrician needs to be aware of what speech is doing, what OT is doing, what physical therapy is doing, what cognitive is doing, what the geneticist is doing, what the ophthalmologist is doing, what the audiologist is doing. We found a pediatrician who reads everything he gets about Laurie, calls me if something doesn't jibe, and really is a coordinator.

We were sort of disappointed in our regular pediatrician. After seeing Josh about four times, he said, "Are you having any special therapy for this boy?" He was just beginning to show signs of a speech delay, and I think the doctor didn't even remember that we were doing everything we could. This pediatrician was strictly inoculations and regular check-ups. He really wasn't prepared to deal with Down syndrome at all.

If the experience is not helpful to you, change it. We had a pediatrician who kept saying "these children," patted me on the head, and told me not to worry, that this is what life was going to be like and I might as well get used to it. But I decided that I wanted to do everything I could and I wasn't getting the impression that this doctor was giving me everything I could do. I had a lot of guilt because I always tend to think a doctor is right—he's the expert. It took me about a month before it dawned on me to go exploring for someone who would be positive.

Sometimes it takes courage to change. Maybe the pediatrician that you have is the one the whole family uses, but doesn't have a clue about dealing with the special problems of handicapped kids. Maybe the person that you picked out isn't suitable. You have to make changes. Never put any of these other considerations, or your own uneasiness about terminating people's services, before the best interests of your child.

Insurance is a major concern. Persistence can have rewards and if the first time you don't succeed in getting coverage for a particular service, keep trying. It could be because the person at that level didn't understand. Or maybe the services are not covered for a particular diagnosis but if you get another diagnosis that really is the same thing but just said in a different way, the policy will cover it. Or if that doesn't work, maybe there is someone else at the next level who has the authority to take it on appeal. Just keep at it. Save all your copies and keep submitting all your documents. Keep going higher and higher up, because once you concede that something is not covered there's no going back. They expect you to give up, but you might get lucky. You may get somebody in the chain of command that will make a reverse decision or you may be perfectly within your rights to expect coverage for a particular service.

FOUR

The Daily Care of Your Baby

ELLIOT GERSH, M.D.* and JOAN RILEY, R.N., M.S.N.**

Many parents of babies with Down syndrome feel that the daily care of their child is very similar to the care of other children. Perhaps for this reason there is very little written about the daily care of a child with Down syndrome. However, because your baby can be different in some ways, her daily care will sometimes require special knowledge and effort. This chapter explores those areas of daily care that are unique to babies with Down syndrome.

A tremendous amount has been written about child care in general. Eating, sleeping, bathing, and diapering are extensively covered in hundreds of baby care books, some of which are included in the Reading List. These general baby care books can be helpful, but their advice must be adapted to your child's special needs. Supplement these books with this chapter's information.

Routine activities—eating, bathing, and diapering—are major events in a baby's or toddler's day. You can tailor your baby's activities to enhance her development simply by being aware of your child's development as you go through each day. But remember: Babies with Down syndrome are babies first and foremost. Care for her as you would any other baby. Follow your instincts, but in those areas where

---

*Dr. Elliot Gersh is Director of Developmental Pediatrics at the Georgetown University Child Development Center in Washington, D.C.
**Joan Riley is a Registered Nurse and a Clinical Instructor at the Georgetown University School of Nursing in Washington, D.C.

your baby has special needs, use the information in this chapter to deal with those needs more effectively.

Routine and Discipline

One of the most important aspects of your baby's daily care is to set a routine. Routines differ for each family because of each family member's schedule and because of each baby's schedule. For example, some families give their babies a bath in the evening in order to help them calm down and relax, while other babies get very excited splashing around and playing in the water. In either case, the consistency of your routine will benefit both you and your baby.

You may also need to reassess your family style in light of your baby's particular needs. Limit-setting and consistency—discipline in general—are important for any child. But for a baby with Down syndrome you may need to be more deliberate about it. For example, if your family routine is very casual, you may have to adjust your methods to your child's special needs. On the other hand, if your family routine tends to be highly structured, you might have to allow for more flexibility. Most likely, your particular style is just fine. Just remember that it is important to be aware of how your daily activities, style, and expectations can affect your baby's development. Other children may manage to get along fine without this higher level of care, but if you optimize your special baby's environment, you will help her reach her full potential.

Don't let your baby's Down syndrome spoil her. Discipline and routine are just as important to her as to any other baby. You will be surprised at how clever she is at manipulating you. Your child will have to learn how to behave, and you won't be doing her a favor if you fail to enforce the do's and do not's.

Eating

From birth onward, mealtime is one of the most important times parents have with their child. Babies are usually alert and attentive while they are eating, and mealtime can be an enjoyable time for all family members to get together. As your child grows, she will enjoy being with the rest of her family, sharing the discussion about everyone's daily activities.

Children with Down syndrome have to learn feeding skills, and this process requires time and patience. It takes practice for your baby to learn to feed herself, and – like other children – there will be plenty of messes. You have to be ready to wipe up spills and clean up faces and hands. But rest assured, all babies with Down syndrome will learn to feed themselves.

Breast or Bottle Feeding

Babies with Down syndrome can breast or bottle feed like other children, but may need a little extra help. It may be harder at first for them to feed in a coordinated way, but most learn quickly to be good breast or bottle feeders. If parents understand their baby's potential feeding problems and how to overcome them, feeding can become a special time for both parent and child.

Babies and children with Down syndrome sometimes have physical characteristics that affect how they eat. The child's mouth may be smaller, allowing the tongue to protrude. The muscles of the lips, tongue, and cheeks may not move in a coordinated fashion due to low muscle tone. Consequently, babies with Down syndrome may have more difficulty getting a tight seal on a nipple. They may have a weaker suck, and later may have more difficulty chewing and moving food around in the mouth. As you work with your baby's teacher or speech therapist, you will be amazed at how complex the act of eating can be and how it is affected by your baby's development.

Some babies require special techniques to strengthen eating skills if their oral motor development is not normal. These techniques stimulate some of the natural patterns your child has for sucking, rooting, and swallowing. Frequently, parents need instruction from someone familiar with these techniques—either your child's therapist or teacher. In general, it is a good idea to have a speech therapist check your baby's eating patterns and oral motor skills to help you provide the best feeding stimulation. Remember, these techniques require time and practice. To stimulate your baby's natural rooting and sucking mechanisms, you can rub her cheeks toward the mouth with your hand or a soft cloth. This should make her pucker. The best time to do this is just before mealtime to stimulate her oral reflexes. You should also encourage her to suck on her hand, fist, or fingers. These normal hand-to-mouth activities will help her develop good oral patterns.

You can also use the nipple of the breast or the bottle to stimulate these reflexes. Gentle pressure on the baby's cheeks or lips will get the baby to turn her head toward the nipple in a rooting reflex. Your baby will need good lip closure on the nipple, and you can help her by holding her in a flexed position, rubbing the cheeks toward the lips, and rubbing upward from the chin and downward from the nose toward the lips.

If you choose to bottle feed your baby, there is quite a wide variety of commercial nipples available. She may respond better to one commercial nipple than to another. In choosing a commercial nipple, you should check to see that there is a nice, even flow of milk. There is also a wide variety of bottles. For a child with a weak suck it may be helpful to use a soft plastic bottle or disposable plastic bag. Either of these will allow you to apply gentle pressure on the bottle or bag to help milk flow out evenly.

Pacifiers can also help strengthen your baby's suck. You may choose from a wide variety of shapes, sizes, and materials. Your baby may respond more positively to one than another, so be ready for some experimenting. The pacifier helps strengthen oral motor control and can help soothe your baby if she is upset. But remember that, just like other babies, your child may not want or need to use a pacifier.

Babies need good support to eat comfortably and efficiently. Low muscle tone makes it more difficult for your baby to hold herself in a good position, which is crucial to proper sucking and swallowing. At first the mother or father must provide good support for their baby. Obviously, the type of support depends on the baby's age and developmental level. When they are tiny, babies should be in a semi-upright position with good head support, and with the head tilted slightly forward. A newborn should be cradled snugly and securely in your arms with her legs supported in your lap.

There are two ways to arrange your baby's mealtimes: You can establish a schedule or you can feed her on demand. With demand feeding you offer the baby food when she shows she is hungry and ready to eat. Scheduled feeding means that you set a routine, usually feeding the baby at three- to four-hour intervals. Babies with Down syndrome generally do best when they are fed on demand. If your baby has difficulty eating, mealtime will go more smoothly when she is hungry and ready to eat. Any baby will concentrate better when awake, alert, and giving signs that she is hungry, such as lip-smacking, hand-to-mouth activity, restlessness, fussing, rooting, sticking out her tongue, or crying. Some babies with Down syndrome tend to sleep through what should be their mealtime. In these cases, parents should monitor their baby's feeding to make sure she is getting enough nutrition and consult with their baby's pediatrician.

Introducing Solid Foods

Your baby can be introduced to solid foods at the same age as other children. This usually occurs from four to six months of age, but some people wait as long as a year. Generally, we recommend that babies with Down syndrome be introduced to solid foods early. Eating solid foods helps develop a number of important skills, including fine motor skills and sensory awareness in the mouth. More importantly, babies with Down syndrome can be extra sensitive to differing textures; if this happens, they may balk at trying different foods. The sooner they can work through this, the better. Check with your baby's doctor or teachers to determine when your child is ready to start eating solid food.

When you do introduce new foods, give your baby a choice of either commercially-prepared, pureed baby foods, or prepare the pureed foods at home. Both options are fine. The commercial baby food companies have emphasized nutrition in the preparation of their foods by limiting the amount of added salt and sugar. The order in which foods are introduced varies, but many people first offer cereal, then yellow vegetables, green vegetables, and fruit, with meats and fish last. Your baby may not like all of these foods, but what baby does? Just strive for a balanced diet.

Give your baby small amounts of new food each day for several days to see that she can tolerate it. Babies will often push food out of their mouth with their tongues. When this happens, you can try putting a small amount of food onto the middle part of the tongue with some downward pressure from the spoon. You can also try applying some gentle pressure on the upper and lower lips to keep the mouth closed around the food.

As babies gain control over solids, they start finger feeding, a very important and enjoyable activity for them. It provides them with independence as well as with another way to explore their environment. In addition, finger feeding develops sensory awareness and fine motor control.

Finger feeding is an extension of the hand-to-mouth activity begun at a very early age. You should offer your baby a large variety of finger foods. Sticky foods are good for children who have not yet developed a good grasp with their fingers. Try cottage cheese, yogurt, or pudding so your baby can dip her fingers into the food and bring it to her mouth. Later on, when the baby develops a better grasp, she can start reaching for small bits of food like Cheerios, cooked pasta, cooked vegetables, and fruits.

When your baby starts to use her own spoon, you will again have to try some of the different sizes and shapes available. Often conventional adult spoons are difficult for a baby to use in the beginning; she will have more success if the spoon is easier to hold and place in her mouth. You can buy baby spoons with a flatter bowl and a wider grip. Some have small holes in the bowl that help keep the food sitting on the spoon until the baby places it in her mouth. Again, it is a good idea to have a therapist check the way your baby takes the food from the spoon and the way she holds and moves the spoon. Proper posture and support are as crucial for eating as they are for breast or bottle feeding. How your baby sits affects how well she can manipulate food and hold a spoon. Your child should be fed in a high chair with her feet well supported, her trunk secure, and the height of the table at elbow level. Sometimes a child will benefit from foam supports in the high chair to keep her in a proper position before she can easily do it herself. You should ask your child's teacher or therapist whether your child needs the extra support and where she needs it.

Mealtimes with your child will be noisy and hectic; they can also be enjoyable. Like all children, your child may often wear more food than she eats. What can you do to prevent mealtimes from becoming too chaotic?

First, consistent discipline is essential. Behavior such as standing on a chair should be discouraged. Set standards for all your children and hold them to it. But remember, mealtimes are excellent opportunities to work on development, language, and self-help skills. Strike a balance and strive for enjoyable mealtimes, knowing that they can be both rewarding and frustrating.

Drinking from a Cup

The transition from breast or bottle feeding to cup drinking depends on your child's ability to reach, grasp, and control the cup. By the time your baby is ready to drink from a cup she already has taken an active role in holding her bottle and can bring it to her mouth. For good cup drinking, your baby has to be able to sip from the cup rather than suck. This can be encouraged by initially having the baby take liquids from a cup with a wide lip or a cup with a lid that allows small amounts of liquid through holes in the lid. Spout cups are not a good idea because they only promote sucking.

While your baby drinks, pay close attention to make sure she is not resting the cup on her tongue instead of on her lower lip. Babies are tempted to do this because it is easier to hold the cup still with the tongue rather than with the lower lip, particularly if the baby is used to sticking her tongue out. This habit is difficult to break when the child is older, so it is a good idea to discourage it early. Giving gentle support under the chin can enable your child to hold the cup

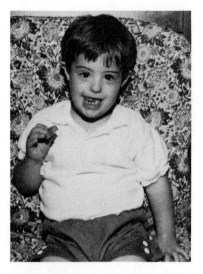

in the right position without using her tongue. Your teacher or therapist can be very helpful in teaching your child to drink correctly from a cup.

Weight Gain

Some babies with Down syndrome have difficulty gaining weight. It is generally a problem among children who have a congenital heart defect. This is usually a concern during the first year of life. These babies should be monitored by their cardiologist and pediatrician. Special diets and other medical treatment can be prescribed to improve weight gain.

Your child should have her growth monitored, using a special growth chart for children with Down syndrome. Figure 1 shows two growth charts with the range of growth for girls and boys with Down syndrome. Children with Down syndrome have a slower rate of growth than children on standard growth charts. The important thing is to maintain balance between weight gain and growth in height. Never settle for the outdated stereotype of the fat and inactive child with Down syndrome.

Parents of children with Down syndrome need to pay particular attention to their child's weight gain. Studies of children with Down syndrome have found that approximately twenty-five percent develop obesity. This obesity is usually caused by a combination of overeating and inactivity due to low muscle tone. An additional factor is that children are frequently rewarded for activities with sweets and high calorie foods. The pattern of excessive weight gain usually becomes obvious as the child reaches two to three years of age.

Constipation

Many children with Down syndrome have difficulty with constipation. This may be due to low muscle tone, which makes it more difficult for the baby to develop a good push for a bowel movement. There are helpful steps you can take. First, control your child's diet.

Figure 1. Growth Charts for Boys and Girls with Down Syndrome

GIRLS WITH DOWN SYNDROME

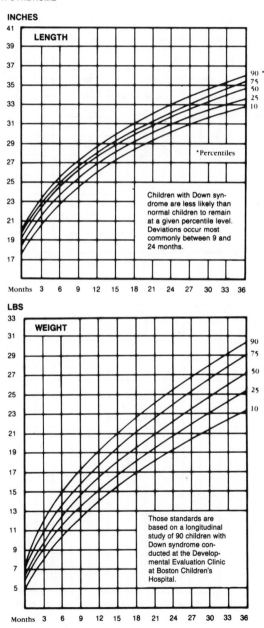

INCHES

LENGTH

90 *
75
50
25
10

*Percentiles

Children with Down syndrome are less likely than normal children to remain at a given percentile level. Deviations occur most commonly between 9 and 24 months.

Months 3 6 9 12 15 18 21 24 27 30 33 36

LBS

WEIGHT

90
75
50
25
10

Those standards are based on a longitudinal study of 90 children with Down syndrome conducted at the Developmental Evaluation Clinic at Boston Children's Hospital.

Months 3 6 9 12 15 18 21 24 27 30 33 36

BOYS WITH DOWN SYNDROME

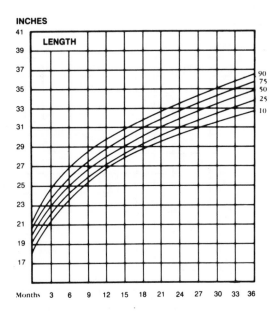

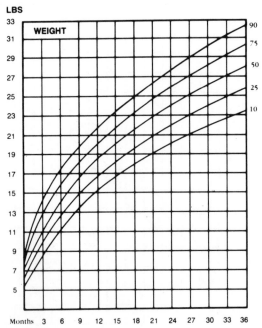

It is important to have a good balance of whole grain cereals, vegetables, fruits, and plenty of liquids. This helps digestion and minimizes constipation. If you notice your child struggling during bowel movements, try flexing her legs up to her abdomen. This puts pressure on the belly and helps your child to push. If additional measures are required, consult your pediatrician.

Hygiene

Good personal hygiene habits are important for children and adults with Down syndrome. The foundation for good hygiene is laid in childhood; getting your child into the pattern of washing, brushing, and caring for herself is a critical skill for the future. This section reviews some of the basics of daily care for your child.

Bathing and Skin Care

Many parents bathe their children daily, but this may not be necessary as long as the child is clean in the diaper area and around the face and mouth. Parents generally give newborns sponge baths using a soft cloth. While the baby is small she is often bathed in a wash bowl, sink, or baby bathtub. When the baby is older and you feel more secure, she can be bathed in a tub.

Children with Down syndrome have a tendency to develop dry skin, with areas of rough, red, flaky, or irritated patches on the legs, buttocks, arms, hands, and feet. To prevent and control this, it is important to develop a good skin care routine. You should use nondetergent soaps, and apply lotions right after bathing while the skin is still moist. Apply lotion more than once a day, particularly on the hands and face after mealtime wiping. If the problem persists, consult your pediatrician. He or she can prescribe more potent skin lotions or suggest other ways to treat dry skin.

Parents often ask about the scalp, which can become crusted and flaky. This cradle cap is quite common in the early months of your baby's life and is part of the scalp's normal way of removing dead skin cells. The best treatment is to gently brush the scalp with your fingers or a soft brush during bathing to remove the dead skin.

It is important to keep the diaper area clean. It may be helpful to routinely use a lubricant such as petroleum jelly to protect the skin from dryness and irritation. Diaper rash can be treated with most over-the-counter ointments. If the rash does not clear up, consult your pediatrician.

Diapering can be an excellent time to incorporate developmental activities. At the very least, it is a good time to be sociable, to talk to your baby, to stroke her body, to help her move her arms and legs. Your baby's teacher or therapist may also have some good ideas on positions and movements during diapering.

Toilet Training

Many children with Down syndrome do not become toilet trained during the first three years of life, although there is a wide range of accomplishments in this area. As with other children, toilet training can be quite a struggle, but your child *will* become toilet trained. It may take longer, but she will do it.

Many books and pamphlets have been published to help parents toilet train their children. There are also books specifically for parents of handicapped or retarded children. As your child grows, she will start to become aware of her bodily functions. At that point, she will need to know how to ask to go to the bathroom. Toilet training requires many areas of development to come together at once—such as communication, muscle control, and awareness of bodily functions. We do not include techniques in toilet training in this chapter, so when your child reaches that stage, refer to the books in the Reading List, and if necessary, seek the help of your baby's teachers, therapists, and doctors.

Eyes

Like other children, babies with Down syndrome sometimes develop blockages in a tear duct, resulting in increased tearing or crusting of the eye. In some children this corrects itself, while in others it may require medical treatment. To help avoid blocked tear ducts, you can clean your baby's eyelids by wiping gently from the inner corner outward toward the ear. This can be done with a clean moist washcloth or cotton ball.

Ears

Barring any ear infections (discussed in Chapter 3), your baby's ears can receive normal care. Earwax builds up naturally in the ears and works its way out of the ear. Therefore, there is no need to insert *any* object into the ear canal. You just need to clean the outer ear and the area behind the ear by gently washing and drying.

Nose

Some children with Down syndrome have more frequent runny noses and thickened secretions due to smaller nasal passages. Usually, the use of a cool mist humidifier in the baby's room is recommended. This will help loosen secretions and make it easier for your baby to breathe.

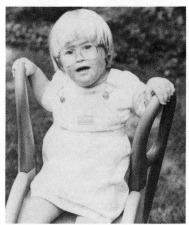

To clean the outside of the nose, wipe it with a warm, moistened cloth such as a diaper or soft cotton washcloth. Occasionally, nose secretions become dry and crusted around the outside of the nose. You can remove these gently with the use of a lotion or a cream. Try not to irritate the nose further by frequent wiping. Petroleum jelly or lotion will also ease the irritation. If the inside of your baby's nose becomes dry and crusty, ask your pediatrician about saline nose drops. Nasal aspirators do not work well and may cause irritation.

Teeth

As with any child, it is important to instill good habits of dental care at an early age. This benefits the child in a number of ways. First, if your baby breathes with her mouth open much of the time, there can be an extra build-up of tartar in her mouth. Second, brushing helps stimulate a number of developmental skills—from getting used to sensory stimulation all around the mouth, to practicing sound production in the mirror, to learning how to handle the toothbrush by herself. To avoid dental problems later, good oral hygiene is essential now.

Holding Your Baby

It is very important to be conscious of how your baby positions herself and how she moves. In addition to low muscle tone, babies with Down syndrome often have very mobile joints. This allows their limbs to settle into positions that might lead to problems when they start to sit, crawl, and walk. Many parents find it helpful to consult a physical therapist soon after birth to ask about positioning. There are simple changes you can make in the way you might instinctively hold your baby, changes that would stabilize her joints and help support her better. For example, it helps to hold your baby so that her legs are together, rather than wrapped around your hips.

Early patterns of movement can influence later development and are crucial to a child's future social acceptance and self-esteem. Children with Down syndrome who move normally can do more of the things other children can do, like climb, run, and play. Good motor development will improve your child's posture, mobility, coordination, and endurance. And how you hold your baby contributes to this.

You may not have given much thought to how you hold your baby. But your baby with Down syndrome has special needs, and how you hold her may affect her development. Consult with your baby's pediatrician and teachers for hints on holding your child. Remember, good development is the product of a lot of small details.

All of this concern about how you hold your child may be intimidating. Unless your baby has a particular medical problem, however, don't handle her as though she were made of glass. She will love "roughhousing" and active play, just as other children do. Not only is this good for sensory stimulation, but it sends to your baby and your other children the message that you intend to treat her as an equal member of the family. If you set this example, family and friends will follow your lead. This will benefit everyone.

Exercise

Exercise is critical to children with Down syndrome. It can break the vicious cycle of low muscle tone leading to inactivity, inactivity leading to obesity, obesity leading to more inactivity, and so on and so on. Because low muscle tone requires your baby to work harder to move, you need to take an active role in monitoring your baby's movements, designing a good exercise program, and motivating her to move around.

A physical therapist, teacher, and selected books can get you and your baby started on an exercise program. Your baby's teacher can also make sure your baby's exercise actually aids development. Strengthening muscles, improving coordination, and learning balance all can help tremendously in many areas of development.

Sleep and Rest

Newborns do not have predictable sleep patterns. They often sleep most of the time and wake primarily to eat. Of course, each child is different, but generally newborns with Down syndrome have normal sleep patterns. As your child grows, the periods of wakefulness and sleep both increase. By two to three months of age, your baby's sleep becomes more organized, and a regular pattern develops.

Parents learn early to interpret their baby's cues for sleep as well as for hunger and attention. Your baby will express her needs for each of these with different cries, movements, and vocalizations. You will come to know when it is time for your baby to sleep–hopefully when *you* want to sleep–and when it is time to be awake. Once asleep, your baby's level of sleep varies, and she frequently will make noises, twitch, and move. These are all normal signs of sleep.

As in all daily care activities, routine is important. Many parents complain that their children won't sleep through the night, or won't settle down without being held or without being allowed to sleep in Mom and Dad's bed. A regular sleep and bedtime routine consistently enforced may help to avoid these problems. Don't assume your child needs comforting any more or less because she has Down syndrome. She will be just as quick as any other child to manipulate you in your attempts to settle her down for the night.

Baby Sitting

Any caring and careful person with whom you feel comfortable can baby-sit your baby. No special training is required. Of course, you will need to spend some time showing the baby sitter how your baby eats, sleeps, or plays, but you would do this for any child. The important thing to remember is that it is good for *everyone* if you get a baby sitter once in a while. You need to take some time for yourself, and your baby needs to learn to deal with people other than family members.

If you feel more comfortable with a trained baby sitter, contact your local Association for Retarded Citizens. They have a list of sitters in your area who specialize in child care for special-needs children.

Selecting a Pediatrician

Most pediatricians are well equipped to care for a child with Down syndrome. If you have selected a pediatrician prior to the birth of your child, you can simply continue to use him or her. It is most important that the pediatrician be able to give you enough time to answer questions, and that he or she be knowledgeable in community resources. Your pediatrician should also have an interest in monitoring your child's development and health, and must be willing to be a part of the team caring for her. It is vital for your pediatrician to work closely with your baby's teachers, therapists, and family. Refer back to Chapter 3 for tips on dealing with doctors.

Conclusion

Caring for a baby–any baby–is quite an imposing challenge. When that baby has Down syndrome and special needs, the task becomes more complicated. Though your baby is special, her daily care will be very much like that of other children. She can adjust to your life and fit in like other children. Information, patience, and persistence will help ease your new baby into a routine that is good for everyone. Use the books in the Reading List and seek the help of doctors, teachers, and therapists. And always remember: Your baby with Down syndrome, like every other baby, needs love, attention, and care.

Parent Statements

We feel it's very important to treat Julie normally. It's having normal expectations for behavior. For example, we put a lot of emphasis on eating properly, using her utensils properly, chewing properly, and things like that. We've had high expectations for her here at home, and her eating has been very good. Expecting normal behavior all the way around, even if you have to work harder at it, is the trick.

As far as little things go, I don't do too much differently with her except just pay more attention to her skin care. Other than that, I treat her like a normal baby; she didn't have any problems that I had to be careful about. As far as working with her goes, that was a major change because I was constantly striving to stimulate her. I was always playing and doing this and that, not only in our normal routine but making time to play with her, whereas before I probably would have done my housework or something. But that's been good too because I learned a lot about how to play with the baby.

The daily care of Josh has always been different from my other kids. It's been more intensive. It's carried a guilt element because we felt that there should be something else we should be doing all the time. We felt we should be making every moment a developmental laboratory.

Our baby has been nursed from when he was an infant so that's very lucky. He always nursed properly and started on solids at four months. He's twenty months now, and he feeds himself with a spoon. My husband is the best person to teach him how to eat because he really can give us the run-around if he wants to. We try not to let mealtimes become a battleground, but he likes testing. He's going through a testing phase, so we find him deliberately holding things over the side of his high chair and watching to see if we're going to say anything before he flings it over. But he can eat properly if he wants to.

When Laurie was two, she was a very plump little child. We put her on a diet, watched every speck she ate, and now she's fine. I think the Down syndrome makes her look heavier than she probably would otherwise. Her muscle tone has improved in the past few months, and she's getting good rotation in her trunk. So she'll be slim as can be in time. But her muscle mass is not good. I just really monitor her food. It's really hard when you have to switch gears after something like heart surgery. Before the surgery it was give, give, give, fortify, fortify— anything she wanted she got. A child gets in those behavior patterns easily.

We do have a hard time leaving her with a sitter. We just haven't felt comfortable doing that. I guess we just felt kind of protective. We didn't even go out for almost two years. Lately we have felt differently. We've left her with more people and she just gets along fine.

FIVE

❖━❑━❑━❖

Family Life
with Your New Baby

MARIAN H. JARRETT, ED.D.*

You have undoubtedly thought about the changes in your life that the birth of your baby will bring. Many of these thoughts are happy ones, and rightfully so, because your baby will bring you great joy. But the arrival of a baby with Down syndrome also brings stress and strain on family members and on family relationships. Having a child with Down syndrome requires coping by the whole family. You will face the challenge of adjusting in your own way, but right from the start you should know that it can be done. Thousands of families can testify to that.

Life today is much brighter for families of children with Down syndrome. So much has been learned to help families successfully raise their child. With early infant education, special schools and programs, better social acceptance, support groups, and vastly improved medical care, family life is dramatically better than it was even ten or twenty years ago. Families are no longer left to struggle on their own.

Most parents worry about what having a child with Down syndrome will do to their families. One of the most common concerns

---

*Marian Jarrett holds a Doctorate in Education and is the Director of the Infant Program at The Glenbrook Day School in Rockville, Maryland.

is how well the child will fit into the family. Parents ask, "Will our child's behavior be so abnormal that everyday family life will be disrupted? Will I or my children be continually embarrassed by our child with Down syndrome? Will normal family fun come to an end?" These questions reflect the common concerns of new parents of babies with Down syndrome.

Parents also worry about how they can meet the challenge posed by a special-needs child. There is a great deal of work involved in raising any child with a handicap, and raising a child with Down syndrome is no different. The challenge of fostering development, independence, and social ability is considerable, and parents naturally wonder how they can do all the work that is required. How can they give their special child all he needs and still meet their other responsibilities: to their other children, to their spouse, to their jobs, to themselves?

A major part of the worry that parents feel is fear of the unknown. But remember, other parents have faced the same fears and worries. They will tell you that it forced changes in their lives that involved hard work and considerable adjustment. They will also tell you that their child was a positive addition to the family and that they cannot imagine life without their special child.

Parents are the key to how well a family adjusts to having a family member with Down syndrome. Children, other family members, and friends follow the parents' cues. How the parents act toward the child sets the pattern for the whole family from the moment the baby is born.

Being the Parent of a Baby with Down Syndrome

Before the birth of your baby, you may have expected child rearing to come naturally. But the parent of a baby with Down syndrome faces unique challenges, and what once seemed easy and natural now seems fraught with complications. You may wonder how this baby can ever be a part of your family as worries about the future invade all your thoughts and activities.

All parents face worries and conflicting emotions in the early stages of their baby's life. They soon learn to depend on love, acceptance, and discipline as the staples of good parenting. You will undoubtedly depend on these also in raising your special child. Although this section focuses on those areas of family life that are *different* because your child is special, the goal for you is the same as for all families: integrating your child into your growing family as a valued, contributing member.

You may turn to your family and friends for help in meeting the challenge of bringing up a special child. Also remember that your child's teacher and other professionals can be a tremendous source of support for you. The parent-professional partnership, which is discussed in Chapter 7, can be a great source of practical information on coping. Just having someone you can ask about problems or questions makes your daily work easier. Nagging uncertainties, worries, and questions can be resolved quickly. More importantly, the advice of teachers and other professionals is based on the collective experience of many children and families. As a result, this advice can be very useful in offering you options for dealing with your own problems and worries.

Becoming Part of the Family

Right from the start, you should expect that your baby with Down syndrome will be a *part* of your family, not the center of it. Just because your child is special does not mean he should dominate family life. This is not good for your baby nor for the rest of the family. Your baby does have special needs and he will demand emotional and physical resources that other children might not demand. But remember, your goal is to balance all the competing demands so that everyone in the family can become an equal and contributing member. This is the same challenge that all parents face, whether they have a handicapped child or not.

The relationship of each family member with the child with Down syndrome will be a reflection of your attitudes as parents. If you hold and cuddle and love your baby, if you voice your feelings of affection, if you face challenges in a positive manner, then other family members will too. As you begin the task of integrating your baby and his disability into your lives, you and all of your family will grow to love your baby more and more. That love will be your strongest ally, your strongest bond. Through patience and understanding your child can be a loved and loving member of your family.

In order for you to guide your family in accepting your baby with Down syndrome, open and honest communication is essential. Encourage everyone in your family to vent his or her emotions and to support one another. Try not to be judgmental. Set an atmosphere of acceptance and allow negative feelings as well as positive ones to be expressed. You as parents need this opportunity to talk about your child; so do siblings, grandparents, and other family members. Frequently, you will find that your feelings are shared by your spouse or other family members.

In addition to open communication and a supportive environment, it is essential that your children have information. Leaving things unsaid will only send a confused and troubling message to your children. Tell them that their sibling has Down syndrome as soon as you think they are ready. Explain it on a level they can understand, and give them more information as they get older. You will be surprised at how much they understand and how easily they accept what most adults receive with shock and sadness. Children have the ability to love their brother or sister unconditionally.

If you accept your child with Down syndrome and are comfortable with him, he will fit into your family and your lifestyle. Your child will enjoy family mealtimes, outings, and going to school with other children. Your child may be able to receive most of his education in a school where he can be mainstreamed with nonhandicapped children for music, art, gym, and special assembly programs. This allows the child with Down syndrome to learn from the example of the children in his regular classes. Working to make your child as much a part of the "normal" world in his school and in your family life will help him tremendously. And the benefits of this are twofold. This exposure will also help others in your child's world become more familiar and more comfortable with Down syndrome and mental retardation.

The medical problems that some babies with Down syndrome have can add stress and hinder family integration. Although your goal is to make your child an integral part of your family, medical needs may make this difficult. Parents sometimes need to focus their attention just on their child with Down syndrome. This is not unreasonable. It can happen in any family when a child is sick or has a special problem. Remember to let your other children be involved with their sibling. Encourage them to make hospital visits and to express their feelings. Above all, keep them informed. They will be concerned and will want to help.

Love and Acceptance

The birth of a baby with Down syndrome comes as a shock to most parents. In addition to the feelings of love and protection they have for their new baby, they also feel sadness and grief. These mixed feelings toward the baby often continue as the child grows. Do not hesitate to recognize these feelings within yourself and accept them without feeling guilty about them. No parent feels good about his or her child all the time.

Get to know your baby. Learn more about Down syndrome. Initially, you may be afraid to love your baby because you know so little about him and his condition. The closer you get to him, the more at ease you will become.

Today you can develop a relationship with your baby with new confidence. Bolstered by the guidance and support of informed professionals, community support groups, and family and friends, you can provide an environment in which your child can grow to be a unique individual supported by your love.

Parents used to be told, "Just put him in an institution and forget about him." But children with Down syndrome have proven how well they respond to a stimulating and loving home. If you put a child in an institution, he will act like he belongs there; if you keep him at home and work with him, he will act like he belongs with you. Your relationship with your child—built on love and acceptance—is the key.

Some parents feel that they cannot keep their baby with Down syndrome at home. But placement in an institution is not the only choice. Another alternative is to place the child for adoption. There are agencies with waiting lists of people who specifically want to adopt a baby with Down syndrome. Foster homes are also a viable alternative because these special children benefit most from family life.

Expectations

Babies with Down syndrome are born with a variety of physical and intellectual abilities. We know that these abilities are more limited than those of other children, but it is not possible to predict any child's full potential at an early age. At this point in your baby's life, do not set limits on what your child will or will not be able to do. Strive for that delicate balance between a realistic assessment of your child's development and the self-fulfilling prophecy of low achievement. Most of all, ensure that your child will lead a happy and useful life by providing appropriate support and training from an early age.

Parents spend more time with their young children than anyone else, and their expectations can affect their children in tangible ways. For example, if you do not expect your child with Down syndrome to dress himself, he may not. This may be due in part to the fact that you unwittingly have not given him the chance. You may dress and undress him or simply help him too much because your expectations are too low.

Do not form your expectations in a vacuum and do not base them on stereotypes. Talk to doctors, teachers, therapists, and other parents of children with Down syndrome. It takes information and exposure to realistically set your expectations. More importantly, try not to look too far into the future. Focus on the next developmental skill; set short-term goals. After all, the future is made up of what your child learns along the way.

Discipline

Discipline is the parents' responsibility. Having a special child does not change that. You do not do your child a favor by failing to demand proper behavior because you feel sorry for him or because you think he cannot understand how to behave. If you allow your child to misbehave, you can be assured he will continue to misbehave. Your child's safety, social integration, and education depend on proper behavior. Parents owe it to their child to demand it.

Disciplining a retarded child may be a difficult thing for you to do. In public and with friends it is even harder. However, the experience of many families is clear: Discipline needs to be enforced *consistently*. Children need to know what is, and what is not, acceptable conduct in *all* situations. Firmness and consistency work best; don't take the easy way out for reasons of convenience, embarrassment, or frustration. Unless you can teach your child safe and acceptable behavior, he may always be dependent on you.

The social development of children and adults with Down syndrome is often more advanced than their level of mental development. Give your child every chance to succeed in life by teaching him to behave the way you expect his brothers and sisters to behave. Set limits and be consistent in enforcing them. And remember, emphasize the positive. Praise and affection are the most powerful motivators for good behavior.

An important consideration is how others will handle your child. With baby sitters, grandparents, relatives, and friends, there is often the opportunity for your discipline to be undermined. It will be necessary for you to politely yet firmly let others know that discipline is important to you and to your child. Explain to them what conduct is acceptable and what is not. Help them understand and enlist their help. Firmness and consistency are not always easy to maintain, but they will pay off.

When setting expectations for your child's behavior, you must learn to give him enough time to process information. Do not expect instant responses or fast transitions from one activity to another. It is possible that he needs a little extra time to understand your wishes and to decide on his own response. What may appear to be resistance or stubbornness may simply be an inability to cope with your demands. If you are faced with a pattern of resistance, you can often break through it by offering a more interesting and exciting alternative. You may have to observe your child and consider his developmental level and his ability to understand in order to distinguish between resistance to reasonable expectations and his inability to process your demands. You as his parent will be in the best position to judge.

Independence

It is natural to feel that your child is particularly vulnerable because he has Down syndrome. It is a natural reaction to feel sorry for your child and to want to protect him. But for the sake of your child's future you must treat him as normally as possible. Your child needs to learn independence and responsibility. He needs to feel good about himself and what he can do.

Your job begins early in teaching your child self-help skills such as dressing and feeding himself. Give your child the opportunity to do things for himself. Don't rush to help him before you give him the chance to try something on his own. Encourage and praise your child along the way and reward him with a big hug for a job well done.

Your child will likely be involved in an education or therapy program at an early age and will need to be "on his own" in many of these situations. Don't let your child's crying tempt you to give up on a new school or program that may be strange to him. Give him time to adjust. Children usually adjust well and really enjoy school.

Expose your child to new situations whenever possible. Provide him with a variety of experiences and help him adjust to what is new and different. Take him to the zoo, introduce him to a sandbox, let him explore the local shopping mall. Give him responsibilities and chores within the family. Think positively about what your child can do. Feel positive about his capabilities. Increase your child's self-esteem by giving him the opportunity to succeed within the secure confines of the family. This will help prepare him to move out into the larger world of friends, school, work, and community.

If your baby has a congenital heart defect, you may not be able to treat him as you would any other baby. Frequent trips to the hospital for cardiac studies, the risk of respiratory infection, and difficulty in feeding will necessitate extra care and caution on your part. Provide this care and protect your baby wisely, but be ready to allow him to move out into the world as soon as he is able. To be sure, this is not easy. Conflicting emotions and real medical concerns intensify the natural urge to protect your child and complicate the necessary process of letting go.

Brothers and Sisters of Children with Down Syndrome

Being the brother or sister of a child with Down syndrome is special. In many subtle and not-so-subtle ways your other children's lives will be different now that they have a special sibling. But do not assume that this difference is all bad. Far from it. Having a sibling with Down syndrome is stressful and enriching, frustrating and fun, worrisome and rewarding. Most of all, it is very much like being the sibling of any other child, complete with all the annoyances and joys. This section reviews the effects—both good and bad—that children with Down syndrome have on their siblings, and focuses on what you, the parent, can do to help all your children build healthy relationships with one another.

Children's Feelings

From the time they are old enough to understand, your other children will have thoughts and feelings about their special sibling. At first, they may perceive only that it takes their brother or sister longer to do things like walk or talk. Later, they will begin to understand that their brother or sister is handicapped. What follows is a summary of the thoughts and feelings typically experienced by siblings of children with Down syndrome.

Pre-School. Children are very perceptive, so it is possible for your other children to react to the anxiety you feel about your baby with Down syndrome. At this age they are unlikely to recognize any difference in their special sibling or understand what Down syndrome is, but pre-schoolers may perceive developmental differences and try in their own way to help teach skills. They want to help. Mostly this is an age when children fall in love with their sibling and want to help take care of him.

Ages Four to Six. As children become more sophisticated they often begin to wonder what is "wrong" with their sibling. They may worry about catching Down syndrome or worry that something is different about them as well. Additionally, they often feel guilty about any negative thoughts they may have toward their special sibling. For example, anger caused by frustration—a perfectly normal response for young children at times—can cause feelings of guilt. Sometimes children try to compensate for their special sibling's problems by trying to be especially exemplary themselves. They become excessively helpful and obedient beyond limits that are good for them, for your family, or for the child with Down syndrome.

Ages Six to Twelve. Children at these ages often have conflicting emotions. On the one hand, they can feel good about being needed by their special sibling, and on the other hand, can consider their sibling a nuisance. They may respond to teasing of their sibling by becoming hostile toward the culprit or by being protective. At the same time they may be resentful of any extra work imposed on them as a result of their sibling's special needs. Parental preoccupation with the special child can be viewed by other children as "babying," which they may consider unfair.

Ages Twelve to Sixteen. During this important period of adolescent development, your child's social life often causes some very normal problems. Teenagers often feel embarrassed by their families. When friends and dates come to your house, your teenager may feel quite embarrassed by your special child. Your teenager will love his or her special sibling and care about him, but just as certainly will want to exercise freedom and independence. This is a time when responsibilities imposed on your other children—including responsibility for your child with Down syndrome—may be resented. Concerns over the future also can arise. Your other children may worry whether they will have to take responsibility for their special sibling in later years and whether their own children will have Down syndrome.

These are just some of the possible emotions your child with Down syndrome may trigger in your other children. Emotions come in every shape and size, and each child's feelings are unique. But some feelings seem universal. Love, fear, jealousy, resentment, anger, pride, and frustration are present at some time in children, as they are in adults. The central challenge for a caring parent is to deal with these many genuine—and conflicting—human emotions.

Dealing with Your Children's Emotions

Just as you experience stress as the parents of a child with Down syndrome, your other children will also find it stressful to be the sibling of a handicapped child. But the strongest factor in their adjustment will be *your* reaction. They will follow your lead in interacting with their brother or sister. But, like you, they will have conflicting emotions about their sibling. It would be easier if children clearly showed their feelings, but often children do not, or cannot, express how they are feeling about life with their special sibling. Parents must be emotional detectives, deciphering their children's emotions from clues in their behavior. First and foremost, dealing effectively with emotions requires observation and listening.

Information. Children can deal better with their sibling with Down syndrome if they have information. You should be the main source of this information. Even if they do not ask, give them information. As with other subjects, give them information appropriate to their age level and expand it as they grow.

Even with an explanation of what Down syndrome is and what it means to be retarded, your children may still be concerned and worried. They may worry about catching Down syndrome, about having children of their own, and about caring for their sibling in the future. Continue to provide information and to reassure your children. Their sibling does not have to be a burden. Be ready to debunk the myths they may hear from friends by giving them the facts.

Communication. It is important that you encourage and even prod your children to talk about the feelings they have for their sibling. Let them know it is normal to feel as they do and that it is healthy to express themselves. If possible, let them join with other siblings of handicapped children to work through their feelings. Sibling groups are sponsored by a variety of organizations. Urge your children to take advantage of the opportunity to sort out what they are feeling and experiencing.

Children get angry, annoyed, frustrated—as we all do. Sometimes they fight. But when a sibling with Down syndrome is the cause of that anger, young children can experience great difficulty. Sometimes out of sympathy for their parents or their sibling, children feel guilty about their anger. As a parent, it is vital for you to let your children know that it is sometimes reasonable to get angry with their sibling and to vent that anger. All of your children need to communicate their anger over things like broken toys or misplaced keepsakes. Protecting your child with Down syndrome from the often well-deserved wrath of his siblings cuts off communication and forces feelings underground. Anger is a natural part of family life. Every member is a target from time to time. Having a child with Down syndrome should not change that.

Balance. It is important that you balance the needs of all of your children. Encourage all of them to succeed and to fulfill themselves. Do not give all of your attention to your child with Down syndrome. It is not healthy for one child to dominate parental attention in family life. Instead, you need to skillfully juggle the many demands on your time and attention.

Do not allow your special child to become overly dependent on his siblings. Rather, encourage your children to take an active part in their special sibling's educational and therapeutic programs. They, too, will become emotionally invested in their brother and will rejoice in each independent step he takes. And, remember to allow them to do this *as a brother or sister*. Do not press them into the role of parent, even if they seem ready to assume it. This is not a healthy situation for them and can breed long-standing resentment.

Organization. With all that is urged upon parents of babies with Down syndrome—early infant education, monitoring for medical problems, all the normal baby-care responsibilities—it is easy to unintentionally overlook your other children. There is only so much of you and only so many hours in a day. Try to organize your time. With a special-needs child, the challenge is a little greater, but it can be done.

Children do not conveniently schedule their crises. They get hurt, upset, or excited on their own time, and when they do, they demand your immediate and full attention. Parents often cannot control their own schedules, but there are a few things you can do to keep things running reasonably smoothly. Here is a short list of ideas:

- Keep track of the amount of time spent with each child. Try to spend some individual time with each child and your spouse. And leave some time for yourself.
- Whenever possible, schedule the time that must be spent exclusively with your child with Down syndrome at times when your other children are not at home or are otherwise occupied.

- When your children are at home, organize group play that includes all your children. Let your older children lead and your younger children follow.
- Keep your children busy. Schedule play times, visits to friends' houses, and outings to the park.
- Don't try to do it all yourself. Organize car pools and play groups. Pay a baby sitter or trade with another mother. If you can, get help with the house.

Individuality. Just as this book encourages you to treat your child with Down syndrome as an individual, it is equally important to do the same for your other children. They need lives outside their family. They need to experience peer friendship, social acceptance, and non-family responsibilities. Their identity cannot be limited just to being the sibling of a brother or sister with Down syndrome. Provide them with activities away from home, with their own friends. Encourage them to pursue their own interests and talents and to exercise their independence. Build their self-esteem just as you would with your special child. Children with balanced lives will be far better adjusted to their special family, as well as more supportive of both you and their sibling.

Your expectations of your children can make a difference. Expect, demand, and work to build and maintain normal family relationships. Allow your other children to act like children. And let them know that you expect your child with Down syndrome to behave appropriately. Siblings resent favored treatment accorded to others. It is important to both your other children and your child with Down syndrome that you require your special sibling to help take care of himself and to contribute in helping with the family chores. Don't settle for less.

Specialness. In addition to encouraging your other children to lead their own lives, it is also very important to give them a sense of their own specialness. Let them know that because their sibling is special, so are they—in a very positive way. Most siblings naturally feel good about being needed by their special sibling. As parents you can reinforce those feelings. Praise their compassion, the extra work they do around the house, and the extra coping required of them. Make them feel that their efforts are recognized and appreciated.

Dealing with Problems

Although society has become far more sensitive and compassionate toward people with handicaps, there is no guarantee that your children will not occasionally be wounded by teasing or cruel remarks. Siblings of children with Down syndrome know their brother or sister is different, and they often are quite protective. When feelings are hurt, parents usually get the job of soothing. Good family communication is a must in these situations.

When adults say insensitive things, siblings of special children can have surprising responses. They may think the adult is ignorant or mean. But if the adult is someone they know and trust, confusion and uncertainty can arise. Parents need to confront these incidents head-on, with facts. Reassure and support your children with information and understanding.

Dealing with the cruel remarks and teasing of children can be more difficult than dealing with those of adults. As children grow, peer acceptance and social interaction increase in importance. Special siblings can sometimes embarrass their siblings, who in turn may alienate their own friends in defense of their special sibling. In addition to encouraging them to express their feelings and offering them reassurance, parents should make sure that their other children have time to be on their own, with their own friends.

Children sometimes repeat the comments and teasing they hear and see at school. When parents overhear teasing or get a report from their children, they sometimes get angry and want to set things right. Children, however, need to learn to cope with life on their own. Fight the urge to rescue. Children can develop their own effective ways of coping and they can do it without losing their love for their special sibling or the friendship of their peers.

Counseling can help children who experience trouble in coping with their special sibling. Talking to someone outside the family, such as an objective, caring professional, can help a great deal. Not all problems need to be solved within the family. Sometimes giving your child room to adjust with the help of a counselor can accomplish what parents cannot. Do not be too afraid—or too proud—to seek help.

The Future

As children grow and mature they will begin to think about their future with their special sibling. Questions about responsibility and care will be asked. Again, parents need to provide facts. Let your children know that they will not need to be responsible for their adult sibling with Down syndrome unless they choose to be. With the increased social integration of people with Down syndrome there are community residential programs available so that siblings need not fear life-long burdens.

Your children and their future will likely be affected by their sibling with Down syndrome. Being the sibling of a child with Down syndrome can cause problems and frustrations, but at the same time it can warm the hearts of your children for a lifetime. Remember that having a handicapped sibling has its good points. Many siblings develop a strong capacity for love and acceptance of someone who is different. They may develop a sense not only of social understanding, but also of social responsibility. They may choose a career in one of the helping professions in an effort to make things better for those who are different. Your children may also develop a sense of specialness about your family and the special ties that bind you together.

This section has emphasized the importance of communication between parents and their children. Remember, parents are not infallible and do not always have all the answers: they hurt, they worry, they feel frustrated. It is not always necessary to put up a cheerful front for the sake of your kids. Let your children know that you do not have all the answers, that you need *their* support, that you are all in this together. Children usually surprise parents with how much they understand and how much they care. In coping with a child with Down syndrome, let your children share in the effort.

Your Child with Down Syndrome and Your Marriage

One of the greatest sources of support you have available as parents of a child with Down syndrome is each other. Although your infant is a source of stress and strain for each of you and for your relationship, you can help one another in dealing with this unexpected event in your lives. The starting place is to identify ways in which you have coped with other difficult situations in your lives. Use these same strategies in dealing with the special needs of your child with Down syndrome.

If your relationship with your spouse is strong, your marriage can withstand the additional stress imposed on it by the birth of your child. In fact, some parents feel that their baby has drawn them closer together. They speak of their awareness of their parental roles and of their responsibility to their child: "We feel we must stick together and support each other in each new crisis related to him."

One of the best ways to support one another is to openly share your feelings about your child with Down syndrome. Remember that you will feel love, hate, anger, fear, guilt—a full spectrum of conflicting emotions. It is perfectly normal to have these feelings, and you should let your spouse know that it is okay for him or her to have them too. If you share and acknowledge these feelings, you can work through them together, or together you can seek the help of others to aid you in this important process. You may find it helpful to talk to a friend, another parent, a priest, rabbi, or minister, a psychologist or a counselor.

When your baby is young, he may be like any other baby in terms of the amount of care and attention needed. But as a toddler, his physical and educational needs will increasingly infringe on the time and energy you can devote to one another. One parent of an infant with Down syndrome spoke about the influence of the infant on his relationship with his wife:

> The most difficult thing has been finding the time to be alone together, to work on our relationship. This is true of all parents with infants, but especially with special-needs infants because we have so many extra doctor appointments. Also, we must work much harder to stimulate our infant. We really don't spend more time playing with her, but more energy. It takes more psychological energy to get her to respond.

Like all parents, you worry about your child's future. You think about his education, his ability to participate in sports and other peer activities, his prospects for employment, and his ability to live independently. Although you will want to find more information about each of these subjects at the appropriate time, you must also learn to live one day at a time. Learn to focus on small steps in your child's development. Learn to enjoy today with your child. Celebrate life's small triumphs.

Earlier in this chapter the statement was made that your special child should not be the center of your family. Neither should he be the center of one parent's life or the sole responsibility of one parent. Each of you should share in the care, stimulation, education, and the pleasure of loving your child. You need to decide what arrangement works best for you. But remember, your marriage and your family can be strengthened and enriched by your child with Down syndrome.

Conclusion

It isn't easy having a child with Down syndrome in the family. In many ways it is richly rewarding, but it is also stressful—on children, on parents, and on marriages. There is no formula for coping perfectly with Down syndrome. Love, communication, acceptance, and the steadfast belief that your family will in the end thrive are your best bets to ensure a healthy and rewarding family life.

There are many books on families with special children. As you begin the task of integrating your child with Down syndrome into your family, reading about the experiences of others can help you a great deal. So can talking to other parents of children with Down syndrome. Their advice, based on what has worked best for them, can be very helpful. Just sharing similar problems and triumphs can help put your life in perspective. Most importantly, remember that you, your spouse, and your whole family are all in this together. Before long, your child with Down syndrome will just be part of the team.

Parent Statements

My relatives were all very good. They were amazing, actually. All my brothers and my sister just concentrated on him; they just responded to him completely. And my mother acted as if there was nothing different about him at all.

Our relatives' reactions have varied. One relative was a little bit condescending about it. He said, "Oh, he's one of God's children; it's okay." He was trying to comfort us, but I think he took the wrong approach.

The first response from people has always affected me very much. But it's not fair to hold them to their first response because they're in shock too, and they don't know anything about Down syndrome either. Most of them come around.

Most of our relatives have been very positive. With a couple exceptions, most of them have more than met our expectations and really looked on their relative just as a new relative. But one did not. One of Josh's cousins must have been told, "This child has Down syndrome, he's different," because the child acted very differently towards him. That hurt us a lot.

Christopher has made us a family. He's a little child and you know, it doesn't really matter that he has Down syndrome. Mothers and fathers and children make families and he's been in every way affectionate and childlike and all the things that children are. That's what makes a family.

We decided that any child would have to fit into our lives. For example, Laurie has so many appointments and needs, but I had originally decided to go back to work. I adjusted it and went back part time. I decided I needed that for myself. We still had to go out at night. We still had to have time alone.

I think every child with Down syndrome should have a person who energizes them, and I don't think it should be a parent. A sibling, an aunt, a next-door neighbor. I've now met three kids who have a person like that and all three kids seem to have a spirit to them.

Our family has been somewhat varied in their reaction. I think there was a lot of sorrow. But I think our own attitude helped a lot of the family work it out. Our attitude of "We're just crazy about this baby" helped everyone a lot.

We treat him generally just like another kid. If we want to go out shopping, okay, he's going to go shopping. He eats what we eat. We don't try to shield him. He has to live in the world. The world's not going to change to accommodate him. The more he is out in the world, the more he will be able to adjust to it.

We had a very interesting experience about three weeks ago. An old friend has a son who is five. We went to visit them for the first time in about two years. They decided not to say anything to their son about Josh having Down syndrome, and to just see what happened. Their son treated him just like a regular kid; it didn't bother him that Josh didn't talk much. They got along great. Maybe if you don't prejudice them, kids accept each other as they are.

We have two kids, and one of them has extremely high intelligence, and the other has Down syndrome. It's tough to switch gears sometimes. It takes a lot of patience, and I don't think I have as much as I'd like to have.

I didn't really feel a sense of mourning or disappointment until recently. It all evolved around placement in schools and integration into the neighborhood. I realized that I was working so much harder to make things easier for this child than with the other two children. It was a mourning; she wasn't a regular kid and I sometimes find myself wishing that it were a little easier.

We like to keep strict tabs on her behavior. We find ourselves saying, "That's cute at four but it's not going to be so
cute at eight."

We use discipline with a lot of consistency, a lot of patience, and never expecting more than they're able to com-
prehend at the moment.

Sometimes I worry about him because he gets so much
attention from adults. He has teachers coming to the house
and fawning on him an hour at a time. And he's charming his
way through school. He's got the director of the school he goes
to just eating out of the palm of his hand. I'm afraid he'll get
away with things just by being cute.

We've tried different things for discipline. First, we tried
the punitive way for misbehavior. We had a relative who was
in special ed who said, "Oh you must try behavior modification and every time he throws his food you have to keep him
from it for five minutes." And so we ended up with him getting very bad tempered and starving and everybody unable to
eat their meal because they were too upset by his screaming.
It didn't achieve a single thing. We discussed the problem with
his educator and decided to try modeling what he should do.
It worked instantly. We picked up all the food he threw down
and put it in his hand and told him to put it back on the table.
He did it and he was so pleased with himself that he started
doing it normally.

I'm kind of a strong disciplinarian and I try to keep the
same standards of discipline for all three kids. But with Julie
you can't let too much time elapse between the event and saying, "No, this is something we don't do."

It's important for Laurie's sister to always be able to express her feelings, and she shouldn't just have to mirror our feelings. Her feelings are going to be different, and we shouldn't feed her our feelings so that those are the only acceptable ones.

There's a lot of sibling rivalry that would be there anyway, I think. But we had the teacher come in every week, and the older one slowly caught on that there was something unusual about his brother. He may have become resentful over the amount of attention his brother got.

Our oldest daughter is a real companion to Julie. But the middle one feels just caught next to this little kid who's a pain in the neck sometimes. But a four-year-old sibling would be a pain in the neck even if she didn't have Down syndrome.

Josh's older brother hasn't seemed to have had problems with teasing from other kids. His friends come here all the time. He's got three or four guys who seem to be here every evening. They take Josh as one of the givens of the house.

The thing that has taken us most by surprise is integrating into the neighborhood. We have very nice neighbors and they think the world of Julie, but they have their own four-year-old children who are normal, competent, capable children who play together real well. There's nothing malicious, you just see the childhood neighborhood going by without her. Unlike fighting to get your kid in the school system, where you become an advocate, you can't do that with the neighborhood. You can't tell the neighbor kids to play with your kid.

I think if you had a weak marriage the Down syndrome would come as a point between you. There were times when it was hard for my husband. Until she was about two, I was really involved in meeting all her needs. It took time away from him.

There are positives and negatives as to the effects on our marriage and family, and on balance it comes out positive. It's more of a workload. It's the struggle with education, a whole new dimension of work that has to be split up. On the other hand, it brought a whole new quality dimension to our life. We both wind up feeling that our family is so much richer. I sometimes think life would be boring if we had all normal kids. Normal seems so boring.

One of the things about marriage is that when you have kids, you assume that those kids are going to be a part of your life for eighteen to twenty years and then you're going to go back to being a couple. But when your kid has Down syndrome, it dawns on you that this kid could be around forever. Then you go through a stage of realizing that that isn't the case—that a retarded kid can grow up and have a life too. Then it's a different emotion, like we don't want her to leave. I know that separation is coming, but it's going to be tough.

Having a baby with Down syndrome didn't diminish the desire to have more children. But the thing was, I had a hysterectomy as a result of her birth. We decided immediately to adopt more children. We definitely would hate the idea of our daughter not having any other siblings. So we have planned an adoption. The baby will come from Honduras and everyone keeps saying, "How do you know it won't have something wrong with it?" And so we say, "Well, we could have produced one ourselves that had something wrong with it."

I can only deal with one day at a time. I have a real hard time planning too far ahead. I don't mean that I muddle through each day, but I can only plan one day in advance. I think some-day I'll evolve out of that and everything will be better and I can plan ahead like I used to.

SIX

Your Baby's Development

FRENCH McCONNAUGHEY, M.Ed.*

One of life's great pleasures is watching your children grow and learn. Sharing in their first steps and first words makes the hard work of being a parent all worthwhile. As babies progress from total dependence to walking out the front door ready for school, parents feel great pride. All of this miraculous change, wonderful growth, and learning is commonly called "development."

Every child learns and grows. So will your baby with Down syndrome. Like every other baby she can provide you with great joy at her growth and development. She may need your help to do it right, and she may develop more slowly, but she will learn, change, and grow. You will be surprised and proud.

This chapter introduces the important subject of "development." It is designed to provide you with an overview along with an introduction to some of the specific developmental needs babies with Down syndrome have. As parents, it is important for you to have a basic understanding of development and to appreciate the important role you can play in enabling your child to maximize her potential.

Parents who get involved in their baby's development truly share in their child's first steps and first words. Studies show that babies whose parents are actively involved in their development make bet-

*French McConnaughey holds a Masters in Special Education and is Director of Development at The Glenbrook Day School in Rockville, Maryland.

ter progress than babies who were either ignored or institutionalized. There is no substitute for direct parental involvement, and with the help of teachers and other professionals, parents can make a tremendous difference. The challenges are great, there is much hard work involved, but the rewards—pride and joy in your child's accomplishments—are great.

What Is "Development?"

Human development is a complex process of growing and acquiring skills. The foundations of development are in a baby's genetic make-up and her environment. Development is a lifelong process that is a result of the interplay of biological, psychological, cultural, and environmental factors. With so many variables, it should not come as a surprise that every individual develops in a unique way.

The endpoint of development is not a predetermined set-point that remains unchanged. Instead, development is an evolving process, subject to both positive and negative influences. If we view development as a process by which an individual realizes her potential, then we are presented with a challenge. How can one foster that process?

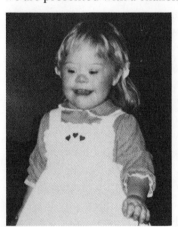

Development can and should be monitored in order to better optimize the positive factors and reduce the impact of negative influences. The developmental process cannot be totally controlled; it can, however, be dramatically affected by positive input. Intervention—direct involvement in an infant's development—can make an important difference.

The development of a baby with Down syndrome will be affected by her extra chromosome. Her genetic make-up establishes a preliminary blueprint for development; it does not predetermine the end result. Genes may create handicaps; growth and learning through positive psychological, cultural, and environmental factors can help lessen the impact of those handicaps.

Development occurs in a sequence that is miraculously organized. Each developmental accomplishment is the foundation for the next step, as increasingly sophisticated skills are acquired. But because each baby's development is the result of many factors, there is great variation in what is viewed as "normal" development. For example, one child may learn to walk three months earlier than another while her first words may be three months later than her peers. One child may move step-by-step through the sitting-crawling-walking sequence while another skips crawling altogether. Each child has her own learning profile that crisscrosses the "normal developmental scale." For parents it is helpful to use developmental milestones and sequences as a guide that helps chart the long range course. The scales and charts are not, however, the only recipe for development. As you watch your child learn and grow you will begin to have an appreciation of her individual learning style, strengths, and weaknesses. With that knowledge you will be better equipped to anticipate where help may be needed to facilitate development.

The Six Areas of Development

Frequently, the process of development is subdivided into six areas: 1) gross motor; 2) fine motor; 3) language; 4) cognition; 5) social; and 6) self-help. All of these areas are closely interrelated, and progress in one area affects progress in others in obvious and subtle ways. Development must be viewed as a whole.

Gross Motor. Through gross motor development a baby learns to move her body by using her large muscles, including the legs, arms, and abdomen. Sitting up, crawling, walking, and climbing are all important gross motor skills. These skills allow your baby to move around, explore her world, and lay a foundation for growth in other areas.

Fine Motor. In fine motor development a baby learns how to control small and detailed movements. Typical fine motor muscles include the muscles in the fingers and hands. Skills like picking up a small object, using the index finger to poke and probe, and squeezing soft objects are all important fine motor skills. In addition to hand skills, the control of eye muscles as well as facial and tongue movements are important parts of the fine motor repertoire.

Language. Learning to communicate is one of the most important and remarkable accomplishments of childhood. Language development is usually divided into two areas: receptive language and expressive language. Receptive language is the ability to understand words and gestures. Expressive language is the ability to use gestures, words, and written symbols to communicate. In the acquisition of language skills, the understanding of a word—its receptive use—precedes the expressive use of the word. It is not uncommon to hear a parent say "the baby understands more than she says." That is as it should be for all children. In analyzing your own language you will realize that you have a far greater receptive vocabulary than the number of words you use in everyday conversation.

Cognition. Cognitive theory has been the subject of many books, its definition the object of debate. In a practical study of development we can view cognition as the ability to reason and solve problems. In babies these skills include the ability to understand object permanence (that objects do not cease to exist when they are out of sight), to understand cause-and-effect, and to draw conclusions from direct experience and later from observation or recall. These complex and abstract concepts take time to learn, but babies can learn them from play. Finding hidden objects teaches object permanence; spilling a container teaches cause-and-effect; stacking blocks conveys the concepts of size and shape and the fundamentals of estimating. Each of these skills helps build the important foundation of concepts a child needs to understand how the world works, how objects relate to one another, and how she can manipulate her environment.

Social. Social development is the ability to function in relationship to others. From birth onward, babies learn how to respond appropriately to themselves and to others. They learn to function in a society of people. For example, they learn how to play with people and objects, become attached to people, and assert their individual independence. These are the important skills that enable babies to mature into functioning members of society.

Self-Help. Learning how to take care of oneself is an important area of development. At birth, babies are totally dependent on others for their care. As they grow and develop, they become able to help take care of themselves. Feeding, dressing, and toileting are all important skills that babies and children learn.

A seventh area—sensory ability—is very important to a child's overall development, but is not usually considered a separate area of development because it acts as an umbrella covering all areas and its

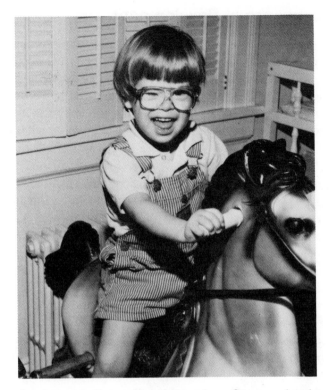

progression is not easily measured over time. Sensory development
is the ability of a child to process sensations like touch, sound, light,
smell, and movement. These skills are refined as babies grow, and
they affect all other areas of development. As explained in Chapters
1 and 3, your baby should be checked regularly to ensure that no hearing or vision problems impede her development. A baby or child can
encounter other sensory difficulties as well. For instance, oversen-
sitivity to touch (known as tactile defensiveness) can interfere both
with her exploration of the world and with a parent's or teacher's attempts to pattern her movements properly.

All areas of development are interrelated and must be viewed as
a whole. Fine motor ability builds on gross motor ability; self-help
skills depend on motor skills, social ability builds on self-help; and
cognitive ability builds on them all. Growth in one area is dramatically
influenced by growth in another. You must view your baby's development as a complete picture. Avoid preoccupation with any single area.
Overall balance is crucial.

The Sequence of Development

Asking questions about development is natural for parents of babies with Down syndrome. "What will my baby do and when should she do it? How can I help my baby learn the skills she needs?" By learning the basic sequence of human development—the progression of learning skills—you can begin to put your child's growth into perspective and play a critical role in aiding her growth and learning.

The First Three Years

The changes that occur during the first three years of life are extraordinary. Your newborn is completely dependent on you and must rely on you for survival. Initially, her behavior is most often the result of reflexes and sensations over which she has little control. By the time of her third birthday, she has developed general control over her body and has become a social being. She can survive somewhat independently, solve problems, and use the complex system of symbols called "language."

During the last ten years the importance of the earliest years has been recognized. More and more studies show that what happens during a baby's early development greatly affects development in later life. Burton White, a leading authority on infant development, states in his book *The First Three Years of Life*:

> After seventeen years of research on how humans acquire their abilities, I have become convinced that it is to the first three years of life that we should now turn most of our attention. My own studies, as well as the work of many others, have clearly indicated that the experiences of those first years are far more important than we had previously thought. In their simple everyday activities, infants and toddlers form the foundations of *all* later development... To begin to look at a child's educational development when he or she is two years of age is already much too late... (Revised Edition, p. v & p. 5)

This chapter divides development in the first three years into four phases. This division is intended merely to show a developmental sequence and not to imply fixed standards. The phases are: 1) birth to eight months, 2) eight to fourteen months, 3) fourteen to twenty-four months, and 4) twenty-four to thirty-six months.

Figure 1 presents developmental milestones in each major area of growth. It does not specify an age for each skill, but places the skill in the developmental phase in which it usually occurs. There is a very wide span of time for "normal" development, and your baby with Down syndrome may experience a different sequence. Use the chart and the section that follows as an overview of development, a general road map. Later in this chapter we will review the conditions babies with Down syndrome may have that can negatively affect their development.

Birth to Eight Months. During a baby's first eight months of life, coping with life outside the womb and gaining the rudiments of self-awareness are the major developmental goals. The skills she will learn are very basic, but very important: getting adjusted to light, sound, touch, smell, taste, and generally to just being alive.

This is a time for laying foundations. Establishing love, security, and trust all help motivate babies to move, explore, and challenge themselves. Motivation itself is vital; this is a period to encourage curiosity and exploration, and to provide new experiences. During this period babies begin to learn the most fundamental aspects of life and their relationship to the world around them: that objects have weight and size, that people look and sound different, that things placed in mouths have a taste and a feel, that they themselves can bring about change. Parents can play a key role in identifying what interests their baby and in fostering those interests.

What skills emerge in the first eight months? A baby learns to roll, sit, and crawl; to interpret light and sound; to manipulate objects; and to relate to different people. She gains some control over her movements, begins to watch and listen, and practices new behaviors. When the baby can sit (at approximately eight months), reach for and hold a toy, and then hand it to her parent, she has learned an extraordinary number of skills. She has left her primitive reflexes behind, has begun to control her body movements, and is aware of herself in relation to others.

Eight to Fourteen Months. Some experts consider this a period of transition. Babies change from passive observers to purposeful doers. The changes that occur at this age are among the most critical

Figure 1. Developmental Milestones

	PHASE I: 0-8 MONTHS	PHASE II: 8-14 MONTHS
Gross Motor	• head control • turns over • sits • crawls	• pulls to stand • cruises • lowers self from standing position • walks alone • climbs upstairs
Fine Motor	• looks at hands • follows with eyes 180° • brings hands together • reaches • explores objects with hands • transfers objects hand to hand	• pincer grasp • scribbles • pushes toys • pokes at objects • one hand helps other
Language	• listens to sounds • turns to sound • babbles • laughs • responds to own name • makes vowel sounds	• recognizes names of common objects • enjoys listening to music • first words spoken
Cognitive	• looks from one object to another • looks after fallen object • pulls string to get object • uncovers toy he has seen hidden	• imitates use of toy • finds hidden toy (emergence of memory) • begins demonstrating cause and effect
Self Help	• reaches for bottle • finger feeds • holds bottle • drinks from cup with help	• drinks from cup with spilling • attempts spoon feeding • takes off socks
Social	• social smile • reaches for familiar person • smiles at mirror image • repeats performance laughed at	• understands "no" • cries when parent leaves • can play alone short periods • understands parent as resource

PHASE III: 14-24 MONTHS	PHASE IV: 24-36 MONTHS
• stoops and recovers • climbs into chairs • stands on one foot • walks up/down stairs holding on • kicks/throws ball • rides mobility toy	• runs, climbs • jumps in place • pulls wagon • rides tricycle
• builds tower of cubes • completes simple puzzles • turns pages of book • turns knobs	• strings beads • works latches and hooks • turns pages of book singularly • snips with scissors
• uses jargon • expands vocabulary • uses some phrases • names pictures • follows simple directions	• names body parts • uses some adjectives (color, size) • asks questions • understands some prepositions
• uses objects as tools • fits related objects together • uses trial and error • can arrange objects by size	• ability to use abstractions • draws recognizable face • understands "1", "2" • names common color • makes associations
• drinks from cup independently • combs hair • uses spoon independently • unzips • removes some clothes • partially toilet trained	• can put toys away • anticipates daily activities • pours • unties and removes shoes • puts on some clothes • toilet trained
• uses dramatic play/pretend • wants to be near other children • parallel play • negativism	• expands imaginary role play • shows sense of ownership • can wait turn • can ask for help • works problems out with less action, more reasoning

in your baby's life. The three major developmental changes that occur during this period are: 1) the start of independent movement; 2) the first understanding of cause-and-effect and object permanence; and 3) the beginning use of language. From eight to fourteen months the ability to move brings about new freedom for exploration. Crawling, climbing, pulling to stand, cruising, and walking are practiced over and over. Refined hand skills will allow your child to pick up and explore small objects with her thumb and forefinger (pincer grasp), to use her hands in tandem to manipulate objects, and to begin to use objects like crayons, hammers, and spoons as tools.

These new motor skills are accompanied by major changes in cognitive ability. The twelve month old knows that when an object is out of sight, it still exists. This concept, known as object permanence, represents a quantum leap in reasoning ability. Research shows that the understanding of object permanence is closely related to a child's ability to use language. Both are abstract processes. These two skills naturally develop simultaneously. During this period, children dramatically increase their ability to understand words (receptive language), and begin to associate sounds with people, food, and objects in their world. Using words (expressive language) begins shortly after.

It is during this time that the strongest social bonds are established, usually to mother and father. Through these relationships the child learns the first *do's* and *do not's* of the family. The first inkling of independence also emerges, as the baby becomes able to play alone for short periods of time. She will also begin to help take care of herself. She will want to drink from a cup and try to feed herself with a spoon. This is the beginning of your child's ability to control her own needs.

Fourteen to Twenty-Four Months. The skills acquired during the first fourteen months launch the toddler into a period of intense skill development for the next ten months. During this part of the second year, the ability to use language seems to explode. Spoken language changes from nonsensical babble to single words and then to phrases. The two year old can follow simple directions and likes to have stories read to her. The establishment of language enables the child to communicate her ideas and feelings to others and to gather information. With this new use of language, the child moves to a much higher level of cognition, as well as into a real sense of personhood.

For the child approaching her second birthday, the world can be an exciting place. Everything is subject to observation and manipulation. All objects are explored in every possible way: feeling, tasting, smelling, poking, throwing. During this period, the testing will gradually shift from analysis to use.

This is a time for solving problems and playing with puzzles. Not only can blocks be stacked; they can be made into a house or fort. The hand skills that were recently established are now put to practice as the child begins to create and build. The child is also able to help feed herself. These new hand skills open new arenas, literally and figuratively.

Socially, this is not an easy period for the child or her parents. During these months, the child struggles with the pushes and pulls of budding independence. Negativism may abound. This period is marked by the child's desire to assert her will and assume a new level of identity and independence. But it is also a time to explore the world of people; she will want to be near other children and will begin what we know as parallel play.

Twenty-Four to Thirty-Six Months. The skills acquired during this phase of development move the child to a dramatic new level of competence. The three year old has mastered most of the elementary gross motor skills. Walking has accelerated to running. Climbing and jumping are established in the motor repertoire. Fine motor, language, and cognitive skills are all expanded and refined. They are now demonstrated in more complex, creative, and constructive behaviors. Toilet training also usually occurs during this time.

Dramatic play now emerges. The child is able to envision herself in the place of another—to imagine, to make believe. Thought is no longer tied to concrete objects. Problem solving can take place by observation and reasoning. The child no longer needs to touch and feel an object in order to learn about it. She can look at an object, remember those she has played with before, and make decisions based on the objects she remembers. In short, the three year old can reason and remember. She also has the ability to make associations and to anticipate the consequences of her actions.

Also, the social competence of three year olds is far more sophisticated. They seek approval in a more dramatic way and are able to use adults as resources. Peers become much more important to them. During this period the child can be a successful part of a small group of two or three other children. Also during this period the child can be quite competitive. It is in this environment that children learn the contrasting roles of leader and follower.

The first three years of life are marked with tremendous growth and development—from absolute dependence to semi-independence. Skills build upon each other so quickly that parents have a hard time keeping track of just what their child is capable of doing at any given time. Parents can only look back and remember when their child— now dressed and ready for nursery school—was utterly reliant on them and on her own instinctive reflexes for survival.

Expectations and Development

Parents of babies with Down syndrome, as well as parents of "normal" children, always want to know how their child will develop compared to other children. First, there is a very wide range of what is considered "normal" development. Some babies crawl at six months, others not until ten months; some skip crawling altogether. Each case is "normal." Your baby with Down syndrome may be within the normal range in some areas; in others she may be slower than "normal." Your child may learn to walk sooner than some other children, while she may learn to talk later.

There is far more to good development than how quickly a baby develops or how many skills she possesses. Quality, not quantity, is the key. Parents should be more concerned that their daughter walks *well* than that she walks *soon*. Parents can be the most important resource for building a good foundation for development. Babies with Down syndrome should be encouraged to explore, learn, and be curious, as all children should. You, as parents, can provide the opportunities.

If a parent steps in too often with an answer or offers only little encouragement, development is hindered. Let your baby take risks. It is far easier to comfort a child who has fallen while trying to climb than it is to stimulate an unmotivated child. Facilitation, the key word, means helping your child perform a skill *and* letting her do it herself.

The Development of Your Baby with Down Syndrome

We have presented a general sequence of development for the

first three years of life. All children will learn skills in each of the six areas of development; their rate and sequence, however, will vary. A child's individual traits will determine her pattern. Some children take longer than others; some children don't master certain skills as well as others. The same is true of babies with Down syndrome.

All children have preferred ways of learning. Most will choose to learn new tasks in the way that is easiest for them. Because of the unique characteristics particular to babies with Down syndrome, they need special guidance to help them master the same skills other babies acquire. You may need to discourage your child from taking the path of least resistance. If you are aware of your baby's strengths and weaknesses you will be better able to give her the help she may need to develop optimally. If you know the stumbling blocks, you have a

better chance of devising ways to overcome or minimize them. For children with Down syndrome there can be specific characteristics that hinder development. This section reviews these traits.

Low Muscle Tone

Low muscle tone, or hypotonia, is very common in babies with Down syndrome. Their muscles feel floppy and flaccid. Although the degree of low tone varies from child to child, it generally affects all the baby's muscles.

How does low muscle tone affect development? The short answer is that its effects are quite extensive, but can be reduced with work. In addition, the low tone usually diminishes with age. As a newborn, your baby may move less. Her posture may be unusual. For example, when lying on her back, her legs may be wide apart and turned (rotated) out. Low muscle tone will slow the rate at which your child will learn the major motor skills. Because muscles are floppier, the attainment of head control, sitting, standing, and walking can be delayed and can also be less coordinated.

The undesirable effects of low muscle tone can, however, be diminished. The earlier you begin to work to improve your baby's muscle tone the better. Seek the help of an infant specialist or physical or occupational therapist if one is available. Techniques to increase muscle tone can begin within the first weeks of life. Intervention directed at improving muscle tone will help your baby acquire motor skills. Everyday routines can be altered to make a difference. For example, you might be taught how to hold your baby in a more beneficial way. If the baby's legs tend to rotate out, it would be more beneficial to hold her with her legs facing forward and held together. Techniques like these can be easily incorporated in your daily routine and they can make a difference in your child's overall development.

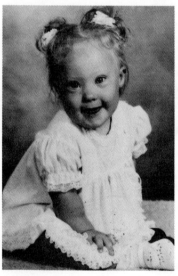

Low muscle tone may also affect the development of both feeding and language skills. The same muscles we eat with are the muscles we use for speaking. When a child eats or talks, she uses muscles in her face, mouth, shoulders, and trunk. Poor muscle tone may make it difficult to form words or to move food around the mouth. Hypotonia throughout the trunk may also reduce the ability of the chest to provide the strong respiration necessary for spoken words. Early intervention will focus on eating and breathing patterns and how they are developing so as to maximize the skills needed for language.

Remember, a professional—a teacher or a therapist—can help devise a plan to minimize the effects of the hypotonia. It is important to get professional help if possible because every baby is different. The amount of low tone itself varies from baby to baby, and how it can affect your baby in particular can vary as well. Children can have lower tone in certain parts of their body than others. That is why parents need instruction on working with low tone using techniques specifically tailored to their baby's needs.

Joint Flexibility

When joints are extraordinarily flexible, they are called hyperextensive. You may notice that your baby's hips and legs are easily rotated outward or that your baby can bend at the waist more easily than other babies. This trait, which is closely related to low muscle tone, also affects motor development. If parents are aware of this excessive joint flexibility, they can provide the extra support the baby needs.

Hyperextensive joints affect development by reducing the stability of your baby's limbs. In order to sit, crawl, and walk, your baby needs a stable foundation. Flexible joints and low muscle tone make this somewhat harder to achieve. Parents, however, can do much to help: something as simple as a firm hold on the hips as your child learns to pull up to a stand, or holding your baby's hips rather than her hands as she learns to walk can be of invaluable benefit. Professional input will, again, be helpful. The input of an infant specialist, occupational therapist, and physical therapist will include intervention to minimize the impact of joint flexibility.

Weak Muscles

Babies with Down syndrome may have weak muscles. Sometimes caused by a heart problem and sometimes by low muscle tone, this condition can be recognized if your baby has difficulty lifting her head, pushing up on her forearms, grasping toys, or pulling up to a stand.

Muscle strength can be improved. Intervention is very much like a general fitness program: Give your baby opportunities to use her muscles in a gradual program. "Roughhousing" will help. Incorporate it into playtime. Hand strength can also be improved by squeezing a sponge during bath time, arms can be strengthened by something as simple as pushing a toy. You want your baby to practice all the usual baby activities. She may just need a little extra motivation and direction because these things may be more difficult for her. Exercises when well planned can serve as play as well as therapy.

In all of these areas—low muscle tone, joint flexibility, and muscle weakness—the effort to minimize their severity and impact is critical because they can slow motor development and diminish the quality of development. Motor development affects growth in every other developmental area. If your baby can't sit, she can't see the world clearly. If she can't sit with stability, she can't really use her hands.

Clearly, the work to improve your baby's muscles and joints is critical and well worth the effort.

Hearing Loss

Many children with Down syndrome have some form of hearing loss. Chapter 3 discusses causes, treatments, and incidence of hearing loss. The percentages stated there are high enough to cause concern: More than half the children tested were found to have at least a mild hearing loss.

The effect of hearing loss on development is severe. Children who hear less, talk less. They can't build their language skills without hearing speech. Because hearing is so vital to development of language, cognition, self-help, and social skills, it must be checked early. With early treatment—using antibiotics, ear tubes, or hearing aids—this potentially major stumbling block can be avoided.

Mental Retardation

In the past, all babies with Down syndrome were considered severely and hopelessly retarded. Not so. Yes, children with Down syndrome are mentally retarded. We often fail to remember, however, that mental retardation affects people very differently. The fact is that the majority of children with Down syndrome function in the mild to moderate range of retardation.

What effect does mental retardation have on development? As with all factors affecting development, the severity of the problem determines the impact. Mental retardation does mean that progress in some areas will be slower. The ability to observe, analyze, and deal with abstract concepts is affected by cognitive ability. Skills that require a child to conceptualize objects or events not directly in front of her eyes can be difficult for the child with Down syndrome. Mental retardation can also cause your baby to have a shorter attention span and lower motivation.

Like other stumbling blocks, mental retardation can be addressed through intervention and its effects can be reduced. It may take a lot of hard work and careful planning with teachers, but the work will pay off. By breaking down tasks and concepts into smaller steps, difficult skills can be mastered. Progress breeds more progress, along with a sense of accomplishment and pride in your child. She will try hard to perform the desired task if it is presented to her in ways she can handle. For example, object permanence–the understanding that objects don't cease to exist when not in view–can be learned gradually, just by providing opportunities to experience it. Try peek-a-boo or other games. Also, concepts are best taught initially with concrete objects that can be touched, seen, and explored rather than with pictures or words.

It is important to monitor your baby's attention span and motivation. New skills need to be practiced in short lesson periods and with a greater number of tries over time. A long lesson period may not work well for your child. Again, your baby's teacher can guide you and work out a complete individual plan for your child.

The coordination of several skills or a series of skills may be difficult for your baby with Down syndrome. Again, by careful evaluation and hard work, each separate part of a coordinated action can be learned. As each small part is mastered, it can be joined with others. For example, learning to use a form box or a shape puzzle will require breaking the task into its different parts (grasping, holding, and putting each piece in place). Over time, however, your baby will learn to combine these separate tasks into one enjoyable challenge.

Parents of babies with Down syndrome often worry about their child's IQ. Skill development, not scores on an intelligence test, should be the goal. There are many children who function much higher than a test score would indicate. There are also many children who test high yet cannot function well. Motivation, pride, security, and love are not measured on an IQ test, though they most certainly and profoundly affect a child's functioning. The goal of parents is to raise children who have maximized their potential. Children with Down syndrome can grow up to do just that–with work. Judge by what your child can do, and leave IQ measurements to the researchers.

Helping Your Child's Development

Although this chapter has pointed out areas of delay in your baby's development, remember that these do not have to be barriers to learning and growing. Some areas of delay will be overcome; others will need to be circumvented. Knowing the problem areas will enable you to help your child better, to work better with her teachers, and to plan the best program for her. Your goal is to maximize strengths and minimize weaknesses so that your child will realize her fullest potential. Your hard work and your knowledge of your own baby's development will be rewarded. Studies show that babies with Down syndrome can develop quite well. Figure 2 shows one study's findings of when babies with Down syndrome generally learn skills, as compared with "normal" development.

Figure 2. Down Syndrome Development Compared to "Normal" Development

	CHILDREN WITH DOWN SYNDROME		"NORMAL" CHILDREN	
	average	range	average	range
smiling	2 months	1½ to 4 months	1 month	½ to 3 months
rolling over	8 months	4 to 22 months	5 months	2 to 10 months
sitting alone	10 months	6 to 28 months	7 months	5 to 9 months
crawling	12 months	7 to 21 months	8 months	6 to 11 months
creeping	15 months	9 to 27 months	10 months	7 to 13 months
standing	20 months	11 to 42 months	11 months	8 to 16 months
walking	24 months	12 to 65 months	13 months	8 to 18 months
talking, words	16 months	9 to 31 months	10 months	6 to 14 months
talking, sentences	28 months	18 to 96 months	21 months	14 to 32 months

(Pueschel, 1978)

Other studies show that early intervention—working with your baby—pays enormous dividends. Marci Hanson of the University of Oregon compared the development of babies with Down syndrome who were part of a program of early intervention with those who were not. The results speak for themselves. As Figure 3 illustrates, some of the children with Down syndrome who were involved in intervention programs developed faster than even the average "normal" child! But most dramatic is the difference between children with Down syndrome who were part of an early intervention program and those who did not participate.

Where to Get Developmental Help for Your Child

Parents can receive help with their baby's development from public or private sources. In some states, babies with Down syndrome are eligible for publicly-funded early infant education through local school districts. In these programs—detailed in Chapters 7 and 8—babies receive early infant intervention aimed at maximizing their potential. Unfortunately, not all states offer services from birth; most

Figure 3. Developmental Milestones

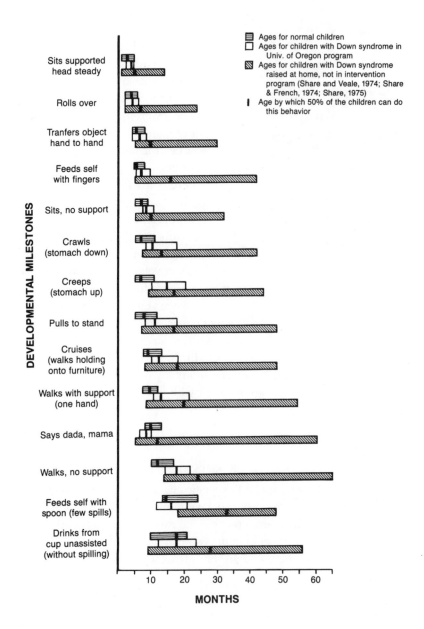

begin between ages three and six. You must check with your local school district and your state department of education. Start with the Resource Guide at the end of the book.

What do you do if public school services are unavailable? First, private teachers and therapists are available almost everywhere, and sometimes their services are covered by medical insurance. Local organizations, advocacy groups, and, of course, other parents are excellent resources for information on what services are available locally. There is a wide variety of alternative arrangements, such as cooperative special nursery schools and private group developmental classes. Also, you can read to learn how to aid your child's development. Lastly, there may even be some federal grant funds available for local school districts to begin infant education. Ask for help: from your local school district, ARCs, advocacy groups, and anyone else who will listen, including your local media. Join with groups who are already lobbying to reduce the starting age for public services to birth, so that infants with Down syndrome can receive the early attention they need. Most importantly, do not let precious time go by; work with your child as much as you can.

Conclusion

This chapter has reviewed the basics of infant development, its sequence, and how your child's specific characteristics can affect that development. Along the way, we have mentioned steps parents can take to help their child develop to the full extent of her potential. With basic knowledge of development, you can now read about teaching your child. Remember, you are her greatest resource.

Parent Statements

I thought there would be a whole lot of things a kid with Down syndrome couldn't do. But he does basically the same things other kids do. It just takes him longer to get there.

I guess the hardest part was waiting for her to roll over, waiting for her to crawl, waiting for her to sit up, waiting for her to walk. I think I had an advantage because I didn't have anyone close to me who had a baby her age, so I wasn't constantly comparing her with anyone. Originally I had this picture in my mind of my baby being a super achiever–doing everything three months early. So it was kind of hard to wait for her to do things.

He has developed exactly like a normal child. It's just that his pace is slower. He's just like any child–he disobeys like another child, and he wants all the things that other little children want.

There really is a wide range of capabilities among kids. You can't know. You can only provide the best kind of stimulation that you can as a parent, and deal with what is there genetically.

With a normal child you just expect the development to happen, but with Chris every milestone is a great success. When he crawls or feeds himself with a spoon we're very happy, and we tell everyone about his progress. Other people might think we're going overboard, but we're very proud of every small victory.

I don't feel anxious about her development right now, but sometimes I wonder what it's going to be like when it's time for first grade and she can't be in first grade, or when she's thirteen and on a fifth grade level. I think about that sometimes, but I try not to spend a lot time worrying about it, because I really don't know how she'll do. She's doing pretty well now; maybe she'll keep it up.

A new parent might wonder, "Will he smile? Will he hug me? Will he play? Will he recognize me?" From our experience, that's not something to worry about. You may feel a little frustrated when he doesn't do what Johnny next door is doing, but you'll find over time that he just reaches those stages a little later, but he'll reach them just the same. The big question after the first three years is "Will he keep up?" My feeling is that his horizons are unlimited. Quite realistically, I don't expect him to be a nuclear physicist, but I do hold out hopes for him to be independent and have a fulfilling life. I think any parent can be happy with that.

I can't say how important it is for parents to know about normal development. You need to know how a child gets into a sitting position to help your child. Otherwise when you plop them down to sit, and they have their legs widespread, you're doing more harm than good. That's why early intervention is just crucial. Also, what comes next? You may see your child starting to do something and not realize it's a move toward the next step, particularly if it's your first child.

There aren't guarantees for any child. Even if somebody is born with a normal set of chromosomes or perfect health, you don't know what's going to happen to that person. They could get sick, or they could grow up perfectly healthy but have some inability to cope with life. There are a lot of people in the world who have normal capabilities but don't know how to use them or who use them for bad purposes.

I still have an unbelievable consciousness of her needs. I know where she is in all areas. But I don't think it's that hard to do. You need to have fun with your child and talk to her, whether you're alone with her or just driving to school.

I used to go to school with her one day a week and come home and feel that I had to push because I wasn't seeing progress in this or that area. I often thought Laurie would never count to ten, and now she can go well beyond that. It can get frustrating when teachers and therapists are reminding you over and over of the things you need to do, and you don't see change from one week to the next. But you're not going to see changes every week, especially when you're monitoring it almost too closely.

Sometimes he won't seem to progress at all for several months and then all of a sudden he'll take off like a rocket, and the progress is extremely noticeable and a real thrill. In our other children, the plateaus are a lot shorter. When he does progress, it's more noticeable.

Sometimes people find that once they have a kid with special needs, they learn a lot about child development. It makes the bringing up of children later extremely interesting. I can watch Josh's younger brother for hours. It's so fascinating because of what I've learned about the learning process—how children learn gross motor skills, fine motor skills, speech. It has deepened our enjoyment of the baby because we know so much more about the process.

SEVEN

Teaching Your Baby with Down Syndrome: An Introduction to Early Intervention

LINDA DIAMOND, M.Ed.*

What Is Early Intervention?

During the past ten years, many types of educational programs for babies, for parents, and for parents and babies together have been developed. In this chapter we examine a special type of educational program designed to aid the development of babies with Down syndrome. Early intervention differs from what you may hear referred to as infant stimulation or "infant stim." Interest in babies and infant development has prompted many groups to offer "stimulating" products, ideas, and classes. Of course, stimulating your baby is a good thing to do. But when a baby has special needs, the stimulation has to be special, too.

Early developmental intervention programs for special-needs children and their families can take many forms and can include a wide

*Linda Diamond holds a Masters in Special Education and is an Infant Development Specialist and Family Coordinator in an early intervention program in the Washington, D.C. area.

133

variety of services. There are, however, many elements that are common to almost all early intervention programs. Thinking separately about "early," "developmental," and "intervention" will help you understand the purpose of these programs. "Early" usually refers to the age range of birth to three years. "Developmental" refers to the growth and development of the baby and to the continual acquisition of new skills. "Intervention" means planned, specific, conscious, and specialized ways of interacting with a baby to enhance development. Together these elements form a program to help children who in some way are not developing normally.

Because your baby has Down syndrome, his development will be different from that of other babies. *Every* baby is unique, possessing both strengths and weaknesses. However, as earlier chapters have explained, your baby is more likely to encounter certain developmental problems due to Down syndrome. Maybe he does not move his arms and legs vigorously; maybe he does not follow objects with his eyes or seems to be disinterested; perhaps feeding is more difficult and slower than it is for other babies. These things are not your fault or your baby's fault, but are examples of how Down syndrome can affect him.

There are many ways of handling and interacting with babies. Some babies prefer certain kinds of handling to others. For example, some babies want and need cuddling while others would rather be placed comfortably in their crib with a mobile in sight. Your baby will also have preferences. His preferences, however, may not always work to his benefit. They might in fact work against good development. For example, your baby's preference to stiffen or "lock" his leg and hip joints as a way to stand can work against good development. Your early intervention program can show you how to minimize this and other tendencies through exercise and proper positioning.

Chapter 6 reviewed how the particular characteristics of Down syndrome affect development. But each baby is different. Learning how *your* baby's development is affected and how to best handle and interact with him to help him grow and develop is the major purpose of early intervention. For instance, if your child has low muscle tone, there are exercises that can help improve it. If your child seems unresponsive, there are many different types of interaction that can be tried to motivate him.

Early intervention requires highly trained specialists who can work with you and your baby to maximize his early development. Remember though, early intervention is a process; it changes as your baby changes and as you and your baby's teachers learn what techniques work best for your baby. The other major purpose of early intervention is to help you in not only learning specific techniques to use with your baby, but also to support you in your efforts to integrate your special new baby into your family.

Early intervention can help your baby develop to the best possible level and it can help you. No one can predict precisely what the future holds for a baby with Down syndrome, and early intervention is not a magical cure, but working at development from early infancy is important in helping your baby reach his full potential.

People and Programs

Early intervention programs can take many different forms and can include a wide variety of services and professionals. In addition, there are significant differences in the quality and quantity of programs in each state, county, and city. Your child needs a program that is designed to meet his special needs. This section reviews the many types of early infant intervention programs and describes the various professionals who work with babies with Down syndrome.

Professionals

Depending on the specific programs in your area and on your baby's needs, you may work with one or all of the professionals described below. These professionals may work as a team in an early intervention program or may work individually to provide particular services in a private practice setting. In any case, they should be highly trained in their area of expertise and specifically experienced with babies with Down syndrome.

Infant Educator. An infant educator is a teacher trained to look closely at your baby's overall development, and specifically at cognitive development. The teacher should be knowledgeable about normal development and about development that is not proceeding normally. The infant educator will focus his or her attention on your baby's responsiveness to stimulation, on how he plays, on his social development, and on the development of his ability to understand concepts. He or she will tailor his or her work with your baby to his age and level of development through infancy and toddlerhood. The infant educator, along with other professionals, may also work with you on the daily care of your baby. The exact role of the infant educator varies greatly from program to program. In some areas, infant educators focus on parents and infants, while in others the emphasis is on the child alone.

Pediatric Physical Therapist. A pediatric physical therapist who works with babies with Down syndrome will focus on helping to minimize physical problems such as low muscle tone. These therapists are trained to evaluate how a baby moves and to assist the baby in using muscles effectively. The physical therapist's goal is to foster the best and most normal movement patterns for your baby.

A physical therapist may work with your child once or twice a week. During these sessions, your baby will work very hard as the therapist uses a series of exercises to help him move. The therapist may have specialized training in neurodevelopmental treatment (NDT), which is a well-accepted and comprehensive approach to physical therapy. Other professionals who work with your baby, such as occupational therapists, speech/language therapists, and infant educators, may also have this specialized training.

Pediatric Occupational Therapist. Occupational therapists are also trained to look at how a baby moves, but concentrate on the positions of shoulders, arms, and hands, and very importantly, how this affects his ability to do activities that involve reaching for and holding objects. These therapists will work with your baby to improve his fine motor skills. This includes assisting you and your baby in developing self-help skills, such as dressing and washing, and even early skills like reaching for his bottle, grabbing a pacifier, or splashing in a bath.

Pediatric Speech and Language Therapist. These therapists are trained to look at how your baby uses the muscles of his mouth and face to eat and to make sounds. From early infancy, the speech therapist can be a resource for concerns or problems with feeding and will work with you and your baby to develop the use and understanding of language. Later he or she will focus on the proper articulation of sounds and words. This therapist can also evaluate your baby's responsiveness to sound and can help spot potential hearing problems.

Mental Health Professional. Some early intervention programs have counsellors, social workers, and mental health professionals who can provide emotional support and counselling to families. At different times, families have found this to be a very helpful service; it can also be sought privately if not available through an intervention program. The service provider can be a social worker, psychologist, family counsellor, or a specially trained infant teacher. Often babies and parents are seen together as part of this service.

Your child's program may also sponsor a parent support group. This group might be led by the mental health professional, by a teacher, or by a parent. These groups offer support, counselling, and an opportunity to share problems with parents who have similar concerns. In addition to your child's early intervention program, many special interest organizations such as your local ARC sponsor parent groups.

Pediatric Nurse. A nurse may be part of the early intervention program in your area, or may be available through your local health department, hospital, or visiting nurse association. He or she may assist with daily medical care and use of equipment, and might also be a resource about early development.

Case Manager. One member of your baby's early intervention team may serve as a case manager or coordinator. It is the case manager's job to gather information and ideas from the team working with you and your baby, and to coordinate the different services being provided. As the primary service provider, the infant educator will be the one to give you an overall picture of your baby's development, to show you how each area of development interacts with another, and to incorporate all of this information into your child's program. Often the case manager is the infant teacher, but any one of the other professionals may also fill this role.

You, however, are ultimately your baby's case manager. As you

learn about his needs and about early intervention, you will become the coordinator of information about your baby; the professionals will become consultants as much as teachers to you. There is simply no substitute for direct parent involvement.

As you can see, there are many professionals who *could* work with your child. Each serves a different function and each has a specialty. But early intervention programs differ from place to place. It is possible that the team could include a different professional for each specialty, or one or two people who provide all of the services, or a combination of professionals working separately. Remember, there is great variety in the way services are provided in different locations. Check out your local programs; many different program models can work. We urge you to find caring professionals to help you obtain the services you and your baby need, especially in the first months after his birth.

Programs

Just as there are different professionals, organizations, and funding agencies who provide services, there are also many types of programs available for babies with Down syndrome. The following descriptions will help guide you in exploring the different programs available to you in many communities.

Family-Centered Service. This kind of program focuses on the family as a whole—parents and children together. Although your baby's special needs are the central focus, this program goes a little further. In addition to working with your baby, the program works with families to integrate the child and the special services he needs into the family. In a family approach, the staff would gear its work with a child to the family's overall circumstances. They would consider such things as family lifestyle, the parents' work schedules, other children, the family's daily routine, other members of the extended family, the baby's health and care requirements, and how the program's recommendations fit into the family's life. By looking at this wide variety of factors, family-centered programs try to help both children and families as a single unit.

Child-Centered Service. This type of program is somewhat more traditional than a family-centered program. In it there is one "client"—the baby. The program usually consists of staff who provide specific suggestions to parents to help the child reach developmental goals. Family life, varying lifestyles, and other family members are not considered as strongly or to the same degree as in a family-centered model.

There is no one ideal type of program. All programs are really a collection of people with a common purpose. You will find that the quality and usefulness of a program depends to a great extent on the staff, the program goals, and how those match with your current needs. Try to find the type of program that works best for you and your baby.

Home- and Center-Based Programs

There are two places babies with Down syndrome receive early intervention services: at home or at a "center." Babies who have health problems such as heart defects require home care, while children with good health can go to a center for their services. This section reviews how early intervention programs work at home or at "school."

In *home-based* services, members of the early intervention team come to your home for regularly scheduled visits to work with you and your baby. They may all visit together once a week, or each may come separately. How many teachers or therapists visit and how often they visit can change as your baby's needs change. Home-based services are generally provided to babies up to two years of age, although some programs provide it until age three. Home-based services are necessary for children who, because of their fragile health, should not to be exposed to other children, and may also work well for many other families.

During a home visit the teacher will work with your baby, focusing on the different areas of development. Each area of development can involve different activities and exercises. The home visitor will likely want you to try the various activities with your child. He or she may work with you and your baby together, or just work with your baby, or perhaps have you do most of the work. The teacher will also ask questions about what you have been observing in your child between visits. Often, at the end of each session, the teacher or therapist will leave suggestions—frequently in writing—about things to try with your baby until the next visit.

In many programs, the teacher may bring a bag of toys and equipment to each session. He or she may leave some of this for you to use with your child or suggest ways to work with your child. For example, a favorite of physical therapists is a big rubber ball that can be used for abdominal exercises as well as for teaching balance.

Home visits are also a time for parents to discuss problems and concerns. For example, if feeding is a problem or if your child's leg movements don't seem right, these can be discussed during a home visit. This exchange of information enables both you and the teacher to work on those areas that need the most work and to continually evaluate your child's progress.

Much of what goes on during a home visit also occurs in *center-based* programs. The major difference between home- and center-based programs is that in a center-based program you bring your baby to a "center," which could be a school, health department, or private office. The "classroom" might look like a typical classroom scaled to the size and needs of babies and toddlers. The center may also have additional rooms for physical therapy with heavy mats on the floor, mirrors, and other equipment.

Center-based programs may be individual, with just you, your baby, and the teacher or therapist, or may include small groups of parents and their babies along with the staff. In group programs, you may receive less individual attention, but you may learn different techniques from the other parents and children. In some cases, home- and center-based services are combined.

The Evaluation

You may be referred to an early intervention program when you receive the diagnosis of Down syndrome. Some programs may start quickly with informal evaluations and initial recommendations, and then later schedule a more formal developmental evaluation. In other cases, before your baby can begin receiving early intervention services, he will need to be evaluated to assess his development and to determine what services he needs. Evaluations are often part of early intervention programs, but they may also be obtained elsewhere, such as through hospitals – usually children's hospitals – as well as health departments and school districts. If these organizations do not provide developmental evaluations in your area, they usually can tell you where to get one.

Developmental evaluations can provide you with important information – sometimes new information, sometimes an objective confirmation of what you already know. The evaluation can tell you the areas of your child's development that are strong and the areas that are weak, so that an effective early intervention program can be designed. An evaluation can also give you an idea of how your baby's skills compare to other babies and enables you to monitor progress through check-up evaluations.

During an evaluation, your child will be given activities to do and may be put through a series of movements. Your baby's performance can provide crucial data, but it is also important for *you* to provide information about your baby to the person assessing him. If the evaluator does not see your baby regularly, he or she may not see everything your baby can do during the evaluation and may interpret your baby's performance differently than you would. That is why your observations about your child are so important. It can make a difference for the evaluator to know that your baby does things at home but not at the evaluation, or vice versa. Generally two to four weeks after the evaluation, a conference or "interpretive" is scheduled. This is a time for you to discuss the results of the evaluation, as well as to ask questions.

The evaluation will usually tell you what your child's developmental strengths and weaknesses are and possibly will result in the recommendation of specific services. This hopefully will assist you in finding a good program for your child. If this testing is part of an early intervention program in which you are enrolled, it will be the basis from which the specific program for your baby is developed. If the evaluation has been done independently, a referral from the evaluating agency can be made to a program in your area. If there is no appropriate infant program, developmental services may be available through a particular hospital department, such as genetics, birth defects, neonatology, or   physical medicine. For parents in

areas without special infant programs, these hospital departments could provide contact with professionals knowledgeable about infant development and could be a good place to ask questions. Private pediatric therapists may also be available and able to provide needed service to you and your baby.

Several types of agencies may have early intervention programs under their auspices. In some areas there may be more than one source for early intervention; in others the resources may be more limited. Generally, services are offered through the following:

1. Public school districts.
2. Private schools that serve children whose special requirements cannot be met by the public school district.
3. Regional children's hospitals.
4. Programs affiliated with universities and university hospitals.
5. State, county, or municipal health departments and divisions of mental retardation or developmental disabilities.
6. Local organizations such as the ARC and local branches of the National Down Syndrome Congress.

If you have difficulty getting the information you need, the local chapter of the ARC, the local or state special education agency, or the local Down syndrome association may be able to steer you in the right direction. The Resource Guide at the end of this book lists the organizations in each state that can help parents of babies with Down syndrome find a developmental program for their baby. Other parents who are already receiving services for their children can also be most helpful.

In choosing a program it is important to obtain information about the programs in your area. Observe a program in operation, interview the staff, and talk to parents whose children are in the program. Then make your choice. Remember though, this field of infant development is new to you, and it is impossible for you to become an expert overnight. But no choice is permanent; if the program you picked does not meet your needs or your baby's needs, find an alternative by making changes with the staff or choosing another program. In this process of choosing a program, the experience of other parents can be invaluable.

Parents as Teachers:
The Parent-Professional Partnership

The essence of early intervention is direct parent involvement. Most programs stress the parent(s) as the primary teacher of their baby. By contrast, in traditional education you may have heard that "parents should not be their children's teacher." But when it comes to teaching your baby with Down syndrome, the parent's role is critical—especially because your baby is starting his education so early.

Parents know their babies best and have the greatest opportunity to work and play with them. Because babies constantly change and are largely unpredictable in how they respond on a particular day and time, working with them every day is necessary. In addition to the scheduled visits of the intervention team, special activities can be incorporated into your baby's daily routine. You will need to understand how to work with your child as you and he go through each day together. In order to do this you need very specialized information. You cannot be expected to know automatically how to meet the special needs of your baby. You need to learn about the special handling techniques, observational skills, and teaching strategies. Early intervention teachers can give you this information.

You are the consumer of a very specialized and very personal service. Someone will not only help your baby to learn, but will also teach you. Establishing a partnership with your early intervention professionals should be a very positive experience. Ideally, it is a two-way relationship: You can learn teaching techniques and hear about new ideas and information, and your child's teachers can learn from you about your baby and your family. For example, a special seat to support your baby and to encourage him to reach may be a great idea, but because of your other children or the layout of your house this may not work for you. Or you may notice your baby trying to hold his head up; the teacher may suggest ways to strengthen neck muscles and new ways to motivate your baby. In a good working parent-professional relationship, both partners should listen to each other and work together to develop ideas that work for you and your child.

The positive aspects of this type of relationship—such as the relief of having someone join you in helping your baby—can be a great help. On the other hand, this kind of service can feel very intrusive and sometimes can trigger feelings of inadequacy in you. You may feel that you are forced to share parenting with a professional whom you may see as competent and knowledgeable while you may feel incompetent and ignorant. Having someone come into your home to work with your baby may make you feel as though you are being taught something you think you should already know. Also, time—already a precious commodity—is further strained by having to fit in visits of the intervention team. The ups and downs just described are part and parcel of the parent-professional partnership. This pull and push is perfectly normal and is to be expected.

Here are some hints for making the parent-professional partnership work for you and your baby:

- There are still professionals with whom you may come into contact who view themselves as "experts" and who think you should be unquestioningly grateful for the help you are receiving. Never forget that this is *your* baby and you are the consumer of these services for both of you. Don't be bullied or intimidated.
- If you don't understand something about your child or the services he is receiving, ask questions. Discuss what is and is not working for you and your baby. Most of all, share your concerns.
- Take good care of yourselves. This means that the goals of the early intervention program should fit into your family's life. The reality of having many responsibilities is that, although the goals for your baby are extremely important, there are times when you cannot work toward them as you would like. This happens to everyone—and it is important to your family that you have a balanced life.
- Keep notes of teaching sessions, the goals and plans of the intervention team, and your concerns and worries. No one can be expected to remember everything.

Teaching Methods and Strategies

In many ways, raising your baby with Down syndrome will be the same as raising any other baby. But there will also be many differences. One facet of being the parent of your special baby is the need to be consciously aware of his development. Babies generally progress automatically from one stage and skill to another. Parents may help them work toward a new goal such as rolling over or reaching out for a toy. But most babies actually direct the efforts and do most of the work. When your baby has Down syndrome, you will have to help direct his development and join him in his "work" to a greater extent. We call this "conscious parenting."

You may not realize it, but you already know a great deal about your baby. Your knowledge will show when people ask you questions about your baby's likes, dislikes, reactions, and schedules. That knowledge will serve as a useful foundation for your work with your baby.

You will also learn about your baby from your work with professionals. Their help will usually take two forms. First, there will be specific instructions for exercises and activities that help your baby reach developmental goals. These may require that you set aside a daily period of time, use particular materials, and follow specific teaching methods. For example, you may need to do exercises with your baby to strengthen his abdominal muscles two times a day for several weeks. Or you may need to sit down at a quiet time and use

small blocks and a box to help your baby learn to sort shapes. These "lessons" are one part of your baby's early intervention program.

The other part of your work with your baby requires incorporating developmental goals into everyday activities. Diapering, waking, feeding, bathing, and just sitting with your baby can all be done in ways that promote your child's development. For example, you can hold your baby with his legs together rather than wrapped around your hips, and you can encourage exploration, reaching out, and communication. This added consciousness in your daily parenting is important to your baby's progress. The types of activities and handling techniques can be designed by you and your baby's teachers. But every baby and every family is different; you will include developmental activities in your child's daily life in ways that fit you, your baby, and your family.

Observing Your Baby

Parents know their children in great detail. As your baby grows and as you learn about development, you will be able to assess your child's developmental strengths and weaknesses, his ways of responding, and his progress. The more you learn about your baby, the better you and your professional partners will be able to develop appropriate ideas for intervention. Observing your baby as you do in his everyday activities, movements, and responses is essential for gathering the information you need. In addition to just spotting problems you will wonder at your baby's many accomplishments and strengths.

The following guide for observing your baby's development will help organize the information you may already possess and will give ideas for additional things to look for. We hope the developmental areas outlined in Chapter 6 and the questions listed below are helpful. Some questions apply to all levels of development; others are more specific to certain stages. Although these questions can serve as a guide in observing your baby's development, there are, of course, additional questions that you and your baby's teacher will ask.

Responsiveness
- Is he aware of his environment and daily routine?
- Does he seem alert?
- How does he "explore" a new toy? By looking, tasting, holding? For a long time or a short time?

- Does he show any change in response to new places, people, or things?
- Is he generally content? Comfortable? Irritable? Fussy?
- Does he get "keyed up," confused, disorganized, unable to settle down? Can you tell what causes this?
- Does he prefer familiar routines or days that include many changes?
- How does he respond to daily activities—bathing, going to sleep, taking naps? Is this predictable or does it vary?
- Does feeding or eating go smoothly? Does it need to be very quiet? How does he respond to new foods—solids, table foods, cup drinking?

Sensory Input
- How does he respond to visual, auditory, tactile, and vestibular (swinging, spinning, and roughhousing) input?
- Does he prefer one type of input to another?
- Does he focus on one kind of input at a time or does he prefer combined activities?

Activity and Energy Levels
- What is his energy level throughout the day?
- Is there any consistent pattern?
- Are there specific types of activities that he prefers at certain times and not at others?

Preferences
- What types of toys—colorful toys, noisy toys, toys to watch, toys to manipulate, small or large toys—does he prefer?
- Does he have favorite people? Do they seem to have a certain manner of approaching or interacting with him (quiet, high energy, or dramatic)?
- How does he prefer to be held?
- How does he play, move, socialize, and interact with children, adults, and objects?
- Does he prefer structured play or independent play?

Learning
- Does he seem to do best when activities are short in duration?

One structured activity at a time with some independent time in between? Several activities in succession but changed frequently? What activities hold his attention?

- How does he seem to accomplish a new skill? Does he keep trying until he succeeds? Does he try something once and then not for a while? Does he reach one developmental milestone at a time or several at roughly the same time after a long waiting period?
- Does he respond best to familiar activities with new wrinkles added one at a time? Or do new activities seem to motivate him?
- When looking at or listening to new activities, does he seem to stay interested longer if he is in a seat? On the floor? Held in your arms?

Movement

- Does he move about freely and easily or does he prefer to get into a position and stay there for awhile?
- How does he position his body during rest and activity?
- What is his preferred resting position – tummy, back, side-lying, sitting?
- How does he position his shoulders, arms, hips, knees, legs, feet, and head during movement, rest, and activity?
- Does he move his legs and arms together or reciprocally (one side and then the other)? When?
- Does he use one side of his body more readily than the other?
- Does he reach for and grasp objects easily? Does he work at it repeatedly until he is able to get it?
- How does he hold objects? Does he transfer the object from hand to hand? Hold it in both hands together?
- Does he use his whole hand or just his fingers?
- What does the rest of his body do when he is trying to play with a toy? Does he move freely or stay in a fixed position?

Communication

- Is he generally quiet or does he make noise most of the time?
- Does he make many sounds or mostly repeat the same sounds?
- Does he change from one sound to another although mostly repeating one sound at a time?
- Does he seem to be quiet at certain times and "noisy" at others?

Do certain activities, movements, or toys (such as mirrors, dolls, and musical toys) motivate "talking?"
- Does he seem to understand very familiar words or names?
- Does he look at you and seem to "talk" to you although he is not saying words? Can you understand his nonverbal communication?
- Does he have different noises for happy, as opposed to complaining, times?

Not all of the questions above may pertain to your baby right now. These are sample questions, but they will give you an idea of what to begin looking for in getting to know the individual developmental "style" of your baby. This may seem overwhelming, but much of it will become natural and routine. You will be able to see more clearly what activities do and don't work for your baby, how many changes really do occur, and where help is needed. Observe and interact with him; your baby will teach you a great deal about himself. But remember, there are no "right" answers to these questions; they are just for guiding you in observing your child, not in measuring his abilities.

Teaching Strategies

Because every baby with Down syndrome is unique, no book can prescribe a precise "curriculum" or teaching program for all children. Based on your own observations, on professional developmental evaluations, and on discussions with the professionals involved, you will develop your own comprehensive program.

In working with your child in any program there are many general strategies that can make your work more effective:

1. Be as *consistent* as possible. Consistency is difficult for everyone to achieve and sustain. But being consistent in your goals for yourself and for your baby will help foster learning.
2. Set *well-defined expectations*. This will help you be consistent and will make things predictable and measurable. It will also allow you to see when your goals have been accomplished, what your baby has achieved, and when to move to the next step.

3. Divide tasks into *small steps*. This will again make your work easier by allowing you to identify what part of a task may be difficult for your baby.

4. *Repetition* is a very important part of your baby's learning process. Although you may, at times, feel that it must be boring and that you should change things, watch your baby for cues. Often repetition is precisely what is needed.

5. Be *patient and persistent*. Many hard jobs lie ahead. Progress in a particular area may take a long time and can be frustrating for all of you. Don't give up. If you lose patience, remember that it happens to everyone. And just when you are most frustrated, another accomplishment will recharge you.

6. A *positive approach* will carry you far. Use of praise and other rewards will motivate your baby and create a positive attitude in both of you. Children with Down syndrome–like all children–respond well to praise. Try to praise your baby as soon as possible after he does what you want. But again, no one can do this one hundred percent of the time; it is meant to be a guide–the optimal situation to reach for as much as possible.

7. Use *prompts or cues* to help your baby learn, but be sure to give him time to respond. There is a variety of prompts you can give. Physically helping your baby to do an activity–called "patterning"–is the most helpful cue you can give. For example, you can hold your child's hands and practice putting a puzzle together. When this kind of help is not necessary, you can try some visual cue or gesture (like pointing) to help your baby begin. A verbal prompt (a reminder of what comes next) can be used with the others from the beginning so that your baby begins to understand what the word or phrase means.

You will undoubtedly find other strategies and teaching methods that work for you and your baby. Be as creative as you can and, most of all, remember that everyone has good times and bad times.

Mainstreaming

In this chapter, we have spoken about the special services your baby with Down syndrome should receive. These special services are usually provided in an infant program separate from other schools and preschools. Parents today, however, are understandably interested in involving their special child in regular schools and classes. This is what is called "mainstreaming."

Mainstreaming is a term that came into use in the field of special education about fifteen years ago, although the concept has been around, in different forms, for much longer. Mainstreaming means being in the main flow of life around you. However valuable and necessary, special education means that a child has less contact with a large peer group. It necessarily results in being "out of the mainstream." Parents and professionals have repeatedly asked how this will affect their children. Frequently the response has been to place special-needs children in regular classrooms in schools and preschools.

Mainstreaming may sound like it applies only to older children, but it relates to children of any age and to their families. In addition to providing special children with exposure to regular classes and peer groups, mainstreaming promotes acceptance from those children and families who do not have the experience of being close to someone with special needs. Being involved with children with special needs and learning to accept them is a valuable social lesson for children of all ages.

Major controversial social questions surround the issue of mainstreaming. But as a parent of a baby with Down syndrome, you need to focus on *your* child's needs first. Mainstreaming may play a part in your baby's education now or may come to play a part in the future. For now, however, your baby's needs take precedence over the debate about mainstreaming.

Mainstreaming can be either formal or informal. In its informal sense, it means including your baby with Down syndrome in your normal activities, vacations, family visits, and contact with neighbors and friends, and it means having your baby exposed to the experiences that naturally come with being part of a family.

In its formal sense, mainstreaming becomes a serious consideration between the ages of two to three years. This is a time when socialization and group experiences become important. It is a time also when you will be looking for a special program with small groups of special-needs children. In addition to a special program, parents often consider placing their child in a regular toddler group or nursery school for part of the week.

Because every child is different, the decision to mainstream is also an individual one. You must assess your child's individual needs and strengths to decide if he would benefit from mainstreaming. How would he benefit from being part of a regular toddler preschool class? What kind of balance might be achieved to serve all of you best? What kind of regular preschool program is best for him? These are some of the questions to be asked.

It is certainly possible to combine services. Many parents do. If your child is sociable, enjoys watching and being around other children, if he likes small groups and responds well to quite a bit of stimulation, you might want to think about a regular preschool toddler group for at least part of each week. Being in the company of children without special needs can often benefit a young child with Down syndrome in many areas of development.

In mainstreaming, your child might be placed in a group of children at a similar developmental level. This generally means your child would be placed with children younger than he is chronologically, but with children who share his favorite activities and abilities. Sometimes, the models of behavior and communication in a regular preschool class can help your child. He may imitate what he sees other children doing, resulting in a great deal of learning. This of course depends on your child, his needs, your feelings, and the specific program at the regular preschool—a lot of considerations to juggle. Ask your early intervention team for advice: they can help you judge your child's needs and determine what mix of special and regular preschool experiences would be best.

There are many ways to mainstream a child with Down syndrome. Often parents can combine a part-time nursery school program with a part-time early intervention program. For example, three mornings a week your child could be in a special program and two afternoons he could go to a regular toddler class. Or individual physical and speech therapy sessions one to two times a week can complement a mainstreamed program in a toddler class. Remember though, the combination of services has to meet your child's *real* needs.

Mainstreaming can have its drawbacks. This is particularly the case if mainstreaming precludes getting other special services that your child needs. Another drawback results if the regular preschool cannot or will not use some special teaching techniques for your child, leading to a loss of skills, slower progress, or frustration. It may be that gains in social skills—one of the primary benefits of mainstreaming—mean that other specific skill areas do not progress as quickly. Your child's progress in *all* areas of development needs to be monitored and addressed by an early intervention program.

Not all preschools will accept a child with Down syndrome. Unfortunately, some nursery school teachers refuse to take on special-needs children. Professionals and parents of babies with Down syndrome may know where to direct you, or you may need to do the searching yourself. Another consideration is that a small neighborhood playgroup might be a good informal alternative to an established preschool program.

If you find a preschool program that will accept your child, it may not be prepared to meet all of your child's special needs and should not necessarily be expected to do so. However, good communication between your child's early intervention team and your child's preschool teachers can be invaluable. Ask your child's teachers if they might talk and exchange ideas. Perhaps each set of teachers can visit the other school (and meet with outside therapists) to learn about how best to handle your child. Sharing ideas about how to best help a special-needs child can be very rewarding for all concerned and can give your child the balanced program he needs. You can also carry information and ideas from one program to another. Whatever will work best in your unique situation is the right thing to do.

Conclusion

Early infant education is a complex, ever-changing field. As the parent of a baby with Down syndrome, you will learn much about it very quickly. The Reading List at the end of this book contains books on teaching your special child and includes several good activity books for parents and children. In addition, the Resource Guide can steer you in the direction of people, agencies, and organizations that can help you get your child started in a program of early intervention.

This book has repeatedly pointed out that parents must be responsible for helping their child with Down syndrome reach his full potential. In early intervention, parents are indeed their child's primary teacher and evaluator. The work involved in constantly aiding good development is substantial, but getting to know the many facets of your baby and assisting him in reaching toward his potential can be an enriching and rewarding experience as well.

Parent Statements

The parent is always ultimately the case manager.

The whole idea of development and teaching my baby was intimidating in the beginning. I had this picture that I was going to have to work with her ten or twelve hours a day. I thought, "Oh, I just can't." I remember at first trying to do that, but I couldn't keep up with it. Finally I got to the point where I could relax a bit and just enjoy her. And she's probably better off now.

It's a good thing to set aside specific work times if you can. But the best approach to teaching is an incidental approach anyway. Whatever comes up in the routine of the day can be made into a learning experience.

I find myself now in the position of being very protective of new parents I talk to. I let them know they still need to be who they are and go for four days if they feel like going for four days without doing a thing. If that's the way they need to react to their child, that's the way it is. You just can't let the special child be the individual around whom you rotate. You just can't give that much energy.

Our county's program serves any child with developmental problems. They set up meetings for parents to meet the co-ordinator and for tours of the school. And they thoroughly test each child. She'll get five or six different evaluations by different therapists and teachers. They have to find developmental delays before she's eligible for special preschool.

I've always felt that Laurie is a low-tone child. I see her as low tone both mentally and physically. To get her to learn well, you have to hype her up. Music is one of the ways we do it. We use music with a purpose—following directions, se-quencing activities, learning concepts. Get her excited and she learns better.

Our little girl is in a center-based program. She started at six weeks old. When it first began, she went three times a week; now she goes twice. They have physical therapists, speech therapists, special education teachers, and occupational therapists. She has speech therapy with a group of four kids once a week, and has an individual appointment another day. She gets all the other different teachers randomly. I go to all the sessions with her. It's not hard fitting it all in. I like it because I get out of the house. And she loves it; she loves seeing other children and she loves the toys.

Often I've wished I had someone I could go to for advice on my "normal" child. I always felt it was a great deal to have someone to turn to when I couldn't figure out how to approach a problem—and my special-needs child wasn't the only one to present me with problems!

I have heard there are a lot of parents who wish they could send their other children to the program, just because it's so good. I visited the classroom and it was cheerful and bright and the teachers seemed genuinely interested; they seemed like they were having a great time.

The teachers in our program were good. I would go to them really frustrated and feeling unable to set aside an hour to do the things they wanted me to do. But the case manager said, "Look, there are ways that you can incorporate these things into your daily routine—when you're changing her, dressing her, when you're bathing her, and feeding her." When I tried to do that, usually it went a whole lot better. I've pretty much given up trying to do therapy-type work with her at home because she's totally turned off to it now. But if we just play—just start fooling around—then she can learn a lot of things. You have to fake her out. We got these wonderful toys—puzzles, pegboards, and blocks—and all she does is ignore them. I guess she figured out that they were educational.

Fortunately, we have lots of family around to give him his therapy and that's made it a lot easier on us. But even so, we do feel under pressure a little. You know, you feel like if you're free and the kid is sitting there, you should do some exercises with him. There was a time when we pressured him too much and he started refusing to do anything and was throwing all his toys around.

When we first understood that he had to have intensive therapy, we really got overenthusiastic. We used to make him do exercises until he cried. And we realized that it was just too much; that we were pushing him too hard. He would reject therapy if we made it so painful for him, so we just stopped to reconsider. Now we try to make it fun for him and that's been much more effective. You get little gems of time when you feel you're effective and over time it adds up.

She tries really hard on some things. On some things she

couldn't care less. She reached a point where she got really turned off about doing certain things–things she didn't like.

These children are called retarded, but they sure can find ingenious ways to avoid having to sit and learn. The old saying that "he may be retarded, but he's not stupid" is really true.

We've had a hard time just leaving him to enjoy his quiet time by himself. I feel I should be holding him, stimulating him, dangling a rattle in front of him. It's like we have a higher standard of care because he has Down syndrome.

With the educators you have to trust your feelings and perceptions because you know your child best. We had one therapist who was very good, but whose voice was very shrill, and our son would get upset. It was interfering with his lesson even though the things she was doing were good. So we changed therapists, and found one who was more compatible.

I feel very strongly that if you have a special-needs child, you need to explore every option, even if it's an option that doesn't appeal to you at first. I checked out every program, and I talked to many therapists. My husband and I sat together and made lists of the advantages and disadvantages of each thing.

Parents shouldn't have any mental barriers in their own minds about what their child can do because you really can't tell. We were constantly finding that Chris could do things that we had no idea he could do. If we hadn't had therapists and people who knew where to look, we just wouldn't have known. The most striking example was when we first had the speech therapist. He was about nine months old. We had no conception that he could understand words. She got him a ball and a telephone and some of his toys, and she asked him, "Where's the ball?" and he pointed to the ball. She said, "Where's the telephone?" and he pointed to the telephone. We were just so amazed and felt very bad that we didn't know he could do that. Kids can really do a lot more than parents imagine.

Every parent should be linked up with a genetic department somewhere, even if they have to travel once a year sixty miles. I think that with our child a physical therapist was vital in the first year. After the first year, a speech therapist was vital, and once she turned three, an OT was vital. A special education can provide a lot of parents with important information that will carry through for the rest of your child's life—especially in terms of teaching you to be your child's advocate.

We have really felt that the work has paid off. The program has been terrific. It was important because we learned too. They really taught me how to help her and I think that was invaluable, just because I didn't know that much about how to play with babies. I just knew the bare minimum. They taught me a lot about how to play but at the same time teach her. I've learned so much. I can't believe how much I've learned.

You have to figure out what's the most important thing to strive for at each development stage like you do in every child's life and give that input regardless of what a thousand professionals are telling you. You are the case manager and have to figure out what is most important, and let the rest roll off your back, which isn't an easy thing to do.

The teachers at my son's nursery school were very interested in working with him and learning about his special needs. They were especially excited over his accomplishments, maybe because he worked harder than the other kids to achieve things. They also felt more protective, perhaps, towards him than the other children.

EIGHT

Legal Rights and Hurdles: Being a Good Advocate for Your Child

JAMES E. KAPLAN and RALPH J. MOORE, JR.*

Introduction

You don't have to be a lawyer to understand the laws that apply to your child, and we don't want to turn you into a lawyer. Because your baby has Down syndrome, however, you and she have many rights about which you may not have been aware. These rights, which include the right to a free appropriate public education, are provided by federal, state, and local laws. They are essential in helping your child reach her potential; they open the door to education and special services. Understanding how to use these laws to ensure that your child receives all the services she needs is crucial for the new parent of a baby with Down syndrome.

It would be impossible to discuss the law of every state. Instead, this chapter provides an overview of the most important legal con-

---

*Ralph J. Moore, Jr. and James E. Kaplan are partners in the Washington, D.C. law firm of Shea & Gardner, and are active in the area of the legal rights of handicapped children. Mr. Moore is the author of *Handbook on Estate Planning for Families of Developmentally Disabled Persons in Maryland, the District of Columbia, and Virginia*.

cepts you need to know, including your child's right to an education as well as to other critical services. There are no federal laws that deal specifically with Down syndrome. Rather, the rights of children with Down syndrome are provided in the laws and regulations for handicapped people generally. In other words, the same laws that protect all handicapped children also protect your child. To effectively exercise your rights and fully protect your child, you need to understand those laws.

In addition to concerns about education, new parents of a child with Down syndrome often worry intensely about the future—especially how to care for their child when they, the parents, are no longer alive. Ironically, even though they worry a lot, parents often avoid or simply overlook planning for the future. This chapter reviews some of the extremely important legal issues parents must face to protect their child's future. Finally, we summarize briefly the disability benefits generally available from federal and state governments after your child is grown.

You should understand that this chapter is designed to provide accurate and authoritative information about the legal aspects of having a child with Down syndrome. The authors and the publisher, however, are not acting as lawyers and are not rendering legal, accounting, or other professional advice. If you need legal or other advice, a competent professional should be consulted.

Your Child's Right to an Education

Perhaps nothing has done so much to improve the education of children with Down syndrome as The Education for All Handicapped Children Act of 1975, better known as Public Law 94–142 or the EAHCA. This comprehensive law has created vastly improved educational opportunities for exceptional children across the country. Administered through the U.S. Department of Education and by each state, the law works on a carrot-and-stick basis.

Under Public Law 94–142, the federal government provides funds for the education of handicapped children to each state that has a special education program that meets a variety of federal standards. To qualify for the federal funds, a state must demonstrate, through a detailed plan submitted for federal approval, that it has a policy assuring all handicapped children a "free appropriate public education." What this means is that states accepting federal funds under Public Law 94–142 must provide both approved educational services and a variety of procedural rights to handicapped children and their parents. The lure of federal funds has been attractive enough to induce all of the states to create special education plans that can truly help children with Down syndrome.

The EAHCA establishes the *minimum* requirements in handicapped education programs for states wishing to receive federal funds. The federal requirements *do not require* states to adopt an ideal educational program or a program that parents feel is "the best." Because states have leeway under Public Law 94–142, there are differences from state to state in the programs or services available. Often parents perceive a difference between the federal minimum provisions and the optimum program for their child with Down syndrome.

States *can* create special education programs that are better than those required by Public Law 94–142, and some have. For babies with Down syndrome this can be important. Parents, organizations, and advocacy groups continually push their states to go beyond the federal requirements and provide the highest quality special education possible. Parents should check with their local school district to find out exactly what services are available to their child.

What Public Law 94–142 Provides

The EAHCA contains many important provisions that can directly affect your child. It is worth knowing what the law says and how it works. This section reviews the important provisions of Public Law 94–142.

Coverage. Generally speaking, Public Law 94–142 requires that states provide special education to handicapped children between the ages of six and eighteen. States may provide services to children between birth and age six and between ages eighteen and twenty-one, even though the EAHCA does not necessarily require it.

There is wide variation among the states as to when they start providing services. Currently seven states provide services from birth onward; two start services at age two; fourteen (including the District of Columbia) begin providing services at age three; twenty-two begin providing services at ages four and five; and, unfortunately, six do not start providing services until age six. Because of state and local laws and regulations, there is great variation *within* each state as to when services of one kind or another are available to babies with Down syndrome.

The chart at the end of the chapter shows when each state begins to provide services to handicapped children. Due to recent amendments, Public Law 94–142 will be applicable to younger children by 1991. In addition, there is another federal law that provides some funds for programs for early infant intervention. Contact your local school district and appropriate state agencies to determine exactly what services are available to your baby and when.

There has never been any question that Public Law 94–142 applies to children with Down syndrome. The law covers children who are mentally retarded, learning disabled, physically handicapped, and seriously emotionally disturbed. A doctor's diagnosis of Down syndrome should be enough to establish that the EAHCA applies to your child.

Length of Services. Currently under Public Law 94–142, states must provide more than the traditional 180-day school year when the unique needs of a child indicate that year-round instruction is a necessary part of a "free appropriate public education." The decision to offer summer instruction depends on whether the child will regress substantially without summer services. If so, the services must be provided at public expense.

Identification and Evaluation. Because the EAHCA applies only to handicapped children, your child with Down syndrome must be evaluated before she is eligible for special education. The law requires the states to develop testing and evaluation procedures designed to identify and evaluate the needs and abilities of each child before she is placed into a special education program. The evaluation procedure is required to take into account the parents' input.

For parents of a baby with Down syndrome, identification is somewhat simpler. School districts almost uniformly recognize that children with Down syndrome need special education. In other words, the challenge is not in convincing a school district that your child is special, but rather in obtaining needed services as early as possible. Doctors, organizations, and – most importantly – other parents can be extremely helpful at this initial stage.

"Free Appropriate Public Education." At the heart of Public Law 94–142 is the requirement that handicapped children receive a "free appropriate public education." The law defines this to mean "special education and related services." In turn, "special education" means specially designed instruction tailored to meet the unique needs of the handicapped child, including classroom instruction, physical education, home instruction, and – if necessary – instruction in hospitals or institutions. "Related services" are defined as transportation and other developmental, corrective, and supportive services necessary to enable the child to benefit from a special education. Services provided by a trained occupational therapist, physical therapist, speech therapist, psychologist, social worker, school nurse, or any other qualified person may be required under Public Law 94–142. Some services, however, are specifically excluded. Most important among these exclusions are strictly medical services that must be provided by a licensed physician or hospital.

The EAHCA does not prescribe a specific educational program, but rather sets a minimum standard for the states to follow. In this way states have considerable leeway in designing special education programs. Let's examine more precisely what "free appropriate public education" means.

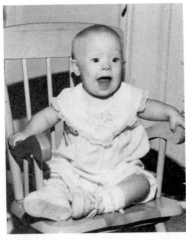

"Free" means that, regardless of the parents' ability to pay, every part of a child's special education program must be provided at public expense. This is true if the child is placed in a program in a public school or, if a suitable public program is not available, in a private school or residential setting. In other words, if a private school or residential placement is necessary to provide an appropriate educational program—not merely the parents' preference— then the school district must place the child in the private school and pay the tuition. In many areas, private schools have programs that are better suited to the needs of children with Down syndrome. Remember, the EAHCA does not provide for tuition payment for educational services not approved by the school district or other governing agency (unless, as is explained elsewhere in this chapter, parents are able to overturn the decision of their school district). Parents who place their child in an unapproved program face having to bear the full cost of tuition.

It often is difficult for parents to understand that the "free appropriate public education" mandated by the EAHCA does not secure for their child either the best education that money can buy or even an educational opportunity equal to that given to nonhandicapped children. The law is more modest; it only requires that handicapped children be given access to specialized educational services individually designed to benefit the handicapped child. A few years ago, the United States Supreme Court decided that a "free appropriate public education" need not be designed to enable a handicapped child to maximize her potential or to develop self-sufficiency. Instead, the basic floor of educational opportunity may be satisfied by a variety of instructional and related services, the extent of which is determined on a child-by-child basis. The law in this area is still evolving, so there are no clear rules as yet for children with Down syndrome.

It is up to parents to secure the most appropriate placement for their child. Under the EAHCA, parents and educators are supposed to work together to design the individualized education program for each child. But to convince a school district to make the best placement for the child, parents must demonstrate to school officials not only that the school district's preferred placement might not be appropriate, but that the parents' preferred placement is. Hopefully in the end there is agreement on the appropriate placement. If not, there are procedures for resolving disputes that we discuss later in the chapter.

"Least Restrictive Environment." In discussing special education, the term "mainstreaming" is often mentioned. Under Public Law 94-142, there is a strong preference for mainstreaming handicapped children, including children with Down syndrome. The law requires that handicapped children must "to the maximum extent appropriate" be educated in the *least restrictive environment* with children who are *not* handicapped.

In practice, the law requires that children with handicaps be integrated into their community's regular schools, if possible. For some this means a combination of special classes, along with physical education, assemblies, and other classes taken with the rest of the school. Special services and additional teaching material can be used to provide the extra educational input special children need. The law was intended to end the historical practice of isolating handicapped children.

Despite the law's preference for mainstreaming, the EAHCA also recognizes that regular classrooms may not be suitable for the education of some handicapped children. In these cases, the law allows for placement in separate classes, separate public schools, private schools, or even residential settings if this kind of placement is required to meet the individual educational—as opposed to medical, social, or emotional—needs of the child. For children for whom placement within the community's public schools is not appropriate, the law still requires that they be placed in the least restrictive educational environment suitable to their individual needs.

"Individualized Education Program." The EAHCA recognizes that each handicapped child is unique. As a result, the law requires that special education programs be tailored to the individual needs of each handicapped child. Based on your child's evaluation, a program specifically designed to address her developmental problems will be devised. This is called an "individualized education program" or, more commonly, an "IEP."

The IEP is a written report that describes: 1) the child's present level of development; 2) both the short-term and annual goals of the special education program; 3) the specific educational services that the child will receive; 4) the date services will start and their expected duration; 5) standards for determining whether the goals of the educational program are being met; and 6) the extent to which the child will be able to participate in regular educational programs.

A child's IEP is usually developed during a series of meetings among the parents, teachers, and representatives of the school district. Even the child herself may be present. The effort to write an IEP is ideally a cooperative one with parents, teachers, and school officials conferring on what goals are appropriate and how best to achieve them. Preliminary drafts of the IEP are reviewed and revised until what hopefully is a mutually acceptable program is developed.

IEPs should be very detailed. Although initially this may seem intimidating, detailed IEPs enable parents to closely monitor the education their child receives and to make sure their child is actually receiving the services prescribed. In addition, the law requires that IEPs be reviewed and revised at least once every year to ensure that the child's educational program continues to meet her changing needs.

Designing a good IEP requires direct parent involvement; no one knows your child's developmental needs better. You cannot always depend on teachers or school officials to recognize your child's unique needs as you do. To obtain the full range of services, you may need to demonstrate that withholding these services would result in an education which would *not* be "appropriate." For example, if parents feel a private school program is best for their child, they must demonstrate that placement in the public school program would not be appropriate for their child's special needs.

Because children with Down syndrome have special needs, it is essential that the IEP be written with care to meet those needs. For instance, low muscle tone requires physical and occupational therapy. Delayed speech requires intense speech therapy, often involving sign language and other language stimulation techniques. Unless parents request these services, they may be overlooked. Make sure school officials recognize the unique needs of your child—the needs that make her different from other handicapped children.

How can parents prepare for the IEP process? First, survey available programs, including public, private, federal, state, county, and municipal programs. Observe classes and see for yourself which program is best suited to your child. Local school districts and local ARCs can provide you with information about programs in your community. Second, collect a complete set of developmental evaluations – get your own if you doubt the accuracy of the school district's evaluation. Third and most importantly, decide for yourself what program and services are best for your child, then request that placement.

To support placement in a particular type of program, parents can collect "evidence" that their child needs special services. Parents can support their demand for a particular type of placement by presenting letters from doctors, therapists (physical, speech, or occupational), teachers, developmental experts, and other professionals. This evidence may help persuade a school district that it would not be appropriate to deny a child the requested placement. Other suggestions to help parents through the IEP process are: 1) don't go to placement meetings alone – bring others for support, such as spouses, doctors, teachers, and friends; 2) keep close track of what everyone involved in your child's case is doing; and 3) *get everything in writing.* For children with Down syndrome, with their unique developmental challenges, parents need to be assertive advocates during their child's IEP process.

Resolution of Disputes under Public Law 94–142

It is usually best to resolve disputes with school districts over your child's educational program *during* the IEP process, before hard positions have been formed. Although Public Law 94–142 establishes dispute resolution procedures that are designed to be fair to parents, it is always easier and far less costly to avoid disputes by coming to some agreement during the IEP process. Accordingly, our first suggestion is to avoid fights when possible; try to accomplish your objectives by persuasion. If there is a dispute that simply cannot be resolved with the school district, however, this section discusses how Public Law 94–142 can be used to resolve that dispute.

In order to protect the rights of handicapped children and their parents, Public Law 94–142 establishes a variety of safeguards. First, prior written notice is always required for any change made in your child's evaluation or educational placement. A school district is prohibited from deceiving parents. School officials must state in writing what they want to do, when, and why.

Beyond the requirement of written notice, the EAHCA allows parents to file a formal complaint locally about *any matter* "relating to the identification, evaluation, or educational placement of the child, or the provision of free appropriate public education to such child." What this means is that parents can file a complaint about virtually any problem they may have with their child's educational program if they have been unable to resolve that problem with school officials. This is a very broad right of appeal, one that parents have successfully used in the past to correct serious problems in their children's educational programs. For information about appeals, you can contact your school district, advocacy groups, and other parents. The appeal process can be started simply by filing a letter of complaint.

The first step in the appeal process is an "impartial due process hearing" held before a hearing examiner. This hearing, usually held on the local level, is the parents' first opportunity to explain their complaint to an impartial person who is required to listen to both sides, and then to render a decision. At the hearing, parents are entitled to be represented by an attorney or lay advocate; they can present evidence; and they can examine, cross-examine, and compel the attendance of witnesses. The child has a right to be present at the hearing. At the end of the hearing, parents have a right to receive a written record of the hearing, of the findings, and of the hearing examiner's conclusions.

Just as with the IEP process, parents need to present facts that show the school district's decisions about a child's educational program to be wrong. To overturn the school district's decision, parents must show that the disputed placement does not provide their child with the "free appropriate public education" that is required by the EAHCA. Evidence in the form of letters, testimony, and expert evaluations are essential to a successful appeal.

Parents or school districts may appeal the decision of a hearing examiner. The appeal usually goes to the state's educational agency. This state agency is required to make an independent decision upon its review of the record of the due process hearing and of any additional evidence presented. The state agency then issues its own decision.

The right to appeal does not stop there. Parents or school officials can appeal beyond the state level by bringing a lawsuit under the EAHCA in a state or federal court. In this kind of legal action, the court must determine whether there is a preponderance of the evidence (that is, whether it is more likely than not) that the IEP-developed program is reasonably calculated to provide educational benefits to the child. In reaching its decision, the court must give weight to the expertise  of the school officials responsible for providing the child's education, but parents can and should also present their own expert evidence.

During all administrative and judicial proceedings, Public Law 94–142 requires that the child remain in her current educational placement, unless the parents and the local or state agencies agree to a move. Parents who unilaterally place their child in a different program risk having to bear the full cost. If, however, the school district is found to have erred, it may be required to reimburse parents for the expenses of the changed placement. Accordingly, parents should make a change of program only after carefully considering the potential cost of that decision.

As with any legal dispute, each phase—complaint, hearings, appeals, and court cases—can be expensive, time-consuming, and emotionally draining. Regarding expenses, federal law now provides that parents who ultimately win their dispute may be awarded attorneys' fees for hearings and appeals under the EAHCA so long as the dispute was either pending or initiated *after* July 3, 1984. Everything considered, however, it is wise for parents to try to resolve problems without filing a formal complaint or bringing suit. For example, parents should consult with other parents who have filed complaints and should talk to sympathetic school officials. When informal means fail to resolve a problem, however, formal channels should be pursued. Your child's best interests must come first. The EAHCA grants important rights that parents need not be bashful about exercising.

The EAHCA is a powerful tool in the hands of parents. It can be used to provide unparalleled educational opportunity to babies and children with Down syndrome. Using it effectively, however, requires an understanding of how it works. The Reading List at the end of this book includes several good guidebooks to Public Law 94–142 and the special education system. With a knowledge of this vital law, parents will be far better able to help their child realize her potential.

The Rehabilitation Act of 1973

Section 504 of the Rehabilitation Act of 1973 eliminates discrimination against qualified handicapped persons and increases their opportunities to participate in and benefit from federally-funded programs. The law provides that "[n]o otherwise qualified handicapped individual . . . shall, solely by reason of his handicap, be excluded from the participation in, be denied the benefits of, or be subjected to discrimination under any program or activity receiving federal financial assistance. . . ." A handicapped individual is any person who has a physical or mental impairment that substantially limits one or more of that person's "major life activities," which consist of "caring for one's self, performing manual tasks, walking, seeing, hearing, speaking, breathing, learning, and working." The United States Supreme Court has determined that an "otherwise qualified" handicapped individual is one who is "able to meet all of a program's requirements in spite of his handicap." Programs or activities receiving federal funding must make reasonable accommodation to permit the participation of such a handicapped person.

Although Section 504 would seem to apply to educational programs receiving federal funds under the EAHCA, the Supreme Court recently decided that parents of a handicapped child with a claim covered by the EAHCA must pursue that claim only under the EAHCA, not under Section 504. In other words, in most disputes involving educational programs for handicapped children, Section 504 adds nothing to the rights and remedies available to you and your child under the EAHCA. As a result, Section 504 generally comes into play to assert rights beyond secondary school or rights other than those directly related to education. A provision exists in the Rehabilitation Act of 1973 for the recovery of attorneys' fees by persons who succeed in their claims under Section 504.

Educational Programs and Services When Your Child Is an Adult

Few children with Down syndrome will be completely independent as adults; some will need support and supervision in employment and daily living. This support and supervision can be provided through employment and residential programs. For example, in some areas there are strong movements toward noninstitutional community residential services and supported employment programs. Regrettably, if these kinds of programs are unavailable, parents are left to provide the necessary support and supervision for as long as possible.

Programs vary from state to state and from community to community. As a result of state and federal budget cuts, these programs typically have long waiting lists and typically are underfunded. The EAHCA generally applies to children until the age of eighteen. After a child reaches age eighteen, her right to a public education ends in many states, even though her needs may continue. Currently, the sad truth is that under Public Law 94–142 thousands of children are receiving education and training that equip them to live as independently and productively as possible, only to be sent home when they complete school with nowhere to go and nothing to do.

Now is the time to work to change this sad reality. As waiting lists grow, your child may be deprived of needed services. Because charitable funds are limited and because most families do not have the resources to pay the full cost of group homes and employment programs, the only other remedy is public funding. Just as parents banded together to demand enactment of the EAHCA, you must band together now to persuade local, state, and federal officials that our nation can afford to allow disabled people to live in dignity. Parents of handicapped *children* should not leave this job to parents of handicapped *adults*, for children become adults—all too soon.

Vocational Training Programs

There is one type of educational program supported by federal funding that is available to adult people with Down syndrome. Operating much like Public Law 94–142, there are federal laws making funds available to support vocational training and rehabilitation. Again, states wanting federal funds must submit plans for approval. Federal law provides that all people who have a mental disability that constitutes a "substantial handicap to employment" and who can be expected to benefit from vocational services are eligible. Unlike the EAHCA, however, handicapped individuals are not granted enforceable rights and procedures under these laws.

The state Departments of Vocational Rehabilitation are sometimes called "DVR" or "VocRehab." People are evaluated and an "Individualized Written Rehabilitation Plan," similar to an IEP, is developed. Under these programs, adults with Down syndrome can continue to receive vocational education after they reach age twenty-one. Parents should contact their state vocational rehabilitation department for specific information on services available to their child with Down syndrome. Despite shrinking federal and state budgets, some states and communities offer their own programs, such as group homes, supported employment programs, and life-skills classes. Contact other parents, organizations, and your local chapter of the ARC for information on what programs are available in your area.

Planning for Your Child's Future

The possibility that your child may be dependent all of her life can be overwhelming. To meet your child's future needs, you need information in areas you may never have thought about before and you must find inner resources you may not believe exist. In most families parents remain primarily responsible for ensuring their child's well-being. Consequently, questions that deeply trouble parents include: "What will happen to my child when I die? Who will look after her? How will her financial needs be met?"

Some parents of children with Down syndrome delay dealing with

these issues, coping instead with the immediate demands of the present. Others begin to address the future. They add to their insurance, begin (alone or with grandparents) to set aside funds for their child, and share with family and friends their concerns about their child's future needs. Whatever the course, parents need to understand in advance some serious problems that affect planning for a disabled child's future. Failure to avoid these pitfalls can have dire future consequences for your child and for other family members.

There are three important issues that families of children with Down syndrome need to consider in planning for the future. These are: 1) the potential for cost-of-care liability; 2) the complex rules governing eligibility for government benefits; and 3) the child's ability to handle her own affairs. Of course, there are many other matters that may be different for parents of special children. For example, insurance needs may be affected, and the important choice of trustees and guardians is more difficult. But these types of concerns face most parents in one form or another. Cost-of-care liability, government benefits, and the inability to manage one's own affairs, however, present issues that are unique to the parents of handicapped children.

Cost-of-Care Liability

When a state provides residential services to a handicapped person, it usually has the power to force that person to pay for them. Called "cost-of-care liability," this power allows states to tap the handicapped person's own funds to pay for the services the state provides. States can reach funds owned outright by a handicapped person and even funds set aside in some trusts. A few states go further. Some impose liability on parents for the care of an adult handicapped person, and some impose liability for other services in addition to residential care. This is an area parents need to look into early and carefully.

The most unfortunate and seemingly unfair aspect of cost-of-care liability is that these payments do *not* benefit the handicapped person. Ordinarily they add nothing to the care and services the individual receives. Instead, the money is deposited into the general funds of the state to pay for roads, schools, public officials' salaries, and so on.

It is natural for parents to want to pass their worth on to their child through their wills or through gifts. The unfortunate effect of allowing a child with Down syndrome to inherit a portion of your estate, however, may be the same as naming the state in your will—something most people would not do voluntarily. Similarly, setting aside funds in the child's name, in a support trust, or in a Uniform Gifts to Minors Act (UGMA) account may be the same as giving money to the state, money that could better be used to meet the future needs of your child.

What, then, can parents do? The specific answer depends on your circumstances and the law of your state. Here are three basic strategies parents use:

First, strange as it may seem, in some cases the best solution is to disinherit your child with Down syndrome, leaving funds instead to siblings in the clear hope that they will use these funds for their disabled sibling's benefit, even though they will be under *no* legal obligation to do so. The absence of a legal obligation is crucial. It protects the funds from cost-of-care claims. The state will simply not be able to prove that the handicapped person owns anything. This strategy, however, runs the risk that the funds will not be used for your child with Down syndrome if the siblings: 1) choose not to use them that way; 2) suffer financial reversals or domestic problems of their own, exposing the funds to creditors or spouses; or 3) die without making arrangements that safeguard the funds.

A second method used in states where the law is favorable to this arrangement is to leave funds intended for the benefit of your child with Down syndrome in what is called a "discretionary" trust. This kind of trust is created to supplement, rather than replace, state benefits. Under discretionary trusts, the trustee (the person responsible for governing the trust) has the power to use or not use the trust funds for any purpose, although the funds can only be used for the benefit of the handicapped child. In many states, these types of trusts are not subject to cost-of-care claims because the trust does not impose any legal obligation for the trustee to spend funds on any purpose, including the expense of care. In contrast, "support" trusts *require* the trustee to use the funds for the care and support of the child. Discretionary trusts can be created under your will or during your lifetime, but, as with all legal documents, must be carefully written.

A third method to avoid cost-of-care claims is to create a trust, either under your will or during your lifetime, that describes the kind of allowable expenditures to be made for the handicapped child in a way that excludes care in state-funded programs. Like discretionary trusts, these trusts—sometimes called "luxury" trusts—are intended to supplement, rather than take the place of, state benefits. The state cannot reach these funds because the trust forbids spending any funds on care in state institutions.

In using all of these estate planning techniques, parents should consult a qualified attorney who is experienced in estate planning for parents of handicapped children. Because each state's laws differ and because each family has unique circumstances, individualized estate planning is essential.

Eligibility for Government Benefits

There are a wide variety of federal, state, and local programs for handicapped persons. Each of these programs provides different services and each has its own complex eligibility requirements. What parents and grandparents do now to provide financially for their child with Down syndrome can have drastic effects on that child's eligibility for government assistance in the future.
future.

There are four major federally-funded programs that can help people with Down syndrome. First, "Supplemental Security Income" (SSI), a public assistance program, and "Social Security Disability Insurance" (SSDI), a disability insurance program, are both applicable to people with Down syndrome. Both are designed to provide a monthly income to qualified disabled persons, and under current rules, people with Down syndrome ordinarily qualify as "disabled." The eligibility requirements, however, do not always end there. Whereas SSDI is not based on financial need, an applicant's resources and other income can disqualify her from receiving SSI. Remember, what your child owns in her own name and what income she is entitled to receive under a trust can prevent her from receiving these government benefits.

Medicare and Medicaid are also potentially important to people with Down syndrome, but each has its own eligibility requirements. Medicaid provides medical assistance to persons who are eligible for SSI and to other people with incomes deemed insufficient to pay for medical care. Because eligibility is based on financial need, placing assets in the name of a child with Down syndrome or providing that child with income through a trust can disqualify the child. Medicare, however, is not based on financial need. Instead, persons entitled to receive benefits under Social Security are entitled to Medicare payments.

It is important for parents to become familiar with the rules governing SSI, SSDI, Medicaid, and Medicare. It is even more important to avoid an unwitting mistake that could disqualify your child from receiving these benefits. Do not set aside funds in your child's own name, create a support trust, or establish a UGMA account. Follow the type of strategies outlined above.

Competence to Manage Financial Affairs

Even if your child with Down syndrome may never need state-funded residential care or government benefits, it is probable she will need help in handling her financial affairs throughout her life. Care must be exercised in giving assets to your child. To do this, there are a wide variety of trusts that can allow someone else to control the ways in which money is spent after you die. Of course, the amount of financial control depends on many different circumstances, such as the child's mental ability, the child's relationship with her siblings, and the parents' financial status. Each family's situation is different. A knowledgeable attorney can review the various alternatives and help you to pick the one best suited to your family.

Estate Planning for Parents of Children with Down Syndrome

More than most parents, you need to attend to estate planning. Because of cost-of-care liability, government benefits, and competency concerns, it is vital that you make plans. Parents need to name the people who will care for their special child in the event of the parents' deaths. They need to review their insurance to be sure it is adequate in light of their child's special needs. They need to make sure their retirement plans are arranged to help their child's education and training beyond the age of eighteen. They need to inform grandparents of cost-of-care liability, government benefits, and competency problems to make sure the grandparents do not inadvertently waste resources that could otherwise benefit their grandchild's future. Most of all, they need to make a will so that their hopes and plans are realized and so that the disastrous consequences of dying without a will are avoided.

Proper estate planning differs for each family. Every will is tailored to individual needs. There are no formula wills, especially for parents of a child with Down syndrome. There are, however, some common mistakes for you to avoid. Here is a list:

No Will. If parents die without first making wills, the law generally requires that each child in the family share equally in the parents' estate. The result is that your child with Down syndrome will inherit property in her own name. Her inheritance may become subject to cost-of-care claims and could jeopardize eligibility for government benefits. These and other problems can be avoided with a properly drafted will. Parents should never allow the state to determine how their property will be divided upon their death. Planning can make you feel uneasy, but it is too important to ignore.

A Will Leaving Property Outright to the Child with Down Syndrome. Like having no will at all, a will that leaves property to a handicapped child in her own name may subject the inheritance to cost-of-care liability and may risk disqualifying the child from government benefits. Parents of children with Down syndrome do not just need any will, they need a will that meets their special needs.

A Will Creating a Support Trust for the Child with Down Syndrome. A will that creates a support trust presents much the same problem as a will that leaves property outright to the child with Down syndrome. The funds in these trusts may be subject to cost-of-care claims and jeopardize government benefits. Have a will drafted that avoids this problem.

Insurance and Retirement Plans Naming the Child with Down Syndrome as a Beneficiary. Many parents own life insurance policies or maintain retirement plans that name a handicapped child as a beneficiary or contingent beneficiary, either alone or in common with siblings. The result: funds may go outright to your child with Down syndrome, creating cost-of-care liability and government benefits eligibility problems. Parents should designate the funds to go to someone else or to go into a properly drawn trust.

Insurance on the Life of the Child with Down Syndrome. Some well-meaning parents and grandparents waste money insuring the life of their handicapped child. This money could be far better used to insure the *parents'* lives. The purpose of life insurance is to protect against the *financial* risk of the death of the insured. The death of a wage-earning parent deprives the family of his or her earnings. The death of a homemaker may require employing household help. In contrast, the death of a child does not have these consequences; typically it creates no financial risk that is appropriate for insurance. As a result, life insurance for your child with Down syndrome helps no one except the insurance agent.

Use of Joint Tenancy in Lieu of Wills. Spouses sometimes avoid making wills by placing all their property in joint tenancies. In joint tenancies, property is owned equally by each spouse; when one spouse dies, the survivor automatically becomes the sole owner. Parents try to use joint tenancies instead of wills, relying on the surviving spouse to properly take care of all estate planning matters. This plan, however, fails completely if both parents die in a common disaster, if the surviving spouse becomes incapacitated, or if the surviving spouse neglects to make a will. The result is the same as if neither spouse made any will at all–the child with Down syndrome shares equally in the parents' estates, creating cost-of-care liability and problems with government benefits. Therefore, even when all property is held by spouses in joint tenancy, it is necessary that both spouses make wills.

Establishing UGMA Accounts for the Child with Down Syndrome. Over and over again well-meaning parents and grandparents of handicapped children set up accounts under the UGMA. When the child reaches age eighteen or twenty-one, the account becomes the property of the child. Once again, problems arise with cost-of-care liability and with eligibility for Medicaid or SSI, just at the time those benefits may be needed to help pay for adult services and programs. Parents should *never* establish UGMA accounts for their child with Down syndrome nor should they open other bank accounts in the child's name.

Failing to Advise Grandparents and Relatives of the Need for Special Arrangements. Just as the parents of a handicapped child need properly drafted wills or trusts, so do grandparents and other relatives who may leave (or give) property to the child. If these persons are not aware of the special concerns – cost-of-care liability, government benefits, and competency – their generosity may go awry and may foil the best laid plans of the child's parents. Make sure anyone planning gifts or bequests to your child with Down syndrome understands what is at stake.

Children and adults with Down syndrome are entitled to lead full and rewarding lives. To do so, they need proper financial support. Planning for the future *now* is the best way to assure they will have that support when they need it. Doing otherwise can tragically short-change their future.

Conclusion

With parenthood comes responsibilities that many people never considered beforehand. Extra responsibilities confront parents of a child with Down syndrome. Knowing and asserting your child's rights are prerequisites to guaranteeing that she will receive the education and government benefits to which she is entitled. Similarly, under-standing the pitfalls of not planning for the future and taking steps to avoid these pitfalls help parents to meet their special responsibilities. In other words, being a good advocate for your child requires more than knowledge; you must also possess the determination to use that knowledge effectively and, when necessary, forcefully.

REFERENCES

Burgdorf, R. & Spicer, P. *The Legal Rights of Handicapped Persons.* Baltimore: Paul H. Brookes Publishing Co. 1980 & Supp. 1983.
Herr, S., Arons, S. & Wallace, R. Jr. *Legal Rights and Mental-Health Care.* Lexington, MA: D.C. Heath & Co. 1983.
Herr, S. *Rights and Advocacy for Retarded People.* Lexington, MA: D.C. Heath & Co. 1983.
Rothstein, L. *Rights of Physically Handicapped Persons.* New York: McGraw-Hill Book Co. 1984 & Supp. 1986.
Children With Special Needs. Law and Contemporary Problems. Vol. 48, Parts 1 & 2, Winter and Spring 1985.

Mandates for Serving Handicapped Children Aged Six and Under by State*

STATE	AGE OF SERVICES	COMMENTS
ALABAMA	5	Local Education Agencies can provide services at age 3.
ALASKA	3	
ARIZONA	6	If Local Education Agencies provide kindergarten, the age is 5.
ARKANSAS	6	If Local Education Agencies provide kindergarten, the age is 5.
CALIFORNIA	3	
COLORADO	5	Many school districts provide earlier services in conjunction with other public agencies.
CONNECTICUT	2.8	Must be 3 by January of school year they want to attend.
DELAWARE	4	Infant stimulation program available from birth through Division for Mental Retardation.
DISTRICT OF COLUMBIA	3	
FLORIDA	5	
GEORGIA	5	
HAWAII	3	
IDAHO	5	
ILLINOIS	3	
INDIANA	6	If at risk, services may begin at at birth. Programs outside school from 3–5. Some districts provide services beginning at 5.
IOWA	0	
KANSAS	5	Some districts have programs beginning at birth. If not, the state funds developmental disabilities centers and other programs.
KENTUCKY	5	
LOUISIANA	3	Services begin at birth for children with serious handicapping conditions that, without intervention, will become progressively more difficult for successful intervention by school age.
MAINE	5	
MARYLAND	0	
MASSACHUSETTS	3	
MICHIGAN	0	
MINNESOTA	3	Some districts provide services at birth.
MISSISSIPPI	5	Some districts provide services at birth.
MISSOURI	5	
MONTANA	6	
NEBRASKA	0	
NEVADA	5	Some services provided at birth. State law allows funding for Local Education Agencies to provide services at 3.

STATE	AGE OF SERVICES	COMMENTS
NEW HAMPSHIRE	3	
NEW JERSEY	0	Programs outside school from birth to 3. Provided by public schools after 3.
NEW MEXICO	5	
NEW YORK	5	
NORTH CAROLINA	5	
NORTH DAKOTA	3	Services offered by Human Service Center's Infant Development Program from birth. Provided by public schools after 3.
OHIO	5	
OKLAHOMA	5	Severely handicapped may receive services from birth.
OREGON	6	
PENNSYLVANIA	4–6	Age at which child is admitted to school, which varies from district to district. Some local programs provide services.
RHODE ISLAND	3	
SOUTH CAROLINA	5	
SOUTH DAKOTA	0	
TENNESSEE	4	
TEXAS	3	
UTAH	5	
VERMONT	6	
VIRGINIA	2	
WASHINGTON	3	
WEST VIRGINIA	5	
WISCONSIN	3	
WYOMING	0	

*There are many different programs available to children with Down syndrome in every state. In addition to Public Law 94–142, states or local school districts may provide early intervention services. There is also a federal law making grants available to local school districts for infant programs. *Even if your state does not start services under Public Law 94–142 until quite late, there may be programs available to your baby now.* Check with your state department of education, your local ARC, and other parents. The Resource Guide at the end of the book contains national and state listings of agencies, organizations, and programs. Call them to find out exactly when services under Public Law 94–142 begin and what other services are available to your child now.

Parent Statements

In getting your child placed in the best program, you have to work your own kid's needs out first. You have to understand your child first of all, and then you have to go in and argue your case. But it's something you can anticipate. You see it coming, and you can start to do some book-learning, and you can get ready.

When we learned that the private therapists were doing an even better job, we just dropped the public program. My feeling was that since we could afford it and this period of time was so crucial, we had to have the best. It was worth it for us. We're spending our time and energy and resources getting him the therapy he needs rather than trying to get the public agency to get them.

Parents need the law explained to them. They've got a club with which they can demand some rights. It helps to find other parents who are slightly ahead of them, and get counsel from them.

The early years are so important to our son that we work very hard to make sure he gets the best education possible. Our school district has good intentions, but sometimes needs to be shown the way. We're polite, but we are also prepared and very persistent.

Under the law [Public Law 94–142], it's all based on what is an "appropriate" education for Mike. When the school district says "appropriate" it may mean just "appropriate;" but when I say "appropriate" I mean "best."

We have a special trust for Chris that is protected from invasion by the state. But we've done more than that. The best insurance that we have for our child is our family and our relatives. I know my family would take care of Chris as much as they could. We named guardians in our will in the event of our deaths. We sent a letter to the relatives who were named in the will and the trust and that gave us an important sense of security.

We think a lot about the boys and how they will be settled in about twenty years or so. We'd like to see Josh in a group home. We make our decisions with that in mind. We always make decisions based on the long term. We don't think too much about the day-to-day stuff.

With estate planning, you just have to grin and bear it and realize you're in for the long haul. You have to start planning for it now. Parents have the obligation to find out what the facts and circumstances are and get competent advice, and then explain the situation to grandparents. It's sometimes difficult to raise the issue, but you have to, or there can be unintended consequences.

We want Josh to grow into a person who can function on his own, with a little structure here and there. We want him to help take care of himself. There may come a day when he has to fend for himself. We want him to be able to do that.

We feel strongly that we don't want her sister to feel in any way responsible in the long term. We feel that what happens will happen, but a lot will come from the attitude of how you bring your children up to care about each other.

I know it sounds selfish, but my greatest worry is that within a few years doctors and scientists will find a way to eliminate Down syndrome so our children might be the last generation of people with Down syndrome. If that happens, there might not be good services any longer.

Getting competent advice doesn't necessarily mean going to a high priced lawyer. It can be as easy as finding whatever advocacy program exists in your community, whether through the ARC or a group who specializes in helping people with

Down syndrome. It really helps to find out if they have advocacy programs for parents, and take a course.

Our hope is that he will be able to be a wage earner and taxpayer, and pay back to the community at least part of what they have given him. I think he can accomplish it. I know his schools have been very expensive for the county, but it's all worthwhile.

Glossary

Adaptive behavior–The ability to adjust to new environments, tasks, objects, and people, and to apply new skills to those new situations.

Advocacy groups–A wide variety of organizations that work to protect the rights and opportunities of handicapped children and their parents.

Alzheimer's disease–A degenerative disease of the brain that causes the gradual loss of mental ability. May affect older people with Down syndrome.

Amblyopia–Loss of vision caused by a variety of eye problems, including nearsightedness, farsightedness, and crossed eyes.

Amniocentesis–A method to test the cells of a fetus for possible genetic defects. A needle is inserted through the mother's belly and a small amount of amniotic fluid is withdrawn. The chromosomes within the cells are then tested.

Amniotic fluid–The liquid that surrounds an embryo in a woman's uterus.

Atlantoaxial instability–Instability in the joints of the upper bones of the spinal column.

Atria–The two upper chambers of the heart.

Atrial septal defect (ASD)–A defect–often a small hole–in the wall between the two upper chambers of the heart.

Attention span–The length of time a child stays on task or is able to pay attention to one thing (attending).

Auditory–Having to do with sounds; the ability to hear.

Babbling–The sound a baby makes when he combines a vowel and consonant and repeats them over and over again (e.g. ba-ba-ba, ga-ga-ga).

Bell curve–A curve on a graph that shows the distribution of characteristics in a population. These curves are used to show the range of human intelligence and developmental skill acquisition, as well as many other characteristics of populations.

Beneficiary–The person designated in a trust or insurance policy to receive any payments that become due.

Bilateral–Both sides of a child's body; of importance in developing skills. For example, banging a drum with two hands.

Bronchitis–Inflammation of the bronchial tubes, the two branches of the windpipe.

Brushfield spots–Light spots on the outer part of the iris of the eyes, often an outward manifestation of Down syndrome.

Cardiac surgeon–A doctor who specializes in heart surgery.

Cataracts–A disease of the eye that causes the lens to become cloudy or opaque, resulting in partial or total blindness.

Cause-and-effect–Understanding the concept that actions create reactions.

Chorionic villus sampling (CVS)–A method for testing the chromosomes of an embryo at nine to eleven weeks of pregnancy. A small number of fetal cells are removed from the chorion through a catheter inserted through the cervix into the uterus. The cells' chromosomes are then tested.

Chromosomes–Microscopic rod-shaped bodies that contain genetic material.

Cognition–The process of perceiving, thinking, reasoning, and analyzing.

Congenital–A condition that exists at the time of birth.

Congenital heart defect–A defect of the heart that a baby is born with.

Coordination–Synchronized, balanced, or harmonious muscle movements.

Cost-of-care liability–The right of a state providing care to a handicapped person to charge for the care and to collect from the handicapped person's assets.

Cradle cap–A patch of crusty dry skin on the scalp of newborns that flakes off over time. This condition is normal in babies.

Cue–Input that prompts a child to perform a behavior or activity.

Cyanosis–A bluish color of skin caused by a lack of oxygen in the blood. This can occur in babies with heart defects.

Cytogeneticist–A doctor or professional who studies chromosomes.

Development–The process of growth and learning during which a child acquires skills and abilities.

Developmental milestone–A developmental goal that acts as a measurement of developmental progress over time.

Developmentally delayed–A baby or child whose development is slower than normal.

Developmentally disabled–A person who has a condition that prevents that person from developing normally.

Discretionary trust–A trust in which the trustee (the person responsible for governing the trust) has the authority to use or not use the trust funds for any purpose, as long as funds are expended only for the beneficiary.

Disinherit–To deprive someone of an inheritance. Parents of handicapped children may do this to prevent the state from imposing cost-of-care liability on their child's assets.

Dispute resolution procedures–The procedures established by law and regulation for the fair resolution of disputes regarding a child's special education.

Diuretics–Drugs that increase the flow of urine, resulting in a decrease in the amount of fluid in the body. They are often used to help children with heart defects to reduce the heart's load because accumulated fluids tend to stress the heart.

Down syndrome—A common genetic disorder in which a person is born with forty-seven rather than forty-six chromosomes, resulting in developmental delays, mental retardation, low muscle tone, and other effects.

Dramatic play—Play involving imagination, role-playing, and games of make believe. Used as a measure of cognitive and social development.

Due process hearing—Part of the procedures established to protect the rights of parents and exceptional children during disputes under Public Law 94-142. These are hearings before an impartial person to review the identification, evaluation, placement, and services by a handicapped child's educational agency.

Early development—Development during the first three years of life.

Early infant intervention—The specialized way of interacting with infants to minimize the effects of conditions (such as Down syndrome) that can delay early development.

Electrocardiogram—A medical technique that measures the electrical impulses of the heart. These measurements show a cardiologist how a heart is functioning and can reveal heart disease.

Embryo—A baby in the earliest stages of development in the uterus.

Endocardial cushion defect—Defects or deformations in the walls between the chambers of the heart.

Epicanthal folds—Small folds of skin in the inner corners of the eyes. Present in babies with Down syndrome.

Estate planning—Formal, written arrangements for handling the possessions and assets of people after they have died.

Eustachian tube—A small tube between the middle of the ear and the back of throat. This tube can become blocked by fluid, resulting in a loss of hearing.

Evaluation—The process of determining the developmental level of a child. Evaluations are used to determine if a child needs educational services, as well as to determine what types of services he needs. The evaluation consists of a series of tests covering all areas of development.

Expressive language—The ability to use gestures, words, and written symbols to communicate.

Extension—The straightening of the muscles and limbs.

Facilitation—A teaching technique of helping a baby or child to perform a task or activity.

FAPE—See Free Appropriate Public Education.

Farsightedness—A condition of the eye that causes near objects to be seen blurred and objects in the distance to be seen clearly. Also called hypermetropia, this condition can be corrected with glasses.

Fertlization—The process of an egg and sperm combining during conception.

Fine motor—The use of the small muscles of the body, such as the hands, feet, fingers, and toes.

Flexion—The bending of the muscles and limbs.

Free Appropriate Public Education–The basic right to special education established under Public Law 94-142, The Education for All Handicapped Children Act.

Genes–Contained within the chromosomes, genes contain the hereditary material. Each gene controls specific traits.

Genetics–The study of genes, chromosomes, and heredity.

Germ cells–A sperm cell (male) or an egg cell (female).

Gross motor–The use of the large muscles of the body.

Hand-eye coordination–The use of the eyes to guide the hands in movements, such as picking up an object.

Handicapped–Refers to people who have some sort of disability, including physical disabilities, mental retardation, sensory impairments, behavioral disorders, learning disabilities, and multiple handicaps.

Heart failure–A condition of the heart in which it is unable to function at the optimal level.

Hyperextensive joints–Joints (such as the hips or shoulders) that are unusually flexible.

Hypermetropia–See farsightedness.

Hypothyroidism–The decreased production of thyroid hormone by the thyroid gland. This condition is more common in babies with Down syndrome than in other children, but is easily treated.

Hypotonia–Low muscle tone; see muscle tone.

Identification–The determination that a baby or child should be evaluated as a possible candidate for special education services.

Imitation–The ability to observe the actions of others and to copy them in one's own actions.

Individualized education program (IEP)–A written report that details the special education program to be provided a handicapped child. Sometimes referred to as IPP or Individualized Program Plan.

Input–Information that a child receives through any of the senses such as vision, hearing, touch, or feeling that helps a child develop new skills.

Intelligence quotient (IQ)–A measure of cognitive ability based on specifically designed standardized tests.

Interactive play–Children playing with each other.

Interpretive–The session during which parents and teachers review and discuss the results of a child's evaluation.

Intestinal malformation–A condition of the intestine, such as a blockage, that prevents the normal function of the gastro-intestinal tract.

Joint tenancy–Property that is owned equally by each spouse; when one spouse dies, the survivor automatically becomes the sole owner.

Karyotype–A picture of human chromosomes. These can reveal the presence of extra genetic material.

Language–The expression and understanding of human communication.

Least restrictive environment–The requirement under Public Law 94–142 that handicapped children receiving special education must be made a part of a regular school to the fullest extent possible. Included in the law as a way of ending the traditional practice of isolating handicapped children.

Leukemia–A type of cancer that attacks the red blood cells. This disease is slightly more common among children with Down syndrome.

Local education agency (LEA)–The agency responsible for providing educational services on the local (city, county, school district) level.

Luxury trusts–A trust that describes the kind of allowable expenses in a way that excludes the cost of care in state-funded programs in order to avoid cost-of-care liability.

Mainstream–The practice of involving handicapped children in regular school and preschool environments.

Medicaid–A joint state and federal program that offers medical assistance to people who are entitled to receive Supplementary Security Income.

Medicare–A federal program that provides payments for medical care to people who are receiving Social Security payments.

Meiotic division–The process of special cell division occuring only in the germ cell during which a sperm or an egg would receive one copy of every pair of chromosomes. The total chromosome count is twenty-three instead of forty-six.

Mental retardation–Below normal mental function. Children who are mentally retarded learn more slowly than other children, but "mental retardation" itself does not indicate the child's level of dysfunction. The level of mental function may not be identifiable until a much later age.

Midline–The vertical center of the body. Development progresses from the midline (proximal) to the extremities (distal). Some important developmental activities occur at the midline (e.g. bringing hands together at the midline) because they allow for other important developmental gains to be acquired.

Mosaicism–A rare type of Down syndrome in which a faulty cell division occurs in one of the early cell divisions after fertilization. The result is that some but not all of the baby's cells contain extra genetic material.

Muscle tone–The degree of elasticity or tension of muscles when at rest. Can be too low (hypotonia) or too high (hypertonia); either condition causes developmental problems, particularly in motor areas. Children with Down syndrome commonly have low muscle tone.

Myopia–see nearsightedness.

Nasal bridge–The bony structure at the top of the nose between the eyes. Usually flatter in babies with Down syndrome.

Nearsightedness – A condition of the eye that causes objects in the distance to be seen blurred and near objects to be seen clearly. Called myopia, this condition can be corrected with glasses.

Neurodevelopmental Treatment (NDT) – An approach to therapy that emphasizes inhibiting abnormal patterns of posture and movement and facilitates the greatest possible variety of innate normal basic motor patterns. Used by physical, occupational, and speech therapists.

Nondisjunction Trisomy 21 – The most common type of Down syndrome, caused by the failure of chromosomes to separate during meiotic cell division in the egg (female) or sperm (male).

Object permanence – The cognitive understanding that objects exist even when they are out of a child's sight.

Occupational therapist (OT) – A therapist who specializes in improving the development of fine motor and adaptive skills.

Oral motor – The use of the muscles in and around the mouth and face. Oral motor skills are important for learning to eat and talk properly.

Orthopedic inserts – Small devices placed in shoes to help stabilize the ankles and feet. Sometimes used to help children with Down syndrome because of low muscle tone and flexible joints.

Parallel play – Children playing near each other and in the same way, but without interacting together.

Parent-professional partnership – The teaming of parents and teachers (or doctors, nurses, or other professionals) to work together to facilitate the development of babies and children with special needs.

Patterning – Physically moving a child through a movement or series of movements with the purpose of teaching the child to do it himself.

Pediatric cardiologist – A doctor who specializes in diagnosing and treating heart conditions in children.

Pediatric geneticist – A doctor who studies genes and the effects of genetic conditions in children.

Pediatric ophthalmologist – A doctor who specializes in the care and treatment of the eyes of children.

Physical therapist – A therapist who works with a baby or child to help him overcome physical problems such as low muscle tone or weak muscles.

Pincer grasp – The use of the thumb and forefinger to grasp small objects.

Placement – The selection of the educational program for a child who needs special education services.

Prompt – Input that encourages a child to perform a movement or activity. See cue.

Public Law 94-142 – The Education for All Handicapped Children Act of 1975, which provides for a "free appropriate public education" for handicapped children. This law applies to children with Down syndrome.

Pulmonary hypertension–High blood pressure in the blood vessels in the lungs. This condition can result from heart defects that cause excessive amounts of blood to be pumped to the lungs, and can be fatal if not corrected.

Receptive language–The ability to understand spoken and written communication as well as gestures.

Reciprocal movement–Moving one side of the body and then the other in a coordinated alternate fashion, such as beating a drum or pedaling a tricycle.

Related services–Transportation and other developmental, corrective, or supportive services needed to enable a handicapped child to benefit from a special education program. Under Public Law 94-142 a child is entitled to receive these services as part of his special education program.

Respiratory infection–An infection, usually viral or bacterial, of the nasal passages, throat, bronchial tubes, or lungs.

Rooting–The instinctive searching for a breast or bottle nipple by a hungry baby.

Rotation (external)–Turning out of the feet, legs, hips, or hands. Seen in babies and children with Down syndrome because of their low muscle tone and joint flexibility.

Self-help–The ability to take care of one's self, including eating, dressing, bathing, and cleaning. Begins early with awareness, responsiveness, and participation in self-help activities.

Sensory ability–The ability to process sensations, such as touch, sound, light, smell, and movement.

Septa (septum)–The wall of cardiac tissue between the chambers of the heart.

Slanting palpebral fissures–The term describing the upward slanting appearance of the eyes of children with Down syndrome.

Social–The ability to function in groups, to interact with other people.

Social Security Disability Insurance (SSDI)–A federal disability insurance system to assist qualified handicapped and disabled people.

Special education–The term commonly used to refer to the education of handicapped individuals.

Speech therapist–A therapist trained to work with people to improve their oral motor skills, and to learn both receptive and expressive language.

Spina bifida–A malformation of the spinal cord that occurs before birth in which the spine does not close properly during fetal development. Its severity and effects vary, but can include paralysis, loss of sensation in the lower limbs, and possibly, mental retardation.

Strabismus–Crossed eyes, when one or both eyes look inward.

Supplemental Security Income (SSI)–A federal public assistance program for qualified disabled people.

Support trust–A trust that requires that funds be expended to pay for the beneficiary's expenses of living, such as housing, food, and transportation.

Tactile – Having to do with the sense of touch.

Tactile defensiveness – An overreaction to or avoidance of touch.

Tear ducts – The glands above the eyes that secrete tears.

The Education For All Handicapped Children Act of 1975 (EAHCA) – Public Law 94–142, which guarantees a "free appropriate public education" to handicapped children.

Therapist – A trained professional who works to overcome the effects of developmental problems.

Thyroid – The gland that secretes the thyroid hormone that controls many important bodily functions.

Tracheo-esophageal fistula – A condition in which the intestinal tract and respiratory system are connected. This condition requires immediate surgical correction.

Translocation Trisomy 21 – A rare form of Down syndrome caused when a part of the number-21 chromosome breaks off during cell division and attaches itself to another chromosome.

Transverse palmar crease – A single crease across the palm of the hands of children with Down syndrome. One of the physical traits used to identify Down syndrome.

Trisomy – The presence of extra genetic material in the cells; three rather than two chromosomes in the cells.

Tympanometry – A test that measures fluid that may be present behind the ear drum or detects a blockage of the Eustachian tube.

Ultrasound – The use of high-pitched sound waves to create a picture of the inside of a body like that of an X-ray. This procedure is used to examine babies before birth and to help guide medical instruments during amniocentesis and chorionic villus sampling (CVS).

Umbilical hernia – A protrusion of the navel caused by incomplete muscle development around the navel. Umbilical hernias usually close by themselves.

Uniform Gifts to Minors Act (UGMA) – A law that governs gifts to minors. Under the UGMA gifts to minors become the property of the minor at age eighteen or twenty-one.

Ventricle – The lower chambers of the heart.

Ventricular septal defect (VSD) – A hole in the wall separating the two lower chambers of the heart.

Vertebrae – The bones of the spinal column.

Vestibular – Pertaining to the sensory system located in the inner ear that allows the body to maintain balance and enjoyably participate in movement such as swinging and roughhousing.

Vocational training – Training for specific job skills.

Reading List

This Reading List is designed especially for parents of children with Down syndrome. The books, articles, and pamphlets recommended meet high standards of quality and usefulness.

The Reading List is divided into each chapter of the book. Because children with Down syndrome are much like "normal" children, child-raising books and general family health books are also included. We have not included books that are outdated or are clinical texts.

This list does not pretend to be complete. There may be many other worthy books available. Check your library and bookstore. Please let us know if we have missed a good book or included a bad one.

Chapter 1

Association For Retarded Citizens. *Mental Retardation: The Search for Cures*. M.R. Research Monograph Series, no. 7. Arlington, TX: Association For Retarded Citizens. 1982. A pamphlet discussing research into the cures of mental retardation, including Down syndrome.

Association For Retarded Citizens. *The Prevalence of Mental Retardation*. Arlington, TX: Association For Retarded Citizens National Research and Demonstration Institute. 1982. A pamphlet discussing the frequency of mental retardation, and the difficulty in measuring intelligence.

Cunningham, Cliff. *Down's Syndrome: An Introduction for Parents*. London: Souvenir Press, Ltd., distributed in U.S. by Brookline Books, Inc. 1982. A comprehensive introduction to Down syndrome written by a British Down syndrome specialist.

Downs, Kay & Judy Marick. *Heaven's Special Children: A Booklet about Down's Syndrome by the Mothers of Cody and Jason*. Vancouver, WA: Parent Education Department, Clark College. An inspirational introductory pamphlet written by the parents of children with Down syndrome.

Edgerton, Robert B. *Mental Retardation*. The Developing Child Series. Cambridge, MA: Harvard University Press. 1979. A brief guide book to mental retardation, its causes and treatment. The book includes a chapter about Down syndrome.

Edwards, Jean & David Dawson. *My Friend David: A Sourcebook about Down's Syndrome and a Personal Story about Friendship*. Portland, OR: EDNICK Communications, Inc. 1983. A warm and endearing book about a person with Down syndrome, partly written by him and partly written by his friend. Also includes basic information about Down syndrome.

Melton, David. *Promises to Keep: A Handbook for Parents of Learning Disabled, Brain-Injured, and Other Exceptional Children*. New York: Franklin Watts. 1984. A good general guide to raising and caring for special-needs children.

Moore, Cory. *A Reader's Guide for Parents of Children with Mental, Physical, or Emotional Disabilities.* Rockville, MD: Woodbine House, 1990. A comprehensive, annotated reading list for all subjects related to developmental disabilities. A valuable resource.

National Down Syndrome Society. *This Baby Needs You Even More.* New York: National Down Syndrome Society. An introductory pamphlet about babies with Down syndrome, filled with quotes from parents. Also available in Spanish.

Prensky, Arthur L. & Helen Stein Palkes. *Care of the Neurologically Handicapped Child: A Book for Parents and Professionals.* New York: Oxford University Press. 1982. A comprehensive, yet clinical, review of the treatment of neurologically handicapped children. Includes a review of professional services.

Pueschel, Siegfried M., M.D., M.P.H., ed. *Down Syndrome: Growing and Learning.* Kansas City: Andrews & McMeel, Inc. 1978. An introduction to Down syndrome written and edited by one of the leading authorities. Covers ages birth to adulthood.

Pueschel, Siegfried M., M.D., M.P.H., ed. *The Young Child with Down Syndrome.* New York: Human Sciences Press, Inc. 1984. A collection of articles by doctors and researchers about specific experimental treatments for children with Down syndrome. Study results are presented along with advanced information about Down syndrome.

Rehabilitation Research Institute. *Dignity.* Washington, D.C.: Institute On Attitudinal, Legal, And Leisure Barriers, The George Washington University. A short pamphlet about mental retardation, debunking myths and giving basic facts.

Ross, Bette M. *Our Special Child: A Guide to Successful Parenting of Handicapped Children.* New York: Walker & Co. 1981. The personal account of a mother and her son with Down syndrome growing up in California. General information and suggestions.

Rynders, John E. & J. Margaret Horrobin. *To Give an Edge: A Guide for New Parents of Children with Down Syndrome.* 2d ed. St. Paul: Colwell/North Central, Inc. 1974. A collection of articles introducing Down syndrome, based on a five-year project at the University of Minnesota.

Special Learning Corp. *Readings in Down Syndrome.* Guilford, CT: Special Learning Corp. 1980. A collection of articles or excerpts from books, some clinical, about Down syndrome.

Chapter 2

Cormack, Barbara Villy. *George.* Toronto: Canadian Association for the Mentally Retarded. 1979. The personal account of a mother and her retarded son.

Featherstone, Helen. *A Difference in the Family: Living with a Disabled Child.* New York: Penguin Books. 1980. A compassionate look into the emotions of having a disabled child, based on the author's experiences and interviews with parents and professionals. Highly recommended reading, but not as one of your first books.

Hunt, Nigel. *The World of Nigel Hunt.* New York: Garrett Publications. 1967. This is the diary of a child with Down syndrome who learned to read and write. In his book he describes the world as he sees it.

Murphy, Albert T. *Special Children, Special Parents: Personal Issues with Handicapped Children.* Englewood Cliffs, NJ: Prentice-Hall, Inc. 1981. A look into the emotions of parents of handicapped children, written with numerous statements by parents.

Perske, Robert. *Hope for Families: New Directions for Parents of Persons with Retardation or Other Disabilities.* Nashville: Abingdon Press. 1981. A compassionate and philosophical book for parents about adjusting to a handicapped child.

Wentworth, Elsie H. *Listen To Your Heart: A Message to Parents of Handicapped Children.* Boston: Houghton Mifflin Co. 1974. A personal book about the emotions of adjusting to a handicapped child.

Chapter 3

American Medical Association. *Family Medical Guide.* Jeffrey R. Kunz, M.D., ed. New York: Random House, Inc. 1982. A comprehensive family medical encyclopedia, covering all aspects of health and medicine. Includes a short description of Down syndrome.

Batshaw, Mark L., M.D. & Yvonne M. Perret. *Children with Handicaps: A Medical Primer.* Baltimore: Paul H. Brookes Publishing Co. 1981. A layman's medical book about birth defects and other medical conditions of children. Good background reading, but not much information specifically about Down syndrome.

Chapter 4

Fredericks, H.D. Bud, et al. *Toilet Training the Child with Handicaps.* Monmouth, OR: Teaching Research Publications. 1975. A program for toilet training handicapped and retarded children. Useful, but somewhat clinical.

Good, Judy. *Breastfeeding the Down's Syndrome Baby.* Franklin Park, IL: LaLeche League International, Inc. 1980. A useful pamphlet about breastfeeding your child with Down syndrome.

Lansky, Vicki. *Toilet Training.* New York: Bantam Books, Inc. 1984. A parents' guide to toilet training children. Useful information, but not focused on toilet training exceptional children.

Leach, Penelope. *Your Baby and Child: From Birth to Age Five.* New York: Alfred A. Knopf. 1981. A good general parents' guide to the first three years, divided into different age groups. Includes all areas of health and daily care. A useful and complete book.

Mack, Alison. *Toilet Learning: The Picture Book Technique for Children and Parents.* Boston: Little, Brown & Co. 1978. A comprehensive toilet training method, written in two parts for parents and children.

Mueser, Anne Marie, Ed.D. & Lynne M. Liptay, M.D. *Talk & Toddle: A Commonsense Guide for the First Three Years.* New York: St. Martin's Press. 1983. A general parents' guide, arranged alphabetically, covering most areas of early child-raising.

Pantell, Robert H., M.D., James F. Fries, M.D. & Donald M. Vickery, M.D. *Taking Care of Your Child: A Parents' Guide to Medical Care.* Revised Edition. Reading, MA: Addison-Wesley Publishing Co. 1984. A general medical guide, utilizing ninety-five decision-making charts for all types of childhood health problems and emergencies.

Princeton Center For Infancy, *The Parenting Advisor.* Frank Caplan, ed. Garden City, NY: Anchor Press/Doubleday. 1977. A general guide, condensing the views of many experts on infants and children.

Chapter 5

Baldwin, Anne Norris. *A Little Time*. New York: The Viking Press. 1978. A book written for children about a family with a child with Down syndrome, written from the perspective of a child.

Brazelton, T. Berry, M.D. *Toddlers and Parents: A Declaration of Independence*. New York: Dell Publishing Co. 1974. A parents' guide for raising children, written by a prominent pediatrician, focusing on the challenges of toddlers.

Brazelton, T. Berry, M.D. *To Listen to a Child: Understanding the Normal Problems of Growing Up*. Reading, MA: Addison-Wesley Publishing Co. 1984. A guide to handling common problems encountered in childhood and adolescence, including bed-wetting, hospitalization, and discipline.

Briggs, Dorothy Corkille. *Your Child's Self-Esteem*. NewYork: Doubleday & Co. 1975. A parents' guide to building a child's self-esteem and feelings of self-worth.

Cairo, Shelley. *Our Brother Has Down's Syndrome: An Introduction for Children*. Toronto: Annick Press/Firefly Books, Ltd. 1985. An excellent book to help parents introduce siblings to Down syndrome. Highly Recommended.

Clifton, Lucille, Thomas DiGrazia, illus. *My Friend Jacob*. New York: E.P. Dutton. 1980. A children's book about a friendship between a mentally retarded child and his best friend who lives next door, written from the viewpoint of the friend.

Dougan, Terrell, Lyn Isbell, Patricia Vyas, comps. *We Have Been There: A Guidebook for Families of People with Mental Retardation*. Nashville: Abingdon Press. 1983. A collection of short, inspiring stories of families coping with mentally retarded children.

Jones, Ron. *The Acorn People*. New York: Bantam. 1976. The endearing story of a summer camp for handicapped and retarded children.

MacDonald, W. Scott & Chester W. Oden, Jr. *Moose: A Very Special Person*. Cambridge, MA: Brookline Books, Inc. 1978. The story of a child with Down syndrome.

Meyer, Donald J., Patricia F. Vadasy & Rebecca R. Fewell, *Living with a Brother or Sister with Special Needs: A Book for Sibs*. Seattle, WA: University of Washington Press. 1985. An excellent introduction to disabilities, including Down syndrome, for siblings. Reviews specific disabilities and discusses what it is like to be a sibling of a special-needs child. Recommended.

Meyers, Robert. *Like Normal People*. New York: McGraw-Hill. 1978. A warm and engrossing story of the life of a mentally retarded person, of his triumphs and failures, and of his impact on the life of his family, written by his brother.

Patterson, Gerald R. *Living with Children: New Methods for Parents and Teachers*. Champaign, IL: Research Press. 1976. A parents' lesson book of techniques for dealing with children.

Perske, Robert. *New Life in the Neighborhood: How Persons with Retardation or Other Disabilities Can Help Make a Good Community Better*. Nashville: Abingdon Press. 1980. A compassionate and philosophical look at handicapped people in the community, beautifully illustrated.

Perske, Robert. *Show Me No Mercy: A Compelling Story of Remarkable Courage*. Nashville: Abingdon Press. 1984. A novel about a father and his son with Down syndrome, written by the author of several nonfiction books about handicapped and mentally retarded people.

Powell, Thomas H. & Peggy Ahrenhold Ogle. *Brothers & Sisters — A Special Part of Exceptional Families*. Baltimore: Paul H. Brookes Publishing Co. 1985. A detailed, yet clinical, examination of the siblings of exceptional children. The book primarily reviews research on the subject.

Pueschel, Siegfried, Jr., Pamela Pueschel & Jeanette Pueschel. *Chris. . . Our Brother*. Providence, RI: Dr. Siegfried M. Pueschel, Child Development Center, Rhode Island Hospital. The account of living with a sibling with Down syndrome, told in pictures and in words by his brother and sisters.

Roberts, Nancy. *David*. Atlanta: John Knox Press. 1974. A book of photographs and stories about a young child with Down syndrome, written by his mother and photographed by his father. Out of print, but available in libraries.

Schleifer, Maxwell J. & Stanley D. Klein, eds. *The Disabled Child and The Family: An Exceptional Parent Reader*. Boston: The Exceptional Parent Press. 1985. A collection of articles from "Exceptional Parent" magazine covering a wide range of topics related to having a handicapped person in the family.

Shalom, Debra Buchbinder. *Special Kids Make Special Friends*. Bellmore, NY: Association for Children With Down's Syndrome. 1984. A picture book for children, introducing Down syndrome.

Turnbull, H. Rutherford & Ann P. Turnbull. *Parents Speak Out: Then and Now*. Columbus, OH: Charles E. Merrill Publishing Co. 1985. A collection of articles by parents of mentally retarded children, focusing on how families learn to cope.

Wright, Logan. *Parent Power: A Guide to Responsible Childrearing*. New York: William Morrow & Co. 1980. Written by a child psychologist, this book focuses on how to discipline children.

Chapter 6

Brazelton, T. Berry, M.D. *Infants and Mothers: Differences In Development*. Revised Edition. New York: Dell Publishing Co. 1983. Written by a prominent pediatrician, this book compares the development of different children during the first year of life.

DeVilliers, Peter A. & Jill G. DeVilliers. *Early Language*. Cambridge, MA: Harvard University Press. 1979. A book describing how a child learns to communicate verbally, including the special challenges of the handicapped child.

Thain, Wilbur S., M.D., Glendon Castio, Ph.D. & Adrienne Peterson, R.P.T. *Normal and Handicapped Children: A Growth and Development Primer for Parents and Professionals*. Littleton, MA: PSG Publishing Co. 1980. A comprehensive review of development and mental retardation, including a chapter on Down syndrome.

White, Burton L. *The First Three Years of Life*. Revised Edition. New York: Prentice Hall Press. 1985. One of the classics of childhood development, covering the first three years of life.

Chapter 7

Amdur, Jeanette R. ed. *Kitchener-Waterloo Infant Stimulation Programme*. Toronto: The United Church of Canada. 1976. A collection of developmental exercises for newborns through age twenty-four months, with exercises and activities in all areas of infant development.

Association For Retarded Citizens. *The Partnership: How to Make it Work.* Arlington, TX: Association For Retarded Citizens National Research and Demonstration Institute. 1977. A short pamphlet about the relationship between parents and the professionals providing services to a handicapped child.

Atack, Sally M. *Art Activities for the Handicapped.* Englewood Cliffs, NJ: Prentice-Hall, Inc. 1982. A practical guide to creative art activities for children with learning disabilities.

Caldwell, Bettye M. & Donald J. Stedman, eds. *Infant Education: A Guide for Helping Handicapped Children in the First Three Years.* First Chance Series. New York: Walker & Co. 1977. An analysis of the value of early infant stimulation programs. Academic.

Cunningham, Cliff & Patricia Sloper. *Helping Your Exceptional Baby: A Practical and Honest Approach to Raising a Mentally Handicapped Child.* New York: Pantheon Books. 1978. A handbook for early infant education, including developmental checklists and activities.

Dmitriev, Valentine, Ph.D. *Time to Begin: Early Education for Children with Down Syndrome.* Milton, WA: Caring, Inc. 1982. A handbook for early infant stimulation for babies with Down syndrome, covering activities in all areas of development during the first years of life.

Goldberg, Sally. *Teaching with Toys: Making Your Own Educational Toys.* Ann Arbor, MI: The University of Michigan Press. 1981. A handbook for making and playing with educational toys.

Gordon, Ira J. *Baby Learning Through Baby Play: A Parent's Guide for the First Two Years.* New York: St. Martin's Press. 1970. A basic general activity book for newborns and infants.

Gordon, Ira J., Barry Guinagh & R. Emile Jester. *Child Learning Through Child Play: Learning Activities for Two and Three Year Olds.* New York: St. Martin's Press. 1972. A basic general activity book for young children.

Hanson, Marci J. *Teaching Your Down's Syndrome Infant: A Guide for Parents.* Baltimore: University Park Press (distributed by Pro-Ed). 1977. A useful guide for parents and professionals to early infant education. Provides lesson plans for all areas of infant development.

Hill, Margaret. *The Retarded Child Gets Ready for School.* Public Affairs Pamphlet No. 349A. New York: Public Affairs Committee. 1982. A brief introduction to sending a retarded child to school.

Houghton, Janaye Matteson. *Homespun Language.* New Richmond, WI: Whitehaven Publishing Co. 1982. A book of practical language lessons based on the objects and concepts of a child's daily routine. Aimed at children over two years old.

Jablow, Martha Moraghan. *Cara: Growing with a Retarded Child.* Philadelphia: Temple University Press. 1982. A personal account of a mother and her child with Down syndrome, following their life during Cara's first seven years of development and education.

Johnson, Vicki M. & Roberta A. Werner. *A Step-By-Step Learning Guide for Retarded Infants and Children.* Syracuse, NY: Syracuse University Press. 1975. A lesson book for early infant stimulation, divided into lessons for each of the areas of development.

Kolucki, Barbara. *Sharing the Street: Activities for All Children.* New York: Children's Television Workshop. 1978. An excellent activity book for children, modeled on Sesame Street.

Levy, Janine. *The Baby Exercise Book: For the First Fifteen Months.* New York: Pantheon Books. 1975. An illustrated handbook of basic exercises for newborns, based on a baby's natural movements.

Long, Kate. *"Johnny's Such a Bright Boy, What a Shame He's Retarded."* Boston: Houghton Mifflin Co. 1978. A sensitive and emotional argument in favor of mainstreaming exceptional children in school. Filled with true stories.

Long, Kate. *Parents Becoming Teachers.* Morgantown, WV: Valley Community Mental Health Center. 1981. A handbook for parents on teaching their baby or young child.

McConkey, Roy & Dorothy Jeffree. *Making Toys for Handicapped Children.* Englewood Cliffs, NJ: Prentice-Hall, Inc. 1981. A guide to making and using toys suited to handicapped and learning disabled children.

Millman, Joan & Polly Behrman. *Parents As Playmates: A Games Approach to the Pre-School Years.* New York: Human Sciences Press. 1979. A creative book of parent-child activities based on everyday life.

Painter, Genevieve, Ed.D. *Teach Your Baby.* New York: Simon & Schuster. 1982. A collection of activities for early infant stimulation for the newborn to the toddler.

Pearlman, Laura & Kathleen Anton Scott. *Raising the Handicapped Child.* Englewood Cliffs, NJ: Prentice-Hall, Inc. 1981. A general guide to raising handicapped children from birth to adulthood.

Simmons, Richard. *Reach for Fitness: A Special Book of Exercises for the Physically Challenged.* New York: Warner Books, Inc. 1986. A guide for exercising and good health for the handicapped written by the T.V. personality. Although its theme is positive, the book contains some inaccurate information about Down syndrome.

Spitalnik, Deborah M. & Irving Rosenstein, eds. *All Children Grow and Learn.* Philadelphia: Temple University Developmental Disabilities Center. 1976. A booklet introducing infant stimulation with words and pictures.

Sternlicht, Manny, Ph.D & Abraham Hurwitz. *Games Children Play.* New York: Van Nostrand Reinhold Co. 1981. Play activities for developmentally disabled children, geared to older children or children able to communicate.

Chapter 8

Anderson, Winifred, Stephen Chitwood, Deidre Hayden. *Negotiating the Special Education Maze: A Guide for Parents and Teachers.* Rockville, MD: Woodbine House, 1990. A guide to helping parents get the best special education for their child through advocacy.

Apolloni, Tony & Thomas P. Cooke. *A New Look at Guardianship: Protective Services That Support Personalized Living.* Baltimore: Paul H. Brookes Publishing Co. 1984. This book reviews the options for providing future support for handicapped persons.

ARC National Insurance And Benefits Committee. *How to Provide for Their Future.* Arlington, TX: Association For Retarded Citizens. 1984. A booklet that explains many of the concerns about wills, estate planning, insurance, and government benefits for parents of retarded children.

Biklen, Douglas. *Let Our Children Go: An Organizing Manual for Advocates and Parents.* Syracuse, NY: Human Policy Press. 1979. A handbook for organizing a grassroots campaign to improve the treatment and education of exceptional children.

Budoff, Milton & Alan Orenstein. *Due Process in Special Education: On Going to a Hearing*. Cambridge, MA: Brookline Books, Inc. 1982. A thorough book that examines due process procedures in special education.

Cutler, Barbara Coyne, *Unraveling the Special Education Maze: An Action Guide for Parents*. Champaign, IL: Research Press. 1981. A guide for parents to dealing with the special education system and to being a good advocate for their child.

Des Jardins, Charlotte. *How To Get Services By Being Assertive*. Chicago: Coordinating Council For Handicapped Children. 1980. A handbook for obtaining services for handicapped children. Contains suggestions on advocating for your child.

Des Jardins, Charlotte. *How To Organize An Effective Parent/Advocacy Group and Move Bureaucracies*. Chicago: Coordinating Council For Handicapped Children. 1980. A handbook on organizing parent advocacy groups and working for change in educational services for handicapped children.

Moore, Ralph J., Jr. *Handbook on Estate Planning for Families of Developmentally Disabled Persons in Maryland, The District of Columbia, and Virginia*. Baltimore: Maryland State Planning Council On Developmental Disabilities. 1981. A guide to estate planning for parents of exceptional children. Although written for the laws of two states and The District of Columbia, the legal principles are generally applicable.

Mopsik, Stanley I. & Judith A. Agard, eds. *An Education Handbook for Parents of Handicapped Children*. Cambridge, MA: Brookline Books, Inc. 1985. A detailed review of the special education process.

Scheiber, Barbara & Cory Moore. *Practical Advice to Parents: A Guide to Finding Help for Children with Handicaps*. Washington, D.C.: Closer Look, Parents' Campaign For Handicapped Children And Youth and Association For Retarded Citizens. 1983. A brief guide to obtaining services for handicapped children, including medical care, education, and financial assistance.

Shrybman, James A. *Due Process in Special Education*. Rockville, MD: Aspen Systems Corp., 1982. A detailed legal guide to the law and special education, including IEP, appeals and due process hearings.

Stotland, Janet F., Esq. & Ellen Mancusco. *The Right to Special Education in Pennsylvania: A Guide for Parents*. Philadelphia: Education Law Center, Inc. 1984. Despite the title, a general booklet about the right to education of handicapped children.

United States Department of Education. *"To Assure the Free Appropriate Public Education of All Handicapped Children:" Seventh Annual Report to Congress on the Implementation of The Education of the Handicapped Act*. Office of Special Education and Rehabilitative Services, United States Department of Education. 1985. The annual report about Public Law 94-142, and about what is being done, or not being done, to carry out its purpose.

Magazines and Journals

"The ARC." Arlington, Texas: Association for Retarded Citizens. The official newspaper of the Association for Retarded Citizens, available to members. Contains articles about the ARC and issues for the retarded and handicapped.

"Down Syndrome News." Chicago: National Down Syndrome Congress. The official newsletter of the National Down Syndrome Congress published ten times a year. One of the best publications for parents, filled with information and news. Available to members.

"Down's Syndrome Papers and Abstracts for Professionals." Baltimore: Down's Syndrome Center, Department of Pediatrics, University of Maryland. Published four times a year, this journal is directed at professionals, but often contains interesting information about the latest in Down syndrome research.

"The Exceptional Parent." Boston: Psy-Ed Corporation & University of Boston School of Education. A useful and informative magazine for parents of handicapped children. Highly recommended.

"People With Special Needs/Down Syndrome Report." Aberdeen, South Dakota, Northern State College Department of Special Education and Communication Disorders. Published quarterly, this journal contains articles on special-needs people with a special supplement on Down syndrome.

"Sharing Our Caring." Caring. P.O. Box 400, Milton, Washington 98354. A magazine written for parents of children with Down syndrome published five times a year. It is "a forum for parental exchange of everyday hopes, joys, problems and sorrows in caring for the child with DS."

Publications of Developmental Charts and Checklists

We do not recommend that parents tackle their child's curriculum on their own. The following checklists can be used for general information, to get an idea of where your child's development should be heading, or to make sure your child's education program is covering everything it should. Remember that it is not always so important that your child develops a skill at a particular time, but that he learn the skill properly and well. Determining this often requires professional judgment.

HELP CHART and HELP ACTIVITY GUIDE © 1979 University of Hawaii at Manoa, Published by VORT Corporation, P.O. Box 11132, Palo Alto, CA 94306. This is a chart and activity guide that tracks developmental milestones up to 36 months. It covers cognitive, language, gross motor, fine motor, social, and self help.

PORTAGE GUIDE TO EARLY EDUCATION © 1976 Cooperative Educational Service, Agency 12, Portage Project, Box 564, Portage, WI 53901. This developmental checklist contains lists of milestones appropriate at various ages up to 5-6 years. It includes socialization, language, self help, cognitive, and motor development.

DEVELOPMENTAL RECORD BOOK, Brigance Diagnostic Inventory of Early Development (Birth to Seven Years), © 1978 Curriculum Associates, Inc., Curriculum Associates, 5 Esquire Road, North Billerica, MA 01862-2589. This booklet is an individualized record of a child's development, covering all areas of development.

Resource Guide

This resource guide contains references to a wide variety of organizations that can help new parents of babies with Down syndrome. We wish to thank the National Down Syndrome Congress and the National Information Center for Handicapped Children and Youth for contributing much of the information in this Guide.

The following list briefly describes the different types of organizations listed in this Resource Guide:

• **STATE DEPARTMENT OF EDUCATION**—The state agency responsible for providing education to children, including special education services to children with Down syndrome.

• **PROTECTION & ADVOCACY SERVICE**—Legal organizations established to protect the rights of handicapped persons, including children with Down syndrome.

• **ASSOCIATION FOR RETARDED CITIZENS (ARC)**—Each state's Association for Retarded Citizens is listed below, but there are many local (city and county) branches. These local organizations and their many programs are essential resources for parents. Because there are so many local (city, county, regional, and state) ARCs, parents should check their local telephone books under "Association for Retarded Citizens," "ARC," or under the name of their city, county, region, state, or state capital (e.g. "Franklin County ARC," "ARC of Smith County," or "Connecticut Association for Retarded Citizens"). Contact your state ARC for information about the local ARC in your area and contact your local ARC for information about their many programs.

• **PRIVATE ORGANIZATIONS**—There are many different types of private organizations that can help parents of children with Down syndrome. They include parent support groups, local groups affiliated with national Down syndrome organizations, and information networks.

• DEVELOPMENTAL CLINICS—There are many pro-
grams that are affiliated with universities that offer developmental
services to parents of special-needs children.

National Organizations

Association for Retarded Citizens
2501 Avenue J
Arlington, Texas 76011
817/640–0204
Contact: Dr. Alan Abeson, Executive Director
A grassroots national organization of retarded persons and their advocates. Publishes information about all types of retardation, advocates on behalf of retarded persons, and supports an
extensive national network of local associations.

Children's Defense Fund
122 C Street, N.W.
Washington, D.C. 20001
202/628–8787
A legal organization that lobbies and brings test cases to expand the rights of children, including
handicapped children.

Clearinghouse on the Handicapped
Department of Education
400 Maryland Avenue, S.W.
Washington, D.C. 20202
202/732–1250
A federal organization that provides information on education, services, support organizations,
federal benefits, medical services, and civil rights.

Commission on the Mentally Disabled
American Bar Association
1800 M Street, N.W.
Washington, D.C. 20036
202/331–2240
An interdisciplinary organization of lawyers founded to foster improvement in the care of the
mentally disabled. Provides lists of lawyers specializing in representing the handicapped.

The ERIC Clearinghouse on Handicapped and Gifted Children
The Council for Exceptional Children
1920 Association Drive
Reston, Virginia 22091
703/620–3660
A clearinghouse of information and publications about handicaps, including Down syndrome.
Performs searches for information and publishes journals and information abstracts.

Joseph P. Kennedy Foundation
1350 New York Avenue, N.W.
Suite 500
Washington, D.C. 20005
202/393–1250
This foundation created and sponsors "Special Olympics." Of special interest for new parents is the foundation's "Let's Play To Grow" program. This excellent program sponsors events for parents and infants that encourage early play activities. Write for "Discover," the newsletter of "Let's Play To Grow."

LaLeche League International, Inc.
9616 Minneapolis Avenue
Franklin Park, Illinois 60131
312/455–7730
A national organization that advocates breastfeeding of infants. Offers information and support for mothers. Publishes a pamphlet on breastfeeding infants with Down syndrome (see Reading List).

National Down Syndrome Congress
1800 Dempster Road
Park Ridge, Illinois 60068–1146
800/232–NDSC 312/226–0416 (Ill. only)
A national organization of parents and professionals. The Congress publishes the "Down Syndrome News" (see Reading List), holds an annual convention, sponsors projects and local events, and coordinates a national network of affiliated local organizations (see entries for each state). An excellent resource for information and support.

National Down Syndrome Society
141 Fifth Avenue
New York, New York 10010
800/221–4602 212/460–9330
A national organization for parents and professionals established to promote a better understanding of Down syndrome and the potential of people with Down syndrome, to fund scientific research related to Down syndrome, and to help families and individuals with Down syndrome. Booklet, NDSS Update, information sheet, and other publications available (see Reading List). Offers an 800 "hotline."

National Information Center for Handicapped Children and Youth
P.O. Box 1492
Washington, D.C. 20013
703/522–3332
This organization operates under an agreement with the Department of Education to provide free information to parents of handicapped children. Parents can send or call in questions or request information on a wide range of subjects, including Down syndrome, early infant education, and national, state, and local resources. Produces fact sheets and "State Sheets" which list each state's resources for handicapped people.

Mainstream, Inc.
1200 15th Street, N.W.
Washington, D.C. 20005
202/833–1162
Provides information about the education and employment of the handicapped.

Siblings For Significant Change
823 United Nations Plaza
Room 808
New York, New York 10017
212/420-0776
An organization for siblings of the disabled. It provides information and referral services, access to legal aid, counseling programs, and community education.

Sibling Information Network
Department of Educational Psychology
Box U-64
The University of Connecticut
Storrs, Connecticut 06268
203/486-4031
A clearinghouse of information on the disabled and their families, with a concentration on siblings. Membership includes professionals, parents, and siblings. Issues quarterly newsletters containing reviews, resource information, and discussions of family issues.

Local Organizations

ALABAMA

State Department of Education
Program for Exceptional Children &
Youth
868 State Office Building
Montgomery, AL 36130
205/261-5099 (In Alabama
800/392-8020)
Contact: Anne Ramsey, Coordinator

Alabama ARC
4301 Norman Bridge Road
Montgomery, AL 36105
205/288-9434
Contact: Douglas Sanford, Executive
Director

Alabama Developmental Disabilities Advocacy Program
918 Fourth Avenue
Tuscaloosa, AL 35401
205/348-4998
Contact: Suellen R. Galbraith, Director

Sparks Center for Developmental &
Learning Disorders
Down Syndrome Project
University of Alabama at Birmingham
1720 Seventh Avenue South
Birmingham, AL 35233
205/934-5471
Contact: J. Wesley Libb

P.A.D.S.
2107 Chestnut Road
Birmingham, AL 35216
205/822-2589
Contact: Charlotte Bell

Association for Down's Syndrome
Citizens
P.O. Box 9083
Mobile, AL 36691
205/344-3948 or 342-1287

ALASKA

Department of Education
Exceptional Children & Youth
Pouch F
Juneau, AK 99811
907/465-2824
Contact: Mary Asper & Kathie
Wineman, Early Childhood Contacts

Protection & Advocacy for the
Developmentally Disabled, Inc.
325 East Third Avenue, 2nd Place
Anchorage, AK 99501
907/274-3658
Contact: David Maltman, Director

Alaska ARC
3605 Arctic Blvd., Suite 323
Anchorage, AK 99506
907/277-6677 or 338-5316
Contact: Benjamin Yerxa, Executive
Director

Alaska Chapter NDSC
c/o Anchorage Infant Learning Program
540 W. International Airport Road
Anchorage, AK 99502
907/561-8060

Bering Strait Infant Learning Program
Box 6
Nome, AK 99762
907/443-2124

AMERICAN SAMOA

State Department of Education
Special Education Division
Pago Pago, American Samoa 96799
Contact: Jane French, Director

ARIZONA

Department of Education
Division of Special Education
1535 West Jefferson
Phoenix, AZ 85007
602/255-3183 (In Arizona
800/352-4558)
Contact: Sara E. Robertson, Preschool
Coordinator

Arizona ARC
5610 South Central
Phoenix, AZ 85040
602/243-1787
Contact: Barry Carson, Executive
Director

Dine Center for Human Development
(Navajo Satellite Center)
Navajo Community College
Tsaile, AZ 86556
602/724-3351
Contact: Loren Sekayumptewa,
Executive Director

Santa Cruz Training Programs, Inc.
P.O. Box 638
Nogales, AZ 85628-0638

District IV Council on Developmental
Disabilities
P.O. Box 5062
Parker, AZ 85344
619/663-3732

"SHARING"-Down Syndrome
Parent Support Group
2451 West Paradise Lane
Phoenix, AZ 85023
602/993-2229 or 275-1426

Pilot Parents
121 East Voltaire Avenue
Phoenix, AZ 95022
602/863-4048
Contacts: Betsy Trombino and Kathy
Pastores

4 CCDD
214 Sierra Drive
Prescott, AZ 96301
Contact: Carol Mumford
602/445-8588

District VI Advisory Council on DD
135 N. Haskell
Willcox, AZ 85643
602/384-2647

ARKANSAS

Department of Education
Special Education Division
Arch Ford Education Building
Room 105-C
Little Rock, AR 72201
Contact: Mary Kay Curry, Early
Childhood Representative

Advocacy Services, Inc.
Medical Arts Building, Suite 504
12th & Marshall Streets
Little Rock, AR 72202
501/371-2171 (In Arkansas 800/482-1174)
Contact: Sherri Stewart, Executive
Director

Arkansas ARC
6115 West Markham Room 107
Little Rock, AR 72217
501/661-9992
Contact: Kathleen Wallace, Executive
Director

Down's Parents of Little Rock
18104 Lawson Road
Little Rock, AR 72210
501/821-2350
Contact: Judy Chunyo

CALIFORNIA

Department of Education
Special Education Division
721 Capitol Mall
Sacramento, CA 95814
916/324-8417
Contact: Nancy N. Obley-Kilborn, Early
Education Consultant

Protection & Advocacy, Inc.
2131 Capitol Avenue, Suite 100
Sacramento, CA 95816
916/447-3324 (In California
800/952-5746)
Contact: Albert Zonca, Executive
Director

California ARC
1515 J Street, #180
Sacramento, CA 95814
916/441-3322
Contact: Theodore E. Johnson

Division of Clinical Genetics &
Developmental Disabilities
Department of Pediatrics
University of California at Irvine Medical
Center
101 The City Drive
Route 81, Building 29A
Irvine, CA 92717
714/634-5791
Contact: Dr. Kenneth W. Dumars

Mental Retardation Program
University Affiliated Facility
University of California at Los Angeles
760 Westwood Plaza
Los Angeles, CA 90024
Contact: Dr. Arturo Torres, Director

Center for Child Development &
Developmental Disorders
University Affiliated Program
Children's Hospital of Los Angeles
4650 Sunset Blvd.
Los Angeles, CA 90027
213/669-2300
Contact: Dr. Wylda Hammond, Director

Down Syndrome Parent Group of Kern
County
7809 Avenida Derecho
Bakersfield, CA 93309
805/832-7964

Ups & Downs
P.O. Box 148
Boulder Creek, CA 95006
408/336-2559
Contact: Carole Schwarzbach

So. Central Down Syndrome Parents
Group
13028 Premiere Street
Downey, CA 90242
213/803-6708
Contact: Bo & Karen Newman

Parents Reaching other Parents
3289 Edgewood Road
Eureka, CA 95501
707/445-8841

Northern California Down Syndrome
Congress
7250 Falcon Road
Fair Oaks, CA 95628
Contact: Dennis Mooney

Infants Development Program
Exceptional Children's Foundation
3750 W. Santa Barbara Avenue
Los Angeles, CA 90008
213/735-1424
Contact: Fran Chesen

Down's Syndrome Parents Group, Inc.
P.O. Box 26127
Los Angeles, CA 90026
818/366-3199

Project Cope
9160 Monte Vista Avenue
Montclair, CA 91763
714/621-3884
Contact: Judy Cook, Joanne Travers

ARC–AC Parent-to-Parent Group
7808 Capwell Drive
Oakland, CA 94621
415/632-4300
Contact: Jacqueline Simoneaux

Proud
P.O. Box 5822
Orange, CA 92667-0822
714/974-6419
Contact: Becky Raabe

Down's Syndrome League
108 Van Ripper Lane
Orinda, CA 94563
415/254-2980
Contact: Virginia Pearce

New Hope Parents Ass'n, Inc.
P.O. Box 2651
Oroville, CA 95965
916/589-1250
Contact: Marsha B. Bernhard

DSPG of PARCA
350 Turks Head Lane
Redwood City, CA 94065
415/595-5590
Contact: Gary Aden

PODS
5190 Howes Lane
San Jose, CA 95118
Contact: June Beck

Down's Syndrome Parents, Teachers &
Friends
1858 Prell Road
Santa Monica, CA 93454
805/928-5093
Contact: Judith A. Lundberg

Parents of Down Syndrome of Northern
California
29865 Westmoore Road
Shingletown, CA 96088
Contact: Sharon Chestnut

Ventura County Down's Syndrome Ass'n
867 Elko Avenue
Ventura, CA 93004
805/647-6047
Contact: Terry Riggs

COLORADO

Department of Education
Special Education
201 East Colfax Avenue
Denver, CO 80203
303/866-6710
Contact: Nancy Sievers, Early Childhood
Consultant

Colorado ARC
1600 Sherman Street, Suite 750
Denver, CO 80030
303/466-1150 (In Colorado
800/332-7690)
Contact: Allan Bergman, Executive
Director

Rocky Mountain Child Development
Center
Down Syndrome Clinic
University of Colorado Health Sciences
Center
4200 East 9th Avenue, Box C234
Denver, CO 80262
303/394-7386
Contact: Dr. Marilyn Krajicek, Project
Coordinator

Parent Education and Assistance for Kids
(PEAK)
3709 E. Platte, Suite 101
Colorado Springs, CO 80909
303/574-2345 (In Colorado
800/621-8385, Ext. 338)
Contact: Judy Martz & Barbara Buswell,
Co-Directors

Western Slope Down Syndrome Ass'n
c/o Effective Parents Project
930 Ute Avenue
Grand Junction, CO 81501
303/434-5071

Mile High Down Syndrome Ass'n, Inc
P.O. Box 620847
Littleton, CO 80162
303/797-1699

CONNECTICUT

Department of Education
Early Childhood Unit
P.O. Box 2219
Hartford, CT 06145
203/566-5225
Contact: Ginny Volk, Coordinator

Department of Mental Retardation
342 North Main Street
West Hartford, CT 06117
203/236-2531
Contact: Amy Wheaton, Commissioner

Office of Protection & Advocacy for
Handicapped and Developmentally
Disabled Persons
90 Washington Street
Hartford, CT 06106
203/566-7616 (In Connecticut
800/842-7303)
Contact: Tina Walts-Gilmore, Director

Connecticut ARC
15 High Street, Room 237
Hartford, CT 06103
203/522-1179
Contact: Peg Dignoti, Executive Director

Special Education Resource Center
275 Windsor Street
Hartford, CT 06120
203/246-8514
Contact: Arnold Fassler

North Central Regional Center Parents
Group
120 Mountain Avenue
Bloomfield, CT 06002
Contact: Mary Leichner

Shoreline Ass'n for Retarded &
Handicapped Citizens
55 Park Street
Guilford, CT 06437
203/453-6531

Meriden Wallingford Society for the
Handicapped
224-226 Cook Avenue
Meriden, CT 06450
203/237-9975
Contact: Justine Gonyea

Tolland Area Ass'n for Retarded &
Handicapped
P.O. Box 2203
Vernon, CT 06066
203/456-2933

Parents & Friends Network
27 Blue Spruce Circle
Weston, CT 06883
203/226-9438
Contact: Maxine Steinberg

LOVARH
3 Marvin Drive
Westbrook, CT 06498
203/399-7431, 566-7569
Contact: Joan M. Hogan, President

DELAWARE

Department of Public Instruction
Exceptional Children/Special Programs
Division
P.O. Box 1402
Dover, DE 19903
302/736-5471
Contact: Dr. Carl M. Haltom, Director

Division of Mental Retardation
449 North duPont Highway
Dover, DE 19901
302/736-4386
Contact: Margo Pollak, Director

Developmental Disabilities Protection
and Advocacy System
913 Washington Street
Wilmington, DE 19801
302/575-0660 (In Delaware
800/292-7980)
Contact: Mary McDonough

Delaware ARC
P.O. Box 1896
Wilmington, DE 19899
302/764-3662
Contact: William T. Wiest, Executive
Director

Delaware Parents of Downs, Inc.
16 Kings Grant Road
Hockessin, DE 19707
302/737-5325

DISTRICT OF COLUMBIA

District of Columbia Public Schools
Preschool/Child Find
Webster Administrative Unit
10th & H Streets, N.W.
Washington, D.C. 20001
202/724-4022
Contact: Robbie Walker King

Information Center for Handicapped
Individuals
605 G Street, N.W.
Washington, D.C. 20001
202/347-4986
Contact: Yetta W. Galiber, Executive
Director

District of Columbia ARC
900 Varnam, N.E.
Washington, D.C. 20017
202/636-2950
Contact: Vincent C. Gray, Executive
Director

Child Development Center
Georgetown University
Bles Building, Room CG-52
3800 Reservoir Road, N.W.
Washington, D.C. 20007
202/625-7675
Contact: Dr. Phyllis Magrab

Children's Hospital National Medical
Center
Department of Genetics
111 Michigan Avenue, N.W.
Washington, D.C. 20010
202/745-2187
Contact: Dr. Kenneth Rosenbaum

District of Columbia Down Syndrome
Ass'n
Parent Child Center
1325 W Street, N.W.
Washington, D.C. 20012
202/462-3375
Contact: Janet Unonu

FLORIDA

Department of Education
Prekindergarten Exceptional Program
Knott Building
Tallahassee, FL 32301
904/488-2054
Contact: Gloria Dixon Miller

Florida ARC
106 South Bronough Street
Tallahassee, FL 32301
904/681-1931
Contact: Kingsley Ross, Executive
Director

Governor's Commission on Advocacy for
Persons with Disabilities
Clifton Building, Room 209
2661 Executive Center Circle W
Tallahassee, FL 32301
904/488-9070 (In Georgia
800/342-0823)
Contact: Jonathan P. Rossman, Director

Child Development Center
Multidisciplinary Training Facility
University of Miami
P.O. Box 016820
Miami, FL 33101
305/547-6635
Contact: Dr. Robert Stempfel

Gold Coast Down's Syndrome Ass'n
3936 Aladdin Avenue
Boynton Beach, FL 33436
305/734-4786
Contact: Ruth Slager

Gold Coast Down's Syndrome Ass'n
3074 N.W. 30th Way
Boca Raton, FL 33431
305/994-6710

Down Syndrome Support Group of Lee
County
2018 S.E. 29th Lane
Cape Coral, FL 33904
813/549-6327
Contact: Bob & Jeannie Glasgow

Down's Syndrome Support Group of
Jacksonville
4308 Sage Oak Court
Jacksonville, FL 32211
904/744-8318
Contact: Jane Aderhold

Parents of Down Syndrome-Parent to
Parent
ARC Dade County
8405-A N.W. 66th Street
Miami, FL 33165
Contact: Sylvia Sanchez

Mothers of Down's Syndrome
3707 Countryside Road
Sarasota, FL 33583
813/921-7245
Contact: Janet Rice

Tallahassee Advocacy Council
3258 Majestic Prince Trail
Tallahassee, FL 32308
Contact: Glenn Garton

GEORGIA

State Department of Education
Program for Exceptional Children
1970 Twin Towers East
205 Butler Street
Atlanta, GA 30334
404/656-2425
Contact: Donna Coleman, Educational
Consultant, Preschool Handicapped

Georgia Advocacy Office, Inc.
1447 Peachtree Street, N.E.
Suite 811
Atlanta, GA 30309
404/885-1447 (In Georgia
800/282-4538)
Contact: Donald Trites, Executive
Director

Georgia ARC
1851 Ram Runway, Suite 104
College Park, GA 30337
404/761-3150
Contact: Mildred Hill

Parents Educating Parents
1851 Ram Runway, D-104
College Park, GA 30337
404/761-2745
Contact: Mildred Hill

Parents of Down Syndrome
Easter Seals
1906 Palmyra Road
Albany, GA 31701
912/439-7061
Contact: Cynthia Fuller

Child & Family Development University
Affiliated Facility
Georgia Retardation Center
850 College Station Road
Athens, GA 30610-2399
404/542-2551, 542-8970
Contact: Richard Talbott, Ph.D

Parent to Parent of Georgia, Inc.
1447 Peachtree Street, N.E.
Suite 522
Atlanta, GA 30309
Contact for referral to local Parent to
Parent groups not listed here.

DeKalb County Parent to Parent &
Fulton County Parent to Parent
1687 Tully Circle
Suite 110
Atlanta, GA 30329
404/321-4646
Contact: Bobbie Stevens

Down Syndrome Ass'n of Atlanta
3765 Moore Road
Ellenwood, GA 30049
Contact: Mrs. Winn Floyd

Troup County Parent to Parent
28 Foirt Drive
LaGrange, GA 30240
404/884-1786
Contact: Betty Clunie

Up With Down's of Cobb County
19 Powder Springs Street
P.O. Box 4453
Marietta, GA 30061

Floyd County Parent to Parent
1300 East First Street
Rome, GA 30161
404/295-6425
Contact: Glen Moye, Client Services
Coordinator

Glynn County Parent to Parent
1004 Beachview Drive
St. Thomas Island, GA 31522
912/264-6220
Contact: Cindy McDonald

GUAM

Department of Education
Special Education Section
P.O. Box DE
Agana, Guam 96910
671/646-8396
Contact: Fidela Limtiaco, Early
Childhood Contact

HAWAII

Department of Education
Special Education Section
3430 Leahi Avenue
Honolulu, HI 96815
808/737-3720
Contact: Miles S. Kawatachi, State
Director

Community Services for the Disabled
Family Health Services Division
Department of Health
741 East Sunset Avenue, Room 209
Honolulu, HI 96816
808/732-0935
Contact: Ethel Yamene

Protection & Advocacy Agency
1580 Makaloa Street, Suite 860
Honolulu, HI 96814
808/949-2922
Contact: Patty Henderson, Executive
Director

Hawaii ARC
245 North Kukui Street
Honolulu, HI 96817
808/536-2274
Contact: Ahmad Saidin, Executive
Director

Down Syndrome Parents Group
Easter Seals
710 Green Street
Honolulu, HI 96817
808/545-7296
Contact: Connie Smith

IDAHO

Special Education Division
Len B. Jordan
650 West State Street
Boise, ID 83720
208/334-3940
Contact: Martha Noffsinger, State
Director

Idaho Coalition of Advocates for the
Disabled, Inc.
1510 West Washington Street
Boise, ID 83702
208/336-5353 (In Idaho 800/632-5125)
Contact: Brent Marchbanks, Director

Up About Down's
2334 Parkside Drive
Boise, ID 83712
208/322-8006
Contact: Brenda Wilson

ILLINOIS

Department of Specialized Educational
Services
100 North First Street
Springfield, IL 62777
217/782-6601
Contact: Lynn Moore, Special Education
Specialist

Department of Mental Health &
Developmental Disabilities
402 Stratton Office Building
Springfield, IL 62706
217/782-7393
Contact: William K. Murphy

Protection & Advocacy, Inc.
175 West Jackson Blvd., Suite A-2103
Chicago, IL 60604
312/341-0022
Contact: Zena Naiditch, Executive
Director

Southern Illinois P.A.D.S.
c/o Archway School
P.O. Box 1180
Carbondale, IL 62901
618/549-4442

Coordinating Council For Handicapped
Children
220 South State Street
Room 412
Chicago, IL 60604
312/939-3513
Contact: Charlotte Des Jardins

Vermilion County Down's Syndrome
Parents' Organization
605 North Logan
Danville, IL 61832
217/442-4840
Contact: Mary Ludwig

Ups for Downs
1041 Cypress Lane
Elk Grove Village, IL 60007
312/364-5031
Contact: Julie Beesley

Down Syndrome Association of
Southwestern Illinois
P.O. Box 685
Granite City, IL 62040
618/656-7074
Contact: R. Hansen

Down's Development Counsel
P.O. Box 118
Grayslake, IL 60030
312/356-7325
Contact: Chuck Walsh

Parent Support Group
P.O. Box 400
Jacksonville, IL 62651
217/245-6113
Contact: Robin Thompson

Central Illinois Down Syndrome
Organization
P.O. Box 595
Normal, IL 61761
309/452-3264

National Ass'n for Down Syndrome
P.O. Box 4542
Oak Brook, IL 60521
312/325-9112

Down's Syndrome Parent Group
Peoria ARC
320 East Armstrong
Peoria, IL 61603
309/672-6308

Down Syndrome Awareness
231 Golf Road
Springfield, IL 62704
217/787-9053
Contact: Ed & Liz Brooks

Knowledge in Down's Syndrome
(K.I.D.S.)
7806 West 165th Place
Tinley Park, IL 60477
312/429-5322
Contact: John Kamphuis

INDIANA

Department of Education
Division of Special Education
Room 229 State House
Indianapolis, IN 46204
317/927-0216
Contact: Sara B. Clapp, Asst. Dir. for
Early Childhood Special Education

Indiana Protection & Advocacy Service
Commission for the Developmentally
Disabled
850 North Meridian Street, Suite 2-C
Indianapolis, IN 46204
317/232-1100 (In Indiana 800/622-4345)
Contact: Ramesh K. Joshi, Executive
Director

Indiana ARC
110 East Washington Street, 9th Floor
Indianapolis, IN 46204
317/632-4387 (In Indiana 800/382-9100)
Contact: John Dickerson, Executive
Director

Developmental Training Center
Indiana University
2853 East Tenth Street
Bloomington, IN 47405
812/335-6508

Riley Child Developmental Program
Riley Children's Hospital
702 Barnhill Drive, 5th Floor
Indianapolis, IN 46223
317/264-2051
Contact: Ernest Smith, Director

Parents & Friends of the
Developmentally Disabled, Inc.
Route 2 Box 183 E
Angola, IN 46703
219/665-7284
Contact: Lowell H. Barker

DeKalb County Parent Group for
Handicapped Children, Inc.
P.O. Box 166
Auburn, IN 46706
219/925-3865

Association for the Disabled of Elkhart
County
P.O. Box 398
Bristol, IN 46507
219/848-7451

Down Syndrome Ass'n of Northwest
Indiana
9330 Idlewild Drive
Highland, IN 46322
219/924-1976
Contact: Nora Billadeau

Parentele
1301 East 38th Street
Indianapolis, IN 46205
317/926–4142

Down Syndrome Support Ass'n of
Central Indiana
3224 Citadel Court
Indianapolis, IN 42628

TOUCH
Parent to Parent
7 Wildwood Drive
Lafayette, IN 47905
317/447–5261
Contact: Marty Meyer

Parents Council for Handicapped and
Retarded Children
3200 South Cleveland Avenue
Michigan City, IN 46360
219/872–6996

Ups for Downs
P.O. Box 385
Newburgh, IN 47630
Contact: Sally Cash

Down Syndrome Support Ass'n of
Central Indiana
1511 Maria Lane
Plainfield, IN 46168
317/839–6201
Contact: Linda Hankins

Council for the Retarded of St. Joseph
County, Inc.
Logan Center
1235 North Eddy
P.O. Box 1049
South Bend, IN 46624
219/289–4831

Wabash County Council for Retarded
Children and Vocationally Handicapped,
Inc.
P.O. Box 400
Wabash, IN 46992
219/563–8411

IOWA

Department of Public Instruction
Division of Special Education
Grimes State Office Building
Des Moines, IA 50319
515/281–3176
Contact: Joan Clary, Early Childhood
Contact

Iowa Protection & Advocacy Service,
Inc.
3015 Merle Hay Road, Suite 6
Des Moines, IA 50310
515/278–2502

Iowa ARC
1707 High Street
Des Moines, IA 50309
515/283–2358 (In Iowa 800/367–2927)
Contact: Mary Etta Lane, Executive
Director

Division of Developmental Disabilities
University Hospital School
University of Iowa
Iowa City, IA 52242
319/353–5972

Iowa has an extensive Pilot Parents
program. The larger support groups are
listed below. For the Pilot Parents group
nearest you contact:

Iowa Pilot Parents
P.O. Box 1151
Fort Dodge, IA 50501
515/576–5870 (In Iowa 800/362–2183)
Contact: Carla Lawson, Director

Pilot Parents
1308 South 15th
Burlington, IA 52601
319/753–2109
Contact: Jim and Lana Frick

Pilot Parents
6112 West Ridgeway
Cedar Falls, IA 50613
319/277–6895
Contact: James & Gayla Hostetler

Pilot Parents of Southwest Iowa
364 Harrison
Council Bluffs, IA 51501
712/322–4514
Contact: Cletus & Nina Baker

Pilot Parents
1102 Higbee
Creston, IA 50801
515/782-4209
Contact: Dale & Joanne Draper

Iowa Pilot Parents
5625 Taylor Court
Davenport, IA 52806
319/386-4099
Contact: Dan & Sandy Elskamp

Pilot Parents
300 East Locust
Des Moines, IA 50319
515/288-6059
Contact: Marsha Laurenzo

Mother's Group
1020 William Street
Iowa City, IA 52240
319/351-5017

Pilot Parents
207 Mahaska Drive
Iowa City, IA 52240
319/337-4467
Contact: Mary & Rich Schmidt

Pilot Parents
725 North 8th
Keokuk, IA 52632
319/524-8353
Contact: Susan & Don Vance

Area VI Pilot Parents
2301 Southridge Circle
Marshalltown, IA 50158
515/752-4528
Contact: Steven & Julie Lang

Pilot Parents
30 South Pierce
Mason City, IA 50401
515/423-5563
Contact: Stephen & Nancy Beavers

Pilot Parents
205 South Fawcett
Sioux City, IA 51102
712/277-8266
Contact: Diane Bobier

Pilot Parents
1203 18th Avenue West
Spencer, IA 51304
712/262-1952
Contact: William & Jane Byrn

The National Down Syndrome Ass'n,
Inc.
P.O. Box 153
Webster City, IA 50595
515/832-4273

KANSAS

Division of Special Education
State Department of Education
120 East 10th Street
Topeka, KS 66612
913/296-7454
Contact: Lucille Paden, Education
Program Specialist

Protection & Advocacy Service for the
Developmentally Disabled
513 Leavenworth Street, Suite 2
Manhatten, KS 66502
913/776-1541 (In Kansas 800/432-8276)
Contact: Joan Strickler, Executive
Director

Kansas ARC
11111 West 59th Terrace
Shawnee, KS 66203
913/268-8200
Contact: Brent Glazier, Executive
Director

Kansas University Affiliated Facility–
Kansas City
Children's Rehabilitation Unit
Kansas University Medical Center
39th & Rainbow Blvd.
Kansas City, KS 66103
913/588-5900
Contact: Dr. Joseph Hollowell, Director

Kansas University Affiliated Facility–
Central Office
Bureau of Child Research
223 Haworth Hall
University of Kansas
Lawrence, KS 66045
913/864-4295
Contact: Dr. Richard L. Schiefelbusch,
Director

Kansas University Affiliated
Facility–Parsons
2601 Gabriel
Parsons, KS 67357
316/421-6550, Ext. 266
Contact: Dr. Joseph Spradlin, Director

Prairie Pilot Parents
Box 451
Colby, KS 67701
913/462-6781

Down's Syndrome International
11 North 73rd Terrace
Kansas City, KS 66111
913/299-0815
Contact: Jessie Bennett

Down's Syndrome Parents
1019 Patricia
Wichita, KS 67208
316/685-4765
Contact: Ruthann Harris

Up With Downs
209 East Butler
Yates Center, KS 66783
Contact: Becky Leis

KENTUCKY

Office of Education for Exceptional
Children
Capital Plaza Tower, 8th Floor
Frankfort, KY 40601
502/564-4970
Contact: Taylor Hollin, State Director

Department of Public Advocacy
Division of Protection & Advocacy
151 Elkorn Court
Frankfort, KY 40601
502/564-2967 (In Kentucky
800/633-6283)

Kentucky ARC
833 East Main Street, Box 275
Frankfort, KY 40601
502/875-5225
Contact: Cecilia Arbuckle, Executive
Director

Human Development Program
University of Kentucky
108 Porter Building
730 South Limestone Street
Lexington, KY 40506-0205
606/257-1714

Citizen Advocacy Program
P.O. Box 302
Covington, KY 41012
Contact: Timothy Heller

B.U.D. (Beginning to Understand Down
Syndrome)
894 Georgetown Road
Lexington, KY 40501
Contact: Growing Together Preschool

Early Education Funding Program
P.O. Box 22552
Louisville, KY 40222
502/893-5446
Contact: Randy Davis

Parent Outreach
1146 South 3rd Street
Louisville, KY 40203
502/584-1239

LOUISIANA

Special Education Services
State Department of Education
P.O. Box 94064
Baton Rouge, LA 70804-9064
504/342-3631
Contact: Irene Newby, State Director;
Ron Lacoste, Section Chief for Preschool

Advocacy Center for the Elderly &
Disabled
1001 Howard Avenue, Suite 300A
New Orleans, LA 70113
504/522-2337 (In Louisiana
800/662-7705)
Contact: Lois V. Simpson, Executive
Director

Louisiana ARC
658 St. Louis Street
Baton Rouge, LA 70802
504/383-0742
Contact: Dave Richards, Executive
Director

Human Development Center
Louisiana State University Medical
Center
Building 138
1100 Florida Avenue
New Orleans, LA 70119
504/568-8386

Children's Center
Louisiana State University Medical
Center
3730 Blair
Shreveport, LA 71103
318/227-5108

Southwest Louisiana Education &
Referral Center, Inc.
P.O. Box 52763
Lafayette, LA 70505
504/232–HELP

Down's Syndrome Awareness Group
P.O. Box 15173
Baton Rouge, LA 70815
504/293–0488

Down's Syndrome Awareness Group
Route 3, Box 368
Gonzales, LA 70737
504/622–2086
Contact: Kathy Edmonston

Down Syndrome Ass'n of Greater New
Orleans
2007 Spanish Oaks Drive
Harvey, LA 70058
Contact: Georgine Rousselle

Acadiana Down Syndrome Ass'n
P.O. Box 32153
Lafayette, LA 70513
318/234–3143

Pilot Parents Program
4302 Canal Street
New Orleans, LA 70119
504/484–6048

MAINE

State Department of Educational &
Cultural Services
Division of Special Education
State House Station 23
Augusta, ME 04333
207/289–5950
Contact: John Hornstein, Early
Childhood Consultant

Advocates for the Developmentally
Disabled
P.O. Box 5341
Augusta, ME 04330
207/289–5755 (In Maine 800/452–1948)
Contact: Dean Crocker, Director

Special-Needs Parent Information
Network (S.P.I.N.)
P.O. Box 2067
Augusta, ME 04330
207/582–2504 (In Maine 800/325–0220)

University Affiliated Handicapped
Children's Hospital
Eastern Medical Center
489 State Street
Bangor, ME 04401
207/947–3711

Down Syndrome Parent Group
Pathways, Inc.
589 Minot Avenue
Auburn, ME 04210
209/786–2406
Contact: Diane Hines

Cerebral Palsy Center
103 Texas Avenue
Bangor, ME 04401
(Serves children with Down syndrome)
Contact: Candace Guerette

York County Parent Awareness, Inc.
P.O. Box 265
Hollis Center, ME 04042

Down Syndrome Guild
P.O. Box 1505
Scarborough, ME 04074
207/772–0561

MARYLAND

Division of Special Education
State Department of Education
200 West Baltimore Street
Baltimore, MD 21201
301/659–2489 or 659–2542
Contact: Martha Irvin, State Director;
Lin Leslie, SIG Project Director

Information & Referral for Handicapped
Department of Education
200 West Baltimore Street
Baltimore, MD 21201
301/383–6523 (call collect)

Maryland Disability Law Center
2510 St. Paul Street
Baltimore, MD 21218
301/383–3400
Contact: David Chavkin

Maryland ARC
5602 Baltimore National Pike
Baltimore, MD 21228
301/744–0255
Contact: Elmer Cerano, Executive
Director

John F. Kennedy Institute for Handicapped Children
707 North Broadway
Baltimore, MD 21225
301/522-2100

Northern Chesapeake Region Down
Syndrome Society
4516 Dresden Road
Baltimore, MD 21208
301/655-9319
Contact: Jay Silverman

Parents of Children with Down's
Syndrome
P.O. Box 2282
Columbia, MD 21045
301/995-1092 or 301/465-4104
Contact: Marilyn Kaufman

Down's Syndrome Parents Group
431 Carrolton Drive
Frederick, MD 21701
301/663-0909
Contact: ARC Frederick County

Early Identification Program
6700 Glenn Dale Road
Glenn Dale, MD 20769
301/262-6122
Contact: June Gallagher

Down's Syndrome Parent Support Group
Route 8, Box 230
Hagerstown, MD 21740
Contact: Carol Alphin

Chesapeake Region Down's Syndrome
Congress
11412 Marbrook Road
Owings Mill, MD 21117
301/363-4141
Contact: Janice & Raymond Starr

MASSACHUSETTS

Division of Special Education
Quincy Center Plaza
1385 Hancock Street
Quincy, MA 02169
617/770-7478
Contact: Rosalie Norman, Coordinator,
Early Childhood

Developmental Disabilities Law Center
11 Beacon Street, Suite 925
Boston, MA 02108
617/723-8455
Contact: William Crane, Executive
Director

Massachusetts ARC
217 South Street
Waltham, MA 02154
617/891-6270
Contact: Matthew Johnson, Executive
Director

Developmental Evaluation Clinic
Children's Hospital Medical Center
300 Longwood Avenue
Boston, MA 02115
617/735-6501

Eunice Kennedy Shriver Center for
Mental Retardation
Walter E. Fernald State School
200 Trapelo Road
Waltham, MA 02154
617/893-3500

Information Center for Individuals with
Disabilities
20 Park Plaza, Room 330
Boston, MA 02116
617/727-5540 (In Massachusetts
800/462-5015)
Contact: Sandy Bouzoukis, Director

Down's Parents of Merrimack Valley
P.O. Box 2
Billerica, MA 01821
617/452-3242
Contact: Pat Griffin

Parent to Parent
34 Sumner Street
Brockton, MA 02401
Contact: Linda Herrmann

Cohasset Support Group for Parents of
Children with Special Needs
36 Atlantic Avenue
Cohasset, MA 02025
617/383-0895
Contact: Taffy Nothnagle

Western Massachusetts Parents of
Down's Syndrome Children
P.O. Box 364
Easthampton, MA 01027
413/527-6070
Contact: Donald & Elaine Light

Parent Group/Down Syndrome
44 Wahooshoc Road
Fitchburg, MA 01420
617/345-5250
Contact: FLLAC Collaborative

North Shore Down's Syndrome Group
184 Lafayette Street
Salem, MA 01970
617/744-1225
Contact: North Shore ARC

Massachusetts Down's Syndrome
Congress
64 Hastings Street
West Roxbury, MA 02132
617/327-8333
Contact: Mark & Kathy Granger

Help for Down's Syndrome
178 Lexington Street
Weston, MA 02193
Contact: Charles Hunt

Martha's Vineyard Special Parents Ass'n,
Inc.
Box 127
West Tisbury, MA 02575
617/693-6270

MICHIGAN

Department of Education
Early Childhood Special Education
P.O. Box 30008
Lansing, MI 48909
517/373-8189
Contact: Dr. Marvin McKinney,
Consultant

Michigan Protection & Advocacy Service
313 South Washington Square, Suite 050
Lansing, MI 48933
517/487-1755 (In Michigan
800/292-5923)

Michigan ARC
313 South Washington Square, Suite 310
Lansing, MI 48933
517/487-5426 (In Michigan
800/292-7851)
Contact: Harvey Zuckerman, Executive
Director

Section of Pediatric Genetics
University of Michigan Hospitals
D1225 Medical Professional Building
Ann Arbor, MI 48109
313/763-5774
Contact: Diane Baker

Parents of Handicapable Children
11421 South Liberty Street
Clio, MI 48420
313/686-8327

Down's Syndrome League
7067 Willow Highway
Grand Ledge, MI 48837
517/627-9467
Contact: Darlene Barker

Parents of Special Tots
10926 Wolf Creek Road
Hubbard Lake, MI 49747
517/727-2411
Contact: Janet Gagnon

Down's Syndrome Awareness Group
705 Chadd's Ford
Kalamazoo, MI 49000

Down Syndrome League of Greater
Lansing ARC
921 North Washington
Lansing, MI 48906
517/484-3068 or 517/485-0737

Mothers of the Handicapped Group
1809 Wilmington Drive
Midland, MI 48640
517/631-1676
Contact: Eileen Finzel

P.O.S.T.
3011 State Street
Ossineke, MI 49766
517/471-5236
Contact: Rose Foster

Friends of Down's Syndrome Children
4265 Halkirk
Waterford, MI 48095
313/623-9660
Contact: Lawrence Hearn

MINNESOTA

State Department of Education
Early Childhood Programs
Capitol Square Building
550 Cedar Street
St. Paul, MN 55101
612/297-3619
Contact: Ann Bettenburg, Specialist

Minnesota ARC
3225 Lyndale Avenue, South
Minneapolis, MN 55408-3699
612/827-5641 (In Minnesota
800/582-5256)
Contact: Emil W. Angelica, Executive
Director

Developmental Disabilities Program
Gillette Children's Hospital
200 University Avenue, East
St. Paul, MN 55101
612/291-2848
Contact: Dr. Richard P. Nelson, Director

Parent Advocate Coalition for Education
Rights (PACER)
4826 Chicago Avenue, South
Minneapolis, MN 55417-1055
612/827-2966
Contact: Marge Goldberg & Paula
Goldberg

TIPS
1235 7th Avenue, North Apt. 5
Anoka, MN 55303
612/427-2152

Parents of Down Syndrome/ARC
18240 Polk Avenue
Hastings, MN 55033
612/645-5020
Contact: Nancy Commerford

MISSISSIPPI

Bureau of Special Services
Department of Education
P.O. Box 771
Jackson, MS 39205
601/359-3490
Contact: Alice Hobson, State Consultant
for Early Childhood Special Education

Mississippi Protection & Advocacy
System for the Developmentally
Disabled
4750 McWillie Drive, Suite 101
Jackson, MS 39206
601/981-8207 (In Mississippi
800/772-4057)

Mississippi ARC
3000 Old Canton Road, Suite 275
Jackson, MS 39216
601/544-4039
Contact: Barbara Caperton, Executive
Director

Parent to Parent: A Down's Syndrome
Support Group
2804 Jamestown Road
Hattiesburg, MS 39401
601/668-9326
Contact: John & Cindy Bivins

Preschool Infant Program
University of Southern Mississippi
Department of Speech & Hearing
Sciences
Southern Station, Box 5092
Hattiesburg, MS 39406-5092
601/266-5116

Down Syndrome Ass'n of Corinth
Route #2, Box 104
Rienzi, MS 38865
601/287-4649
Contact: Johnie & Clara Bennett

MISSOURI

Department of Elementary & Secondary
Education
Division of Vocational Rehabilitation
P.O. Box 480
Jefferson City, MO 65102
314/751-2965
Contact: Karen Campbell, Early
Childhood Representative

Department of Mental Health
Division of Mental Retardation and
Developmental Disabilities
P.O. Box 687
Jefferson City, MO 65102
314/751–4054
Contact: Kenneth Dowden, Coordinator

Missouri Protection & Advocacy
Services, Inc.
211 B Metro Drive
Jefferson City, MO 65101
314/893–3333 (In Missouri
800/392–8667)
Contact: Carol D. Larkin

Missouri Coalition of Child Advocates
1018 Bedford Lane
Ballwin, MO 63011
314/227–1391
Contact: Madeline Wendland

University of Missouri at Kansas City
University Affiliated Facility for
Developmental Disabilities
2220 Holmes Street, 3rd Floor
Kansas City, MO 64108
816/276–1770

Missouri LINC
University of Missouri at Columbia
609 Maryland
Columbia, MO 65211
314/882–2733 (In Missouri
800/392–0533)

Down's Syndrome Ass'n of Southeast
Missouri
P.O. Box 475
Cape Girardeau, MO 63701
314/335–1871
Contact: Faith True

Pilot Parent Program
4649 South Kelly Lane
Springfield, MO 65807
417/883–4065 or 417/887–0226

Region VII Council on Developmental
Disabilities
Rolla Regional Center
P.O. Box 1098
Rolla, MO 65401
314/364–5510
Contact: Patti Koon, Coordinator

Down Syndrome Ass'n of St. Louis
42 Middlesex Drive
St. Louis, MO 63144
314/567–6042 or 314/961–2504 (24 hr.)
Contact: Kathleen Marafino

MONTANA

Special Education Unit
Office of Public Instruction
State Capitol
Helena, MT 59620
406/444–4429
Contact: Judith Johnson, Early Childhood
Representative

Montana Advocacy Program, Inc.
1219 East 8th Avenue
Helena, MT 59601
406/444–3889
Contact: Kristin Balula, Executive
Director

Montana ARC
2025 South Billings Blvd.
Trailer Village, Lot #70
Billings, MT 59101
406/248–8249

Montana University Affiliated Program
University of Montana
Missoula, MT 59812
406/243–5467

Parents, Let's Unite for Kids
P.O. Box 30935
Billings, MT 59107
406/657–2039 (In Montana
800/821–8360)

NEBRASKA

Special Education Branch
State Department of Education
P.O. Box 94987
Lincoln, NE 68509
402/471–4318
Contact: Jan Thelen, Early Childhood
Consultant

Nebraska Advocacy Services for
Developmentally Disabled Citizens, Inc.
522 Lincoln Center Building
215 Centennial Mall, Room 422
Lincoln, NE 68508
402/474-3183
Contact: Timothy Shaw, Executive
Director

Nebraska ARC
3100 North 14th Street, Lower Level
Lincoln, NE 68521
402/475-4407
Contact: Dave Powell

Meyer Children's Rehabilitation Institute
University of Nebraska Medical Center
444 South 44th Street
Omaha, NE 68131
402/559-6430

Scottsbluff Northeast Chapter, Panhandle
Pilot Parents
Route 1, Box 10
Harrisburg, NE 69345
308/235-2500
Contact: Charles & Gwelda Carlson

Pilot Parents Program
410 Lincoln Center Building
Lincoln, NE 68508
402/477-6925
Contact: Elaine Rod, Director

Clinical Genetics Center
8301 Dodge Street
Omaha, NE 68114
402/390-5488
Contact: Beth A. Fine, Genetic
Counselor

NEVADA

Nevada Department of Education
Special Education Branch
400 West King Street, Capitol Complex
Carson City, NV 89710
702/885-3140
Contact: Sharon Palmer, Early Childhood
Consultant

Developmental Disabilities Advocate's
Office
2105 Capurro Way, Suite B
Sparks, NV 89431
702/789-0233 (In Nevada
800/992-5715)
Contact: Holli Elder

Nevada ARC
1520 Maine Street
Fallon, NV 89046
702/423-4760
Contact: Frank Weinrauch, Executive
Director

Southern Nevada Down Syndrome
Organization
5135 Gray Lane # C
Las Vegas, NV 89119
702/739-3628 or 702/739-6872
Contact: Marilyn Lamascus

NEW HAMPSHIRE

State Department of Education
Special Education Section
101 Pleasant Street
Concord, NH 03301
603/271-3741
Contact: Barbara D. Bourgeine

Division for Community Developmental
Services
Health & Welfare Building
Hazen Drive
Concord, NH 03301
603/271-4706
Contact: Richard Lepore, Assistant
Director

Developmental Disabilities Advocacy
Center, Inc.
6 White Street
P.O. Box 19
Concord, NH 03301
603/228-0432 (In New Hampshire
800/852-3336)
Contact: Donna Woodfin, Director

New Hampshire ARC
244 North Main Street
Carrigan Commons
Concord, NH 03301
603/228-9092
Contact: Karen Cowen

Parent Information Center (P.I.C.)
P.O. Box 1422
Concord, NH 03301
603/224-7005
Contact: Judith Raskin

NEW JERSEY

Department of Education
Division of Special Education
Bureau of Programs & Services
225 West State Street, CN 500
Trenton, NJ 08625
609/292-0147
Contact: Dr. Noreen Gallagher

Division of Mental Retardation
Department of Human Services
222 South Warren Street
Capitol Place One
Trenton, NJ 08625
609/292-3742
Contact: Eddie C. Moore, Director

Statewide Computerized Referral
Information Program (SCRIP)
108-110 North Broad Street, CN 700
Trenton, NJ 08625
609/292-3745 (In New Jersey
800/792-8858)

Department of Public Advocacy
Division of Advocacy for the
Developmentally Disabled
CN 850
Trenton, NJ 08625
609/292-9742
Contact: Herbert Hinkle

New Jersey ARC
99 Bayard Street
New Brunswick, NJ 08901
201/246-2525
Contact: John Scagnelli, Executive
Director

Rutgers Medical School
Department of Pediatrics
Busch Campus
P.O. Box 101
Piscataway, NJ 08854
201/463-4447

SCRIP—Self-Help Group Clearinghouse
of New Jersey
800/452-9790

Down Syndrome Support Group of
South Jersey
401 4th Avenue
Haddon Heights, NJ 08035
Contact: Joanne McKeown
609/547-6773; Paul Williams
609/424-1231

New Jersey Down's Syndrome Chapter
Department of Special Education
Jersey City State College
2039 Kennedy Blvd.
Jersey City, NJ 07305
201/547-3023
Contact: Professor George Voller

Down Syndrome Ass'n of Central New
Jersey
7 Fieldston Road
Princeton, NJ 08540
Contact: Joan Nester

NEW MEXICO

State Department of Education
Division of Special Education
300 Don Gasper Avenue
Santa Fe, NM 87501-2786
505/827-6541
Contact: Ruth Fletcher, Educational
Services Specialist

Protection & Advocacy System
2201 San Pedro, N.E.
Building 4, Suite 140
Albuquerque, NM 87110
505/888-0111 (In New Mexico
800/432-4682)
Contact: James Jackson, Executive
Director

New Mexico ARC
8210 LaMirada, N.E., Suite 500
Albuquerque, NM 87109
505/298-6796
Contact: Kermitt Stuve, Executive
Director

NEW YORK

State Department of Education
Office for Education of Children with
Handicapping Conditions
Education Building Annex, Room 1073
Albany, NY 12234
Contact: Lawrence Gloecker, Assistant
Commissioner

Office of the Advocate for the Disabled
Agency Building 1, 10th Floor
Empire State Plaza
Albany, NY 12223
518/473-4129 (In New York
800/522-4369)
Contact: Frances Berko, State Advocate

New York State ARC
393 Delaware Avenue
Delmar, NY 12054
518/439-8311
Contact: Marc N. Brandt, Executive
Director

Developmental Disabilities Center
St. Lukes-Roosevelt Hospital Center
Columbia University-College of
Physicians & Surgeons
428 West 59th Street
New York, NY 10019
212/870-6844

Rose Kennedy Center
Albert Einstein College of Medicine
University Affiliated Facility
Yeshiva University
1410 Pelham Parkway South
Bronx, NY 10461
212/430-2440

University Affiliated Diagnostic Clinic for
Developmental Disorders
University of Rochester Medical Center
P.O. Box 671
601 Elmwood Avenue
Rochester, NY 14642
716/275-2987

Mental Retardation Institute
New York Medical College at Valhalla
Valhalla, NY 10595
914/347-5400

Down Syndrome-Aim High, Inc.
P.O. Box 12-12212
Albany, NY 12212
518/377-7368

Association for Children With Down's
Syndrome
2616 Martin Avenue
Bellmore, NY 11710
516/221-4700
Contact: Fredda Stimell

Rockland Parents Assistance Committee
on Down's Syndrome
P.O. Box 210
Blavett, NY 10913
914/358-6321
Contact: Martha Zambri

Project H.O.P.E. Ltd.
8206 15th Avenue
Brooklyn, NY 11228
212/331-9006
Contact: Jean Gregoli

Down's Syndrome Awareness Group of
St. Lawrence County
P.O. Box 642
Canton, NY 315/344-7066

Down's Syndrome Parent Group
7 Warrington Drive
Fairport, NY 14450
716/377-2132
Contact: Pat Marshall

The Mid-Hudson Valley Down's
Syndrome Congress
RT. 1 Box 403B
Highland, NY 12528
914/691-6334
Contact: Roger Dodge

Down Syndrome Parent Support Group
of Queens, New York
209-14 82nd Avenue
Hollis Hills, NY 11427
718/465-6261
Contact: A.S. Harris

Down Syndrome Family Group
217 Snyder Hill Road
Ithaca, NY 14850
607/273-6966
Contact: Regina Billman

The Down's Syndrome Parent Group
547 Englewood Avenue
Kenmore, NY 14223
716/832-9334
Contact: Carol Hetzelt

Manhatten-Bronx Parent Support Group
145 Central Park West
New York, NY 10023
Contact: June Eichbaum

Pre-Kindergarten Center
Box 87, Thorndike Hall
Teachers College
Columbia University
New York, NY 10027
Contact: Elaine Gregoli

Down Syndrome Parent Support Group
of Long Island
191 Atlantic Street
North Great River, NY 11722
Contact: G. Widmann

Parent Assistance Committee on Down's
Syndrome
208 Lafayette Avenue
Peekskill, NY 10566
914/739-4085
Contact: Barbara Levitz

Down Syndrome Parent Group
116 Willow Bend Road
Rochester, NY 14618
716/442-9268
Contact: Mrs. Leigh Little

Syracuse Parents of Down Syndrome
Children
116 Doll Parkway
Syracuse, NY 13214
315/446-5332
Contact: Susan Judge

NORTH CAROLINA

Department of Public Instruction
Division of Exceptional Children
Early Childhood Program
114 East Edenton Street
Raleigh, NC 27611
919/733-6081
Contact: Janice Dellinger, Consultant

Governor's Advocacy Council for Persons
with Disabilities
1318 Dale Street, Suite 100
Raleigh, NC 27605
919/733-9250 (In North Carolina
800/662-7030)

Information and Referral Program
Department of Human Resources
325 North Salisbury Street
Raleigh, NC 27611
919/723-4261 (In North Carolina
800/662-7030)
Contact: Susan Crocker, Director

Advocacy Center for Children's
Education and Parent Training
(ACCEPT)
P.O. Box 27952
Raleigh, NC 27611
919/821-2048 (In North Carolina
800/532-5358)
Contact: Jennifer Seykora

North Carolina ARC
P.O. Box 18551
2400 Glenwood Avenue
Raleigh, NC 27619
919/782-4632
Contact: Carey S. Fendley, Executive
Director

Biological Sciences Research Center
Division for Disorders of Development
& Learning
The University of North Carolina at
Chapel Hill
Chapel Hill, NC 27514
919/966-5171

Concerned Parents of the Handicapped
2542 Turnberry Lane
Charlotte, NC 28210
704/554-0185
Contact: Joanne Longo

Catawba Valley Down Syndrome Ass'n
Family, Infant & Preschool Program
Morganton, NC 28655
Contact: Janet C. Weeldreyer

B.A.B.I.E.S.
650 North Highland Avenue
Winston-Salem, NC 27010
919/725-7777
Contact: Bruce Halverson, Director

NORTH DAKOTA

Department of Public Instruction
Special Education Division
State Capitol
Bismark, ND 58505
701/224-2277 (In North Dakota
800/932-8974)

Protection & Advocacy Project for the
Developmentally Disabled
State Capitol Annex, 1st Floor
Bismarck, ND 58505
701/224–2972 (In North Dakota
800/472–2670)
Contact: Barbara C. Braun, Director

North Dakota ARC
418 East Broadway Avenue
Bismarck, ND 58501
701/223–5349
Contact: Dan Ulmer, Executive Director

North Dakota Down Syndrome Interest
Group
844 6th Street
Devils Lake, ND 58301
701/662–5734
Contact: Sam Johnson

Parents of Down Syndrome Children
Southeast Human Service Center
15 Broadway
Fargo, ND 58102
701/237–4513
Contact: Peg DuBord, Developmental
Disabilities Coordinator

OHIO

State Department of Education
Division of Special Education
933 High Street
Worthington, OH 43085
614/466–2650
Contact: Jane Weichel, Early Childhood
Consultant

Special Education Regional Resource
Centers (SERRC)
Ohio operates special education centers.
These agencies provide assistance to
parents, teachers, and educational
agencies. Contact the State Department
of Education or your local telephone
book for the SERRC in your area.

Ohio Legal Rights Service
8 East Long Street, 8th Floor
Columbus, OH 43215
614/466–7264 (In Ohio 800/282–9181)
Contact: Catherine Worley, Executive
Director

Ohio ARC
360 South 3rd Street, Suite 101
Columbus, OH 43215
614/228–4412
Contact: Carolyn Sidwell, Executive
Director

University Affiliated Cincinnati Center
for Developmental Disabilities
Pavilion Building
Elland & Bethesda Avenues
Cincinnati, OH 45229
513/559–4623

Nisonger Center
The Ohio University
McCampbell Hall
1580 Cannon Drive
Columbus, OH 43210–1205
614/422–8365

Southwestern Ohio Coalition for Persons
with Disabilities
3333 Vine Street
Cincinnati, OH 45220
513/861–2400
Contact: Thomas Murray, Director

Citizens Advocacy Coalition
824 East 5th Street
Dayton, OH 45402
513/461–5600
Contact: Thomas Lindstrom

Parents Who Care
Metzenbaum Center
8200 Cedar Road
Chesterland, OH 44026
Contact: Pat Cigoi

Down Syndrome Ass'n of Greater Cincinnati
Down Syndrome Center
1821 Summit Road, Suite G-30
Cincinnati, OH 45237
513/761-5400

Caring Parents of Children With Down
Syndrome
4428 West 53rd Street
Cleveland, OH 44144
216/871–7292
Contact: Maureen Lynn

Down Syndrome Ass'n of Central Ohio
3104 Kellner Place
Columbus, OH 43201
614/239-1871
Contact: Sherrie Andrus

Miami Valley Down Syndrome Ass'n
1444 Beaver Creek Lane
Kettering, OH 45429-3704
513/294-1240
Contact: Mrs. Patti Ann Dixon

St. Rita's Down Syndrome Parent Group
St. Rita's Medical Center
730 West Market Street
Lima, OH 45801
419/226-9019
Contact: Jane D. Schmidt

Ohio Valley Down Syndrome Ass'n
27 Sylvan Way
Marietta, OH 45750
614/373-5603
Contact: Carole Hoff

Handi-Parents of Clark County
2430 Van Buren
Springfield, OH 45505
513/323-4944
Contact: Jeanne G. McLean

Down Syndrome Parent Support Group
P.O. Box 502
Toledo, OH 43693
419/666-8842

North East Ohio Down Syndrome
Organization
6983 Pinewood Drive
Youngstown, OH 44512
216/758-0343
Contact: Susan Bartalo

OKLAHOMA

State Department of Education
Section for Exceptional Children
2500 North Lincoln, Suite 263
Oklahoma City, OK 73105
405/521-3351
Contact: Joann Gordoni, Coordinator,
Early Childhood

Protection & Advocacy Agency for the
Developmentally Disabled
9726 East 42nd Street
Osage Building, Room 133
Tulsa, OK 74146
918/664-5883
Contact: Dr. Bob M. Van Osdol,
Director

Down's Syndrome Ass'n of Northwest
Oklahoma
Box 676
Laverne, OK 73848
405/921-5157
Contact: Viola Duncan

Parents of Children with Down's
Syndrome
4510 Beckett Court
Norman, OK 73069
Contact: Jan Watts

Tulsa Parents of Children with Down
Syndrome
P.O. Box 54877
Tulsa, OK 74155
918/665-6650

Parents of Children with Down's
Syndrome
Route 3, Box SA 65
Tuttle, OK 73089
405/381-2778

OREGON

Department of Education
Special Education & Student Services
Division
700 Pringle Parkway, S.E.
Salem, OR 97310-0290
503/378-3782
Contact: Terry Kramer, Early Childhood
Specialist

Oregon Developmental Disabilities
Advocacy Center
400 Board of Trade Building
310 Southwest 4th Avenue
Portland, OR 97204
503/243-2081 (In Oregon 800/452-1694)

Oregon ARC
1745 State Street, N.E.
Salem, OR 97301
503/581-2726 (In Oregon 800/452-0313)
Contact: Janna Starr, Executive Director

Center on Human Development
University of Oregon
Clinic Services Building, 3rd Floor
Eugene, OR 97403
503/686-3591

Genetics Clinic
Crippled Children's Division
Oregon Health Sciences University
707 S.W. Gaines Road
Portland, OR 97202
503/225-8364
Contact: Diane Plumridge

Pilot Parent Program
718 West Burnside #316
Portland, OR 97209
503/223-7279
Contact: ARC Multnomah County

Committee for Down's Syndrome
2251 Hazel, N.E.
Salem, OR 97303
503/581-5034
Contact: Niki Smith

PENNSYLVANIA

Bureau of Special Education
333 Market Street
Harrisburg, PA 17109-0333
717/783-6913
Contact: Joyce Wilder, Special Education
Early Childhood Coordinator

Developmental Disabilities Advocacy
Network, Inc.
3540 North Progress Avenue
Harrisburg, PA 17110
717/657-3320 (In Pennsylvania
800/692-7443)
Contact: Edwin Frownfelter, Executive
Director

Pennsylvania ARC
123 Forster Street
Harrisburg, PA 17102
717/234-2621
Contact: William A. West, Executive
Director

Developmental Disabilities Program
Temple University
9th Floor Ritter Annex
13th Street & Columbus Avenue
Philadelphia, PA 19122
215/787-7000

Down's Syndrome Parent Group
1388 Argyle Way
Bensalem, PA 19020
215/638-2277
Contact: Paul Scott

Down's Parenting Group
Easter Seal Society Building
6410 4th Street
Bloomsberg, PA 17815
717/784-9495

Down Syndrome Parents' Support Group
of Chester County
6 Wildlife Drive
Chester Springs, PA 19425
215/935-7809
Contact: Bernedette Krzywicki, President

Down Syndrome Today
481 Baker Road
Freedom, PA 15042
Contact: Linda Uhernik

Down Syndrome Group
1001 Brighton Road
Pittsburgh, PA 15233
412/322-6008
Contact: ARC Allegheny, Gaynell
Markowski

Parents of Down Syndrome
R.D. 2, Box 497
Slatington, PA 18080
215/767-7736
Contact: Sheila Stasko

Down's Syndrome Interest Group
27 West Cherry Avenue
Trappe, PA 19426
215/489-7670
Contact: Cathie Van Alstine

RHODE ISLAND

Department of Education
Special Education Unit
Roger Williams Building, Room 200
22 Hayes Street
Providence, RI 02908
401/277-3505

Rhode Island Protection & Advocacy
System, Inc.
86 Weybosset Street, Suite 508
Providence, RI 02903
401/831-3150
Contact: Elizabeth Morancy, Executive
Director

Rhode Island ARC
2845 Post Road
Warwick, RI 02886
401/738-5550
Contact: James Healey, Executive
Director

Child Development Center
Rhode Island Hospital
593 Eddy Street
Providence, RI 02902
401/277-5681
Contact: Dr. Siegfried Pueschel

Down Syndrome Society of Rhode
Island
P.O. Box 9221
Providence, RI 02940
401/463-7425

SOUTH CAROLINA

Office of Programs for the Handicapped
100 Executive Center Drive
Santee Building, Suite A-24
Columbia, SC 29210
803/758-6122
Contact: Millie Fournier, Early
Childhood Specialist

South Carolina Protection & Advocacy
System for the Handicapped
2360A Two Notch Road
Columbia, SC 29204
803/254-1600 (In South Carolina
800/922-5225)
Contact: Louise Ravenel, Executive
Director

South Carolina ARC
7412 Fairfield Road
Columbia, SC 29202
803/754-4763
Contact: Dr. John E. Beckley, Executive
Director

Human Development Center
University Affiliated Facility Program
University of South Carolina
Winthrop College
Rock Hill, SC 29733
803/323-2244
Contact: Francys Travis

Center for Developmental Disabilities
University Affiliated Facility
University of South Carolina
Benson Building, Pickens Street
Columbia, SC 29208
803/777-4839 (In South Carolina
800/922-1107)
Contact: Richard Ferrante

South Carolina Down's Syndrome
Conference
P.O. Box 50466
Columbia, SC 29250
803/256-7394
Contact: Kay I. Richardson

Parent to Parent
103 Pinehurst East
Hartsville, SC 29550
803/332-4765
Contact: Robert Kearns

SOUTH DAKOTA

Division of Education
Section for Special Education
700 North Illinois Street
Pierre, SD 57501-2292
605/773-3315
Contact: Deborah Barnett, Early
Childhood Representative

South Dakota Advocacy Project
221 South Central Avenue
Pierre, SD 57501
605/224-8294 (In South Dakota
800/742-8108)

Center for the Developmentally Disabled
University of South Dakota
Julian 208
414 East Clark Street
Vermillion, SD 57069
605/677-5311
Contact: Charles Anderson, Director

South Dakota ARC
222 West Pleasant Drive
P.O. Box 502
Pierre, SD 57501
605/224-8211
Contact: John Stengle, Executive
Director

People With Special Needs/Down
Syndrome Report
1409 North First
Aberdeen, SD 57401
Publishes a newspaper about Down
syndrome

South Dakota Parent Connection
McKennon Hospital, Room 4509
P.O. Box 5045
800 East 21st Street
Sioux Falls, SD 57117-5045
605/338-3009
Contact: Jan Van Veen

A New Beginning-Parent Support Group
305 North Buchanan
Pierre, SD 57501
605/224-5193
Contact: Olena Gooding

TENNESSEE

Division of Special Programs
132 Cordell Hull Building
Nashville, TN 37219
615/741-2851
Contact: Dr. Joeta Reynolds

Children Services Commission
James K. Polk Building, Suite 1600
505 Deaderick Street
Nashville, TN 37219
615/741-5274
Contact: Pam Frakes, Preschool Services
Coordinator

Effective Advocacy for Citizens with
Handicaps
P.O. Box 121257
Nashville, TN 37212
615/327-0697 (In Tennessee
800/342-1660)
Contact: Harriette Darryberry, Executive
Director

Tennessee ARC
1700 Hayes Street, Suite 200
Nashville, TN 37203
615/327-0294
Contact: Roger Blue, Executive Director

Child Development Center
University of Tennessee
711 Jefferson Avenue
Memphis, TN 38105
901/528-6511

Support Group for Parents of
Handicapped Children
Route 8, Box 280
Johnson City, TN 37601
615/928-1940
Contact: Toni Bell

Down's Parents of Memphis, Inc.
P.O. Box 3777
Memphis, TN 38173-0777
901/683-9667
Contact: Jane Morgret

Down's Parents Ass'n, Inc.
P.O. Box 120832
Nashville, TN 37212
615/776-5420
Contact: Debbie Bommiciwo

TEXAS

Special Education Program
William Travis Building
1701 North Congress Avenue
Austin, TX 78701
512/463-9414
Contact: Joene Grissom, Early Childhood
Coordinator

Advocacy, Inc.
7700 Chevy Chase Drive, Suite 300
Austin, TX 78752
512/475-5543 (In Texas 800/252-9108)
Contact: Dayle Bebee, Executive
Director

Texas ARC
833 West Houston Street
Austin, TX 78756
512/454-6694
Contact: Carmen Quesada, Executive
Director

University Affiliated Center for
Developmentally Disabled Children
Department of Pediatrics
University of Texas Health Science
Center at Dallas
6011 Harry Hines Blvd.
Dallas, TX 75235
214/688-2883
Contact: Dr. Norman Keele

Parents of Persons With Down
Syndrome
2818 San Gabriel
Austin, TX 78705
512/476-6410
Contact: Austin ARC

Down Syndrome Guild
P.O. Box 821174
Dallas, TX 75382-1174
214/239-8771

HANDS
502 North Trinity
Glimer, TX 75644
Contact: Doug & Lynnnette Soape

Parents of Children With Down
Syndrome
P.O. Box 35268
Houston, TX 77035
713/931-7586

Up With Downs–MARC
2701 North "A"
Midland, TX 79705
915/682-9771

Up With Downs, Inc.
271 East Lullwood
San Antonio, TX 78212
512/826-4492

UTAH

State Office of Education
Special Education Section
250 East 5th South
Salt Lake City, UT 84111
801/533-5982
Contact: Dr. R. Elwood Pace

Legal Center for the Handicapped
254 West 400 South, Suite 300
Salt Lake City, UT 84101
801/363-1347 (In Utah 800/662-9080)

Utah ARC
455 East 400 South, Suite 300
Salt Lake City, UT 84111
801/364-5060 (In Utah 800/662-4058)
Contact: Ray Behle, Executive Director

Developmental Center for Handicapped
Persons
Utah State University
UMC 68
Logan, UT 84322
801/750-1981

Utah Parent Information and Training
Center
4984 South 300 West
Murray, UT 84107
801/265-9883 (In Utah 800/468-1160)
Contact: Jean E. Nash, Director

Utah Down's Syndrome Foundation
3340 North 425 East
North Ogden, UT 84404
801/782-7343

Parents for Down's Syndrome
134 North Quincy
Ogden, UT 84404
801/394-7502

Down's Syndrome Parents Group
4037 Foothill Drive
Provo, UT 84604
801/225-5030

VERMONT

State Department of Education
Special Education Unit
120 State Street
Montpelier, VT 05602
802/828-3141
Contact: Kristen Hawkes, Early
Education Consultant

Vermont Developmental Disabilities Law
Project
6 Pine Street
Burlington, VT 05401
802/863-2881
Contact: William J. Reedy, Director

Vermont ARC
Champlain Mall, #37
Winooski, VT 05404
802/655-4014
Contact: Joan Sylvester, Director

Center for Developmental Disabilities
University Affiliated Facility Satellite
449C Waterman Building
University of Vermont
Burlington, VT 05405
802/656–4031

Vermont Coalition of the Handicapped
73 Main Street
Montpelier, VT 05602
802/223–6149

VIRGINIA

Department of Education
Early Childhood Program for the
Handicapped
P.O. Box 6–Q
Richmond, VA 23216
804/225–2873
Contact: Andrea M. Lazzari, Supervisor

State Advocacy Department for the
Developmentally Disabled
9th Street Office Building, Room 527
Richmond, VA 23219
804/786–4185 (In Virginia
800/552–3962)

Virginia ARC
6 North 6th Street, Suite 102
Richmond, VA 23219
804/649–8481
Contact: Lewis H. Zieske, Executive
Director

Virginia Institute for Developmental
Disabilities
Virginia Commonwealth University
1015 West Main Street
Richmond, VA 23284
804/257–8485

Parent Educational Advocacy Training
Center
228 South Pitt Street
Alexandria, VA 22314
703/836–2953
Contact: Winifred Anderson, Director

Special Programs
100 North Washington, Suite 212
Falls Church, VA 22046
703/532–4898
Contact: Kathleen Kestner, Director

Rappahannock Down's Syndrome Parent
Group
103 Butler Road
Fredericksburg, VA 22405
703/371–2712
Contact: Thelma Dietrich, Parent Education Infant Development Program

Riverside Hospital Infant Development
Program
Parents of Down's Syndrome–Support
Group
J. Clyde Morris Blvd.
Newport News, VA 23601
804/599–2065
Contact: Marilyn Johnson

Down's Syndrome Ass'n of Greater Rich-
mond, Inc.
P.O. Box 11585
Richmond, VA 23230
804/262–7933
Contact: Judy Scott, President

PODS of Northern Virginia
451 Orchard Street
Vienna, VA 22180
703/281–1211

Down Syndrome Parent Support Group
3525 Royal Palm Arch
Virginia Beach, VA 23452
Contact: Richard B. Murphy

PODS of Shenandoah Valley
P.O. Box 3172
Winchester, VA 22601

WASHINGTON

Superintendent of Public Instruction
Old Capitol Building, F–G 11
Olympia, WA 98504
206/753–0317
Contact: Joan Gaetz, Early Childhood
Education Coordinator

Division of Children & Family Services
Office Building, Two MS: OB–41
Olympia, WA 98504
206/753–1233
Contact: Susan Baxter, Early Childhood
Interagency Coordinator

The Troubleshooters Office
1550 West Armory Way, Suite 204
Seattle, WA 98119
206/284-1037
Contact: Katie Dolan, Executive Director

Washington ARC
1703 East State Avenue
Olympia, WA 98506
206/357-5596
Contact: Judith Devine, Executive
Director

Child Development and Mental
Retardation Center
University of Washington
Mail Stop WJ-11
Seattle, WA 98195
206/545-1242
Contact: Dr. Donald Farrel, Acting
Director

Resource Center for the Handicapped
20150 45th Avenue, N.E.
Seattle, WA 98155
206/362-2273 (In Washington
800/22-SHARE)

Special Education Coalition
Parent Advisory Council Training
1703 E. State Street
Olympia, WA 98506
206/357-5596
Contact: Laila Adams, Director

Whatcom Infant Stimulation Program
5217 Northwest Road
Bellingham, WA 98226
206/676-2215
Contact: Bea Prill

Caring, Inc.
P.O. Box 400
Milton, WA 98354
206/922-8194
Publishes newsletter

Father, Infants & Toddler Program
1510 Debrelon Lane
Mukiltea, WA 98275
206/355-5663
Contact: Dave Jones

Parent to Parent
2230 8th Avenue
Seattle, WA 98121
206/622-9324
Contact: Pat Condie, PPS Coordinator

Down's Syndrome Support Group
5523 NE Chateau Drive
Vancouver, WA 98661
206/694-1284

WEST VIRGINIA

Office of Special Education
Administration
Capitol Complex
Building 6, Room B-309
Charleston, WV 25305
304/348-8830
Contact: Ghaski Lee, Early Childhood
Representative

West Virginia Advocates for the
Developmentally Disabled, Inc.
1200 Quarrier Street, Suite 27
Charleston, WV 25301
304/346-0847 (In West Virginia
800/642-9205)
Contact: Nancy Mattox, Executive
Director

West Virginia ARC
700 Market Street
Union Trust Building, Room 400
Parkersburg, WV 26101
304/485-5283

University Affiliated Center for
Developmental Disabilities
West Virginia University
College of Human Resources &
Education
509 Allen Hall
Morgantown, WV 26506-6122
304/293-4692

West Virginia Genetics Evaluation &
Counseling Center
West Virginia University School of
Medicine
Morgantown, WV 26506
304/293-7331

Early Intervention Program
Valley Community Mental Health Center
301 Scott Avenue
Morgantown, WV 26505
304/296-1731
Contact: Jan Nash, M.S.W.

BUDS
20 Heather Drive
Morgantown, WV 26505
304/599-4929

WISCONSIN

Division for Handicapped Children &
Pupil Services
Early Childhood Section
125 South Webster Street
P.O. Box 7841
Madison, WI 53707
608/266-6981
Contact: Betty J. Rowe, Chief

Developmental Disabilities Office
Bureau of Community Programs
Division of Community Services
P.O. Box 7851
Madison, WI 53707
608/266-2862
Contact: Kary Hyre, Director

Wisconsin Coalition for Advocacy, Inc.
30 West Mifflin Street, Suite 508
Madison, WI 53703
608/251-9600
Contact: Lynn Breedlove, Executive
Director

Wisconsin ARC
5522 University Avenue
Madison, WI 53705
608/231-3335
Contact: Merlen Kurth, Executive
Director

Harry A. Weisman Center on Mental
Retardation and Human Development
University of Wisconsin
1500 Highland Avenue
Madison, WI 53706
608/263-5776

Parent Education Project (PEP Coalition)
UCP of Southeastern Wisconsin, Inc.
152 West Wisconsin Avenue
Milwaukee, WI 53202
414/272-4500 (In Wisconsin
800/472-5525)
Contact: Liz Irwin, Director

Fox Valley Down Syndrome Parent
Support Group
808 East Atlantic
Appleton, WI 54911

Down Syndrome: Parent to Parent
Down Syndrome Support Group
1119 Black Oak Trail
Deerfield, WI 53531
Contact: Lanam F. Koclanes

Down Syndrome Division, Wisconsin
ARC
5522 University Avenue
Madison, WI 53705
608/231-3335 (In Wisconsin
800/362-5455)
Contact: Mary Murphy

Southwest Wisconsin Parents of Down
Syndrome
R.R. #1
West Mount Road
Platteville, WI 53818
608/348-8651

Down's Syndrome Parent Group of
Racine
5636 Freedy Avenue
Racine, WI 53406
414/886-3523
Contact: Mrs. Marion Hauser

WYOMING

State Department of Education
Program Services Unit
Hathaway Office Building
Cheyenne, WY 82002
307/777-7417
Contact: Carol Nantkes, Director

Developmental Disabilities Protection &
Advocacy System, Inc.
2424 Pioneer Avenue, Suite 101
Cheyenne, WY 82001
307/632-3496
Contact: Jeanne A. Kawcak, Executive
Director

Wyoming ARC
P.O. Box 1205
Cheyenne, WY 82003
307/632-7105
Contact: Lorinda Vetter, Executive
Director

Child Development Services of Fremont
County
P.O. Box 593
Lander, WY 82520
307/332-5508
Contact: Fran Cadez

CANADA

UPS and Downs
447 Abadan Place, N.E.
Calgary, Alberta
Canada T2A 6W3
403/235-4798
Contact: Lin Hermanson

Early Intervention Program
65 Brunswick Street
Fredericton, New Brunswick
Canada E3B 1G
506/454-8698
Contact: Anne Luiely

Down's Syndrome Parents Group
19 Hickery Place
Brantford, Ontario
Canada N3S 3C7
Contact: Murray MacDonald

K.I.I.D.S.
102 Dovercliffe Road
Guelph, Ontario
Canada N1G 3A6
Contact: Brenda Nancarrow

Parent to Parent for Down's Syndrome
17 Rexway Road
London, Ontario
Canada N6G 3C1
519/472-9769
Contact: Mrs. Lorraine Hewett

The Down Syndrome Ass'n for the
Region of Halton
129 Riverview Street
Oakville, Ontario
Canada L6L 5P6
416/827-1025
Contact: Karen Ireland

Pilot Parents
2 Baldwin Avenue
Roxboro, Quebec
Canada H8Y 2W8
514/684-9346
Contact: Susan Daigle

Down Syndrome Ass'n of Metropolitan
Toronto
96 Brooklawn Avenue
Scarborough, Ontario
Canada M1M 2P6
416/691-1712
Contact: Margaret Herd

"UP WITH DOWNS"
214 Sylvian Way
Saskatoon, Saskatchewan
Canada 57H 5G2
306/374-8100
Contact: Ronalyn Bradshaw, Coordinator

Durham Down Syndrome Ass'n
P.O. Box 231
Whitby, Ontario
Canada L1H 5S1

INTERNATIONAL

Down's Children Ass'n
Quinborne Centre
Ridgeacre Road
Birmingham B32 England
021/427-1374

National Centre for Down's Syndrome
9 Westbourne Road
Edgbaston
Birmingham B15 England
021/454-3126

Dr. Julio Abdo
Hospital Herrern Llerandi
Fac. de Medicina
University Francisco Marroquin
6th Avenue 8-71
Guatemala 10, Guatemala

Watchdog, Ltd.
GPO Box 6667
Hong Kong
Contact: K. Sharman

YATED
42 Gaza Street
Jerusalem, Israel 92384
631728
Contact: Rivka Friedman

Association Bambini Down
Via Giannone 25
Rome, Italy
Contact: Giorgio Albertini

HOPE
35 Malcolm Road
Singapore 1130 Japan
2515472
Contact: Elizabeth Tan

Down's Association
P.O. Box 4142
Auckland, New Zealand
5341090

APPADM
Tv. Santa Quiteria, 87
1200 Lisbon, Portugal

Sociedad Puertorriquenadel Sindrome de
Down
Azules del Mar J-15
Dorado del Mar-Dorado
Puerto Rico 00646
137/796-2698
Contact: Miriam P. Martinez

Associacion de Padres Pro Bienestar de
Ninos Impedidos, Inc.
Box 21301
Rio Piedras, Puerto Rico 00928
809/765-0345

Puerto Rico ARC
G.P.O. Box 1904
San Juan, PR 00936
809/767-6718
Contact: Roxanna De Soto, Executive
Director

Scottish Down's Syndrome Ass'n
3 North Balmossie Street
Monifieth
Dundee, DD 5 4QJ Tayside
Scotland, UK
Tel: DUNDEE 532654
Contact: Mrs. Teresa Stewart

The Down Syndrome Ass'n
P.O. Box 221
Wendywood
2144 TVL
South Africa

Fundacio Catalana Per A La Sindrome
De Down
Calle Valencia 229
Barcelona 08007 Spain
Contact: Mrs. Montserrat Trias

William & Karen Hagerman
Jahnstrusse 16
6365 Rosbach V .dH1
Federal Republic of West Germany
Tel: 06003-1545

Index